WHERE TIME STOOD STILL

ALSO BY THE DUCHESS OF ST ALBANS

Green Grows the Oil
Le Théâtre en Classe (2 vols.)
The Mimosa and the Mango
The Road to Bordeaux
Uncertain Wings

Where Time Stood Still

A Portrait of Oman

The Duchess of St Albans

QUARTET BOOKS

LONDON   MELBOURNE   NEW YORK

First published by Quartet Books Limited 1980
A member of the Namara Group
27 Goodge Street, London W1P 1FD

Copyright © 1980 by The Duchess of St Albans

ISBN 0 7043 2247 1

Typeset by Input Typesetting, Wimbledon, SW19
Printed in Great Britain by
The Anchor Press Ltd, and bound by
Wm. Brendon & Son Ltd, both of Tiptree, Essex

FOR BRIGADIER PETER THWAITES,
WITH GRATITUDE

Contents

Acknowledgements

Among all the people who have helped me in my quest, I am most indebted to Brigadier Peter Thwaites, who was not only my host in Ruwi, but made it possible for me to get into Oman in the first place. His solid backing and constant encouragement made it easier to dig out the necessary information and background, without which I could never have attempted this book.

The Sultan's Armed Forces provided transport wherever I wanted to go, by land or by air: helicopters whisked me up to the top of inaccessible mountains; the Air Force shot me across the desert in their jets; the Ministry of Information provided all the books, the cars and the help I needed. For all this I particularly want to thank Mr Tony Ashworth in Muscat and Mr John Ward in Salalah.

Major Martin Robb, his wife Jenny and their little daughter Lucy who took me into their home and treated me like an old friend, although we had never met before, turned my stay in Dhofar into a delightful family affair. Lt-Colonel Jonathan Sallsbury-Trelawny, who was my host on my second visit to Oman, and who had fought in the Dhofar War, made all his personal notes on the campaign available to me. Brigadier Colin Maxwell, Colonel Michael Loyd and Lt-Colonel Richard John, whose fund of knowledge about Oman is apparently inexhaustible, patiently answered all my questions. With his valuable introductions and the loan of his own books, Colonel Peter Kemp smoothed my way in academic circles in London; and Major Peter Bennett gave permission for his unique photographs of the Dhofar War to be reproduced in the text. I am also most grateful to Captain Anthony ffrench Blake for his careful checking of the manuscript.

Captain Richard Morley and Captain Andrew Bruce acted as indefatigable guides in the hot and dusty interior of Oman Proper and, where horses are concerned, Commander and Mrs Jay Frazier and Captain Jamie Mackie put their mounts through their paces for my benefit. And there are many more, both Omani and British, who helped me more than they realized with their hospitality, their friendliness and their unfailing kindness.

Illustrations

All photographs not otherwise attributed were taken by the author

An oasis in Wadi Sumayl (*Peter Thwaites*)
The fortress of Jalali, Muscat
A house built of brain coral
A silver stall, Matrah *souq*
A fort in Wadi Sumayl (*Peter Thwaites*)
Falaj in Fanja oasis
Stranded in Wadi Bidbid
Storm clouds over Wadi Bidbid (*Peter Thwaites*)
There were few places which couldn't be reached by truck (*Peter Bennett*)
Early morning chores in camp (*Peter Bennett*)
Dawn ambush on Jebel Akhdar (*Peter Bennett*)
Exchanging 'the news', soldiers of S.A.F., Jebel Akhdar (*Peter Bennett*)
The rebel leader's house after the bombardment, Jebel Akhdar (*Peter Thwaites*)
An oasis in the heart of the Hajar range (*Ministry of Information, Dubai*)
The peaks of Jebel Akhdar which were scaled by the S.A.S. during the tribal.rebellion (*Peter Thwaites*)

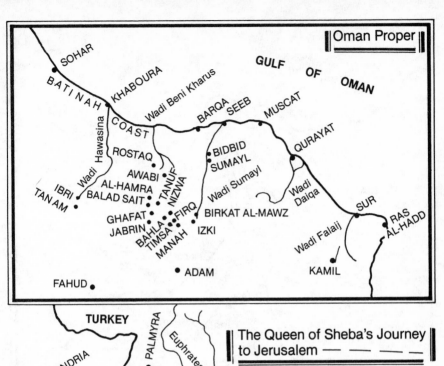

Oman Proper

The Queen of Sheba's Journey to Jerusalem

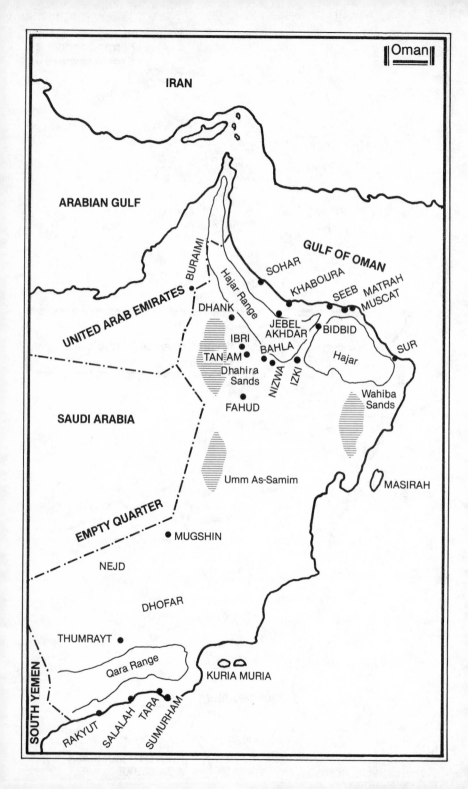

WHERE TIME STOOD STILL

1   A Goodly Land

Until 1973 the ceremony of *dum-dum* took place in Muscat every evening after sunset: the cannon boomed on top of Fort Mirani and the great doors of Bab el-Kebir in the town wall closed for the night. After this, no one was allowed out in the dark narrow streets without an oil lantern swinging from the fist. This was one of the rules imposed by ex-Sultan Said bin Taimur who was deposed in 1970 and succeeded by his son, the present young Sultan Qaboos.

Under the new monarch's régime, Oman is emerging from the Middle Ages and fast growing into a modern State. Avoiding the mistakes of some other Arab countries out of which exploded all the steel and concrete tokens of the materialistic culture on the tidal wave of the new oil wealth before their people were quite ready for it, Oman is wisely controlling the construction side of its development, and concentrating very much more on education, the health services and civil aid.

Sultan Qaboos has done away with the restrictions imposed by his father. In the old days, no foreigner was allowed into the country without the ruler's personal authorization. With curious foresight, Sultan Said, who had a horror of smoking, forbade the use of tobacco throughout the land. There was another very odd taboo, more difficult to understand, against the wearing of dark glasses. But however eccentric the repres-

3

sive measures may have seemed, there was usually a reason for them: basically, behind all the repressive measures, was the Sultan's conviction that his people were not yet ready for Western civilization, and that its impact would only unbalance and corrupt them. Although it seems difficult to imagine those friendly, hospitable and un-arrogant beings undergoing such a total change of character, prevention is better than cure, and Sultan Qaboos is taking no chances either. An uncontrolled flood of tourists from the West is no part of the development plan.

Before 1970, travelling was limited to the usual camel-caravans, plodding their way along from the interior to bring supplies to Muscat; there was no gadding about the country-side for pleasure or even on business. People had to stay at home, whether they liked it or not. There were precisely three schools in the land. There was one hotel for those intrepid enough to brave the very lukewarm reception awaiting them in Oman. The only tarred road was five miles long. So, before anything else, an extensive programme of road-building had to be set up.

Schools have now been built in most of the villages and all the towns. There are two very large, up-to-date hospitals. Health centres, clinics and dispensaries are dotted throughout Oman. One of the main problems is the lack of qualified nationals, making it essential to employ teachers from other Arab countries at very high rates of pay, to lure them into the more remote and inaccessible districts. This heavy drain on the resources of the Ministry of Education will not ease up until the newly-built training colleges begin to turn out home-grown men and women teachers. The same problem besets the health services. Most of the doctors and nurses at present come from India and Pakistan. Omani medical students are being trained abroad, so in time these will return as fully-fledged medical staff.

There are now two major airports, and several other smaller ones in various parts of the country. Airstrips and helipads have been laid out in the most unlikely places, including the very top of otherwise inaccessible mountain peaks. The pilots of Oman are fearless performers who think nothing of snaking their way into the deepest and narrowest of canyons, climbing up the face of perpendicular cliffs several thousand feet high, and executing faultless landings on the rough gravel beds of dry wadis. It says a good deal for the skill and confidence of these men that I for one, anyway, have never felt the slightest twinge of alarm in any of those nimble little aircraft.

If no more oil strikes are made the present wells will eventually dry out, a fact to which the Government seems resigned. Since geologists have declared that new finds are unlikely, efforts are being made to establish alternative sources of income. Extensive surveys have revealed that the soil holds other riches only waiting to be brought to light. Copper mines, for which Oman was known all over the ancient world, could still be made to yield a couple of thousand tons a year. Near Saham, asbestos has been discovered in sufficient quantities to make further imports unnecessary. Coal apparently lurks in substantial amounts at the south-eastern tip of the country, in as yet inaccessible places. Some means of reaching them will have to be devised before mining can start. Apart from that, there is marble and limestone in the mountains and unexpected minerals such as nickel, zinc and chrome. Iron and manganese have also been spotted here and there as well.

With a 2,000-mile coastline, fishing has always been one of the country's main occupations. The surplus which wasn't consumed on the spot was dried and traded with limes and dates in the interior, but now a more scientific approach is being developed. Research has revealed the incredible fecundity of the waters in the Kuria Muria Bay and the Gulf of Masirah; a consortium of Japanese companies have been granted a concession by which they keep sixty per cent of the haul, while the rest is handed over to the Government.

Agriculture is another potential source of revenue. Several research stations are at work testing crops, seeds and pesticides; when proved successful, they are put into practical use on Government farms. Extension centres are dotted all over the agricultural areas. Seeds and advice are handed out to the farmers, and there is a very popular scheme for the loan of agricultural machinery. The aim of all these efforts is to make Oman not merely self-supporting in fruit and vegetables, but also to enable it to export to other Gulf States.

And so, with unflurried calm and dignity, Oman has been translated in seven brief years from a feudal State into a progressive, confident, outward-looking society, anxious to catch up with the rest of the world, but intensely conscious of its own intrinsic qualities, and fiercely determined to preserve its independence, its traditions and the faith of Islam.

2 Clanking Chains in Cable Bay

'When a sinner goes to Muscat, he gets a foretaste of
what to expect in the afterlife' — An Arab saying

'Only a few years ago I could hear the prisoners' chains
clanking as they hobbled about inside the fort,' says the
Ambassadress, as we stand on the enormous terrace of the
British Embassy overlooking the little cove of Cable Bay, at
the foot of the forbidding fortress of Jalali in Muscat. 'And
although their hands were shackled and their feet hobbled
with a heavy iron bar which had to be lifted with a cord
whenever they wanted to move,' the Ambassadress goes on,
'they seemed a cheerful lot.'

This I had already heard tell before. The prisoners, though
so heavily loaded with chains, would happily spend the time
of day drinking coffee with the guards in the porch of the
main gate of the fortress.

Twice a month, Sultan Said's own doctor is said to have
visited them in their dungeon, although other sources describe
it as the most grim, inhuman and cruel prison in the world.
Crouching on top of its rock, with its impregnable grey stone
walls and massive towers, it certainly does its best to look as
inhospitable as it can. It was one of Colonel David Smiley's
duties to visit the prisoners while he was Commander-in-

Chief of the Sultan's Forces, and in his book *Arabian Assignment* he describes the place as a veritable hellhole, housing about a hundred inmates, political prisoners and ordinary criminals all indiscriminately herded together, one of them an incurable alcoholic who was only there to keep him away from the bottle. The worst feature at that time was the cruelly short water-ration on which the prisoners were kept as punishment for their crimes.

These contradictory reports are probably the result of the different policies which changed according to each new governor's disposition and temperament. In Smiley's time the reigning incumbent was a ruthless, sadistic monster who enjoyed watching the prisoners' pitiful agony in the fearful heat of summer, and who countered all the colonel's pleas for mercy by saying they had done wrong and deserved their punishment. In the end Smiley managed to get his own soldier guards' water-ration increased, and the surplus secretly smuggled to the prisoners.

Until recently, Jalali was the only jail in town. Only once did anyone ever escape from its grim hospitality: in 1963 some forty prisoners managed to get clean away, nobody quite knows how, but probably by knotting rice sacks together. However, they didn't get far. Everything went wrong from the start: the moon rose too late, the tide didn't behave as expected, guards were lurking when they should have been fast asleep. The result was, everybody on that particular jaunt was recaptured and made to feel sorry for ever trying to get away. On another occasion, when a lone prisoner decided to try his luck on his own, he was so horrified at the sight of the dagger-like rocks sticking straight out of the sea all around that he turned tail on the spot and bolted back into the safety of the fortress. Surrounded by this terrifying jumble of razor-sharp vertical rocks, the steep flight of steps cut into the cliff face on the sea side provides the only access to the fortress, and it is difficult to imagine anyone ever getting away from it.

Having read and heard so much about the horrors of the prison, I was considerably surprised by the unexpectedly open and cheerful look of the place when I went to visit it. The whitewashed cells, which are all shapes and sizes, are above ground and equipped with ceiling fans – looking more like aviaries awaiting the next batch of exotic tropical birds than prison cells. Built on top of the rock, the lay-out of the fort follows the formation of the outcrop, with the two great towers perched on the highest points, one facing out to sea, the other inland. Steps lead up from one level to the next in various directions: to the governor's tower, the battlements, the rooftops, and a long gallery overlooking the bay of Muscat. Here, pointing at the harbour, are the huge cannons which were installed to protect the town against all invaders. The floor, made of enormous uneven boards, looks as if it might cave in under the weight of the guns at any moment. Unused now for many years and encrusted with rust and dust, they all came originally from England or India in the eighteenth and nineteenth centuries. The beautiful Portuguese guns for which the gallery had been built were pitched into the bay in a fit of irrepressible relief and high spirits by the soldiers of the Imam when the hated invaders were finally evicted in 1654.

'The Sultan wanted to have these guns in front of his palace, but they were too heavy to move,' our guide informs us as we try to decipher the date on one of the great barrels. How on earth were they brought here in the first place, up those steep narrow steps on the side of the cliff? Nobody knows and nobody cares – it was a long time ago, and how the problem was solved at the time is irrelevant now. The guns are too heavy to be moved and that is all there is to it, so they will have to stay where they are till kingdom come.

A profusion of exotic weeds blooms in the dust of the central courtyard, where a large Gulf almond is growing out of the rock with nuts the size of gulls' eggs. Cracking some with a stone I find a minute kernel at the centre, half an inch long. 'Eat it, eat it,' says the guide. 'Very good.' And so it is. But no Arab, either here or anywhere else in the Gulf, would ever trouble to pick them.

As we return to the Embassy terrace for a cooling drink after our hot climb, a delicious little breeze is blowing off the smooth bottle-green waters of the harbour below, where great dhows from India, Madagascar, Zanzibar, Mombasa and the

Gulf ports stand loaded half-way up the mast with bundles of every shape and size.

The Embassy had originally been built by the Indian Government as a consulate-general in 1880; in the middle of the courtyard in front of it stands the famous flagpole which was 'home' to fleeing slaves. If they could reach and clasp it with both hands before being caught, they would gain their freedom and a certificate of manumission, which was solemnly presented to them on the spot. In the Embassy you can still see examples of this document, although no one has claimed it for some time now. Any slaves remaining in the country have been born into their estate in the land of Oman, and are treated as members of the family.

In their present form, the two great fortresses on either side of Muscat harbour date from the sixteenth century. Jalali was built in 1587 and Fort Capitan, later renamed Mirani, was designed by one Manuel do Souza Coutinho in 1588. His name can be seen to this day engraved over the main gateway. Below it lies the small harbour of Mukalla, described by a contemporary mapmaker as a 'hole for shippes'. Today, surrounded by hopeful herons perched on top of the rocks all around, the Sultan's navy lies peacefully at anchor. Except for the year 1743–4, when it was occupied by the Persians, Fort Mirani, which is said to contain more cannon than any fortress ever, has been in Omani hands ever since. In his book *Muscat and Oman, the end of an era*, Ian Skeet writes: 'an official salute fired by four of these ancient cannon is a semi-social event of Victorian melodrama: a lighting of fuses, swabbings, explosions, smoke rings and a sergeant ever more wildly leaping from one gun-team to another giving action signals.' Nowadays, this only happens when ships from foreign navies drop in on courtesy calls, when they get practically blasted out of the water by the wildly exuberant explosions.

The rocks on both sides of the bay are decorated with the names of ships which have called here in the last three centuries. When he visited Muscat as a midshipman, Nelson is supposed to have scaled the cliff to paint it with his own ship's name, *Seahorse*. The latest to be added to his 'marine autograph book', as Sultan Said used to call it, is *Britannia*, riding peacefully at anchor at this very moment in the bay round the corner.

The summer months are excessively scorching in Muscat, and the commercial capital of Matrah next door was described by Colonel Smiley as 'a vast pressure cooker simmering in the damp suffocating heat'. The burning rays of the sun, stored all through the day in the naked rocks which form a rampart all around, turn the place into a furnace. To make matters worse, the *gharbi* (west wind) gathers up the throbbing waves of heat off the scalding rock face and sweeps the lot down into the sweltering town. At midnight the temperature can reach over 50° Centigrade (120° Fahrenheit). With air conditioning, this is no longer a problem. The present Ambassador enjoys the best of health. But between 1800 and 1810 the first four British Residents all swiftly perished, carried off by the rigours of the climate.

Seen for the first time, either from land, sea or air, Muscat is an unforgettable spectacle. Lieutenant Wellstead, writing about it in his *Travels in Arabia*, at the time of Sultan Said the Great, claimed that 'no part of the world presents a wilder or more romantic aspect than Muscat Cove'. And Lord Curzon described it as the most picturesque harbour in the East.

Crowned at either end by the formidable piles of its twin fortresses brooding menacingly on top of their forbidding rocks, and crammed together by the crescent-shaped peaks of the Hajar range, the crowded little town is unable to spread any further and takes up every inch of available space. The jumbled white houses, often leaning against one another for support, used to straggle right down to the sandy shoreline. An elegant Corniche (frequently signposted as Cornish) now sweeps along the front, dividing the town from the often less than salubrious beach. The Queen's present visit has done much for the general appearance of the place. Subjected in the last three days before Her Majesty's arrival to a vigorous face-lift, Muscat is now gleaming white with fresh paint. Mud huts, wooden hovels, *barasti* (palm-frond) shelters and disintegrating dwellings of one kind and another were all cordoned off behind hastily constructed palisades. The graveyard is concealed by an elaborate cardboard screen of castle-wall decorations. Whole settlements of shanty-town shacks were

11

bulldozed and flattened overnight. Peering behind some of the sugar-loaf peaks which jut out of the ground all round the town, I spied most of the shacks hastily re-erected out of sight, decently hidden away from view by the rocks. The less tottering residences which were allowed to stand were painted over during the third night of those feverish three days.

The architecture of Muscat is a mixture of Arabian, Indian and Persian influences. Dating from the eighteenth and nineteenth centuries, some of the grander houses of Muscat are very handsome indeed. There are very few of the really old Arabian type left, built of mud and encrusted with elaborate decorations and beautifully carved doorways, and these are mostly in Sur and Hamra. One thing which surprised me, bearing in mind all this Persian influence around, is the total absence of wind towers, those draught-conductors which suck down into the rooms below any breeze which might be lurking in the upper layers. The landscape of many Gulf towns, which also came under the domination of Persia, is dotted with these attractive, exotic architectural features. However, to make up for the non-existent towers, houses in Muscat are built with walls three or more feet thick, and this does succeed in keeping out some of the sizzling fires of hell which roast everything outside in the furnace of high summer. Although there is now a certain amount of air conditioning, many people still prefer to sleep on the roof, under the shooting stars and tinsel moon of the glittering oriental sky.

It is the day of the Queen's arrival, and the wind has freshened a good deal. By three o'clock the seas are running high under a stiff south-easter. Setting off from Qurm we are heading straight into it, with great waves washing right over the boat every time we dive into a trough. After a good hour of plunging and bucketing about, we finally arrive, soaked to the marrow, as *Britannia* is steaming slowly into Muscat harbour. The bay is thronged with boats of every shape and size, all bouncing about on the swell, with flags and yards of bunting fluttering in the wind. A large dhow chugs around ponderously, and an identical pair of green tugs, encrusted with barnacles and festooned with tyres and trailing seaweed, churn about spewing sulphurous, stinking fumes and making a terrible racket with their engines. Another boat draped in bunting is brimming with tiny boy scouts who cling unsteadily to the white rope of their gangway. The Muscat Divers are there in their fibreglass nutshell, and all the private launches are milling around, loaded to capacity with loyal, cheering Britons. As the noble yacht, all gleaming with brass and brand-new paint, edges in slowly among the hooting, teeming skiffs, a couple of police launches swish about like sheep dogs, clearing the way, eventually ramming each other, the only collision of the whole afternoon.

Setting off from the palace steps, the Sultan's launch comes skimming through our ranks with the British Ambassador, his wife and the Under-Secretary for Defence on board. The Queen comes tripping down the gangway, followed by Prince Philip and their entourage, almost blasted off their feet by the wild honking and hooting of the little boats. As the Royal party steams along towards the palace, the cannon of Mukalla bang off their twenty-one-gun salute.

After dinner, the Sultan treats the good people of Muscat to a firework display. As this starts with unexpected punctuality and we, being used to Arab hours, set off late, we manage to miss the show.

The State banquet and the fireworks being over, we watch the Queen and Prince Philip come down the palace steps and wave to the cheering expatriate Britons along the sea wall. A child shouts 'Have a good trip', and the show is over. Everybody drifts away through the brightly lit streets, and I can't help thinking that only seven years ago we would have been clutching smelly, smoking lanterns and creeping cautiously through the dark, narrow lanes of the town, hustled along by ferocious *askars* bristling with *khanjars* and old desert rifles.

The Sultan wanted to make sure of having a nice clean city in which to welcome the Queen. Apart from the repainting of Muscat, an enormous amount of trouble has been taken all round. Everywhere triumphal arches span the town streets and the country roads, decorated with touching little messages such as 'Qaboos welcomes Elizabeth II. May the doves of peace flutter all over the globe'. And elsewhere, 'With education and confidence the Omani people develop their nation'. An enormous plasterboard cut-out of Windsor Castle stands across the road on the way to the airport and, among the barren rocks of the Corniche, a windmill, outlined in red electric-light bulbs, keeps a lonely watch. From a golden clockwork pot hanging in the sky pours a perpetual stream of blood-red coffee (as black would be lost in the night) into a waiting cup perched upon a lonely crag along the deserted cliff. The wide flaring spout withdraws, bends over again to refill the cup, then returns to its upright position in the sky.

Along with the dark and dirty streets and the compulsory oil lamps, Progress has done away with much of the more exotic side of Muscat. Bab el-Kebir (the great gate) was the end of the road and final meeting-place for the great caravans which had travelled across the desert from the north, from Syria, Jerusalem and Alexandria, and from the southern regions of Yemen. Marib, the unforgettable capital city of the Queen of Sheba, was at that time the main collecting centre for frankincense, which grew in natural forests, protected by brightly-coloured winged serpents nestling in the foliage of the precious trees.

Until the early 1920s, the Sultan's palace was guarded by a couple of caged lions. One of these beasts was reputed to be quite tame and could be seen roaming the streets, calling on friends. An elephant shambled along to the British Embassy every day at the same hour for his sugar ration, and an ostrich was another town pet which spent many a happy hour pecking its way through the refuse of the fruit and vegetable *souq*. I much regret that none of these intriguing Muscateers were still about on my recent visits to Oman. When Theodore Bent was there in the nineteenth century, he reported that beside the lion's cage was a cell for first-offence prisoners. If they were ever sentenced a second time, they were locked in with the lions at lunchtime.

A few bays along to the north of Muscat you come to Matrah, a big straggly town with some fine old houses along the waterfront in the Indian Ocean style, for those who know what that is. On the heights a Portuguese fort, smaller and less imposing than the Muscat monsters, and a string of fighting towers overlook the town. The *souq* sits astride the bed of a wide wadi which floods from time to time, washing out to sea all the accumulated rubbish whose rich aroma pervades the air. The Matrah *souq* with its constant clatter, its lively, incessant bustle and its smells is probably much the same as it looked two or three thousand years ago. The narrow streets are neither paved nor cemented. Presumably on account of the occasionally gushing wadi, the merchants' shop-holes (there is no other description for these rabbit warrens) are perched about three feet above street level. Some are furnished with one or two steps made of stone or mud, others with a rolling palm log, but most of them have nothing at all, so that you have to be heaved up into his shop by the merchant himself. Omani housewives, all bundled in their *abbas* and their veils, can sometimes be quite a challenge to hoist on board. I have watched with hypnotized fascination a hauling operation immobilized in mid-air, and on one or two occasions it was touch and go, like a tug of war, which side would eventually pull it off.

The milling throng in the narrow streets is constantly being squashed and flattened against the walls by little donkeys, trotting down the middle with heavy square tins slung on either flank like panniers. The water man who follows close behind whacks the tins with a camel-stick to draw attention to his precious load and cut himself a way through. On street corners, small letterboxes stand off the ground on high, thin, metal legs, no doubt to keep the mail dry. Ian Skeet tells a tale about one of the banks incautiously hoarding its paper money in the vaults and having it all reduced to pulp by one of these tumultuous floods. But when I later met the bank manager concerned in Muscat, and asked him about the incident, he assured me that the notes had remained perfectly dry in their watertight vaults, and that it was the customers' files which had floated away on the furious waters, never to be seen again.

As in the City of London, there are specialized streets for jewellery, silver, spices, tailors, shoe-makers and plastic merchants. The latter stock anything from polythene aprons to buckets and fly swats. Some of these shops go in for imaginative names, such as 'The Good Friends' Welcome' and 'The God Help Us Taylor'. At one scent emporium into which I venture, a drop of real, wildly expensive essence of musk is generously dabbed on my hand. 'This is a real turn-on, Memsahib,' the Indian merchant assures me earnestly, as he holds the nasty stuff up to my nose.

The fish *souq* conducts its noisy, odoriferous activities in a long covered building, the interior divided into stalls by iron bars. Within each cage the merchant sits cross-legged on a table swimming in fish blood, just behind and level with the counter. Fish of every kind surround him on all sides; large torpedo-shaped tunas, huge fleshy groupers with milky, jelly eyes, chinless, silver-skinned sharks, kingfish with razor-blade teeth, trumpet and parrotfish, and the long, thin, delicate garfish, whose bones turn bright fluorescent green when cooked.

Schoolchildren, all dressed in white, scuttle along, weaving in and out among the teeming crowd, the girls in white veils and long white dresses like tiny tropical nuns, the boys in calf-length tunics and little, white, lace prayer-caps. Like any European schoolchild each swings a satchel, but instead of bubble-gum and bars of chocolate, they buy twists of roasted melon seeds or puffed-up chick peas which look just like sweet corn.

The narrow, twisting streets swarm with Omanis dressed in their midi-length tunics, a *khanjar* proudly stuck through the belt in the middle of their anatomy, and a Kashmir turban, each one done up with its own individual twist, some smooth and round, all ends tidily tucked in, hugging the head like a bathing cap, but more often flat on top of the head, with fringes sticking out all round like the spikes of a sea-urchin. There are Indians, neat and clean and soulful, Baluchis with vast rolling bellies and popping eyes and, of course, English housewives doing their shopping in the *souq* like everybody else.

Most important of all the foreign elements assimilated into the daily life of Oman are the Indians. They work in banks, commercial offices, shops of every kind. They own and operate with impressive efficiency all the supermarkets and 'cold stores' in the land, and they keep import-export businesses in thriving order. Without them the economy of the country would soon grind to a cosy, lotus-eating halt.

Driving inland through the mountains from Matrah, you eventually hit Bait al-Falaj, the House of the Canal, the headquarters of the Sultan's Armed Forces. The old fort, which is now a barracks, stands beside a dry wide wadi and is surrounded by vast open spaces over which trucks and lorries wheel around in all directions, and helicopters land and take off throughout the day. In the compound all round the fort is an outcrop of bungalows, as well as the building from which the Staff officers operate and control the army. The Sultan, who trained as an officer at Sandhurst, and is tied to the British Government by long-standing treaties of friendship, is actually very pro-British himself. The atmosphere at Bait al-Falaj, with its complement of seconded officers and others on contract, is cheerful, brisk and, above all, efficient. A comforting feeling of reliability and competence reigns over the whole place. Here, you feel, the old values still hold good: a gentleman never breaks his word or cheats at cards. Discipline is the framework of daily life but there is nothing oppressive about it. The feeling which emanates from the walls of the fort is one of integrity and rectitude, a sensation I have never experienced in France, which used to be taken for granted in England, but no longer is. Oman must be one of the few places where it still exists.

A short drive away from Bait al-Falaj is Ruwi, a bedraggled town which straggles on among dusty tracks and parking lots. Here and there the odd volcanic peak sticks straight up out of the sand. Some streets bite right into these astonishing outcrops, and you can see the raw stone, dark red like congealed blood, rising right behind the shops' back-doors where the plastic dustbins stand.

Arabs (Omanis included) take a great deal of trouble with the inside of their dwellings, but they don't give a damn about the approaches, so you may be going to visit one of the top sheikhs, shuffling through acres of hot soft sand, with a hole or two where the heavy machinery has left a mark and a few casual planks thrown across the really rough spots. Straight from this chaotic wilderness you step into the coolest, most civilized palaces, all tinkling fountains, rare Arabian antiques, pet gazelles and veiled women flitting past through potted pomegranate trees and slender colonnades. That is if you are lucky. As often as not it is a bit of Knightsbridge or Park

17

Lane which has been flown out to the desert, complete with wall-to-wall Wilton and fake crystal chandeliers.

It is here in Ruwi, surrounded by a large patch of bumpy, uneven, oil-stained ground which serves as a car park that my host, Brigadier Thwaites, Chairman of the Joint Staff, has a flat of surprising comfort and elegance. It all begins to make sense when you learn that the place has been done up by his wife Jacqueline who owns and runs the Inchbald School of Design, no less.

Besides myself, the other guests in residence are Rosie and Patrick Brook, who fought and was wounded in the Dhofar War. Rosie, I am told, is my chaperone. I am tickled pink at the thought of having a chaperone at my age, and with three grandchildren! Rosie is pretty tickled herself.

Although Sultan Qaboos has opened up the country a great deal since he succeeded his father in 1970, the lush and tantalizing land of Oman is still very difficult to visit. You can't just turn up in order to wander about and look around. Tourists are not encouraged. Visas are granted for specific reasons only. But once you are there, you are welcomed like nowhere else in the western world. Wherever you go, total strangers come up to shake your hand and invite you into their hut or cave or fareeg (tree-tent) or wherever they happen to be living at the time. Within seconds you are being chatted up like a long-lost friend. Hospitality, always generous and profuse throughout the Middle East, is less formal and more spontaneous here than in many other Arab countries. There are no long involved rigmaroles such as I was once treated to as I watched a boat being built among rotting fishbones and liquefying jellyfish on the seashore, when the blessings of Allah were called down upon the heads of my great-great-grandchildren's progeny by a proud and noble-looking elder all bundled up in an extraordinary assortment of tattered rags and old sacks. Here in Oman, particularly inland, away from the languid airs of the coast, it is all very much brisker and more vigorous. Old men never creep. They stride along with impressive speed and purposefulness, leaping from stone to stone in the wadi beds, their cotton-wool beards flapping in the breeze, with dagger-straight backs and sharp eyes darting everywhere, missing nothing. In this manner they happily cover astonishing distances, marching from one end of a province to the other, intent on their own private affairs.

Throughout history Oman has kept herself to herself and, in spite of innumerable invasions, has managed somehow to keep her independence. The Omani way of life survives to this day, no doubt helped by the massive mountain range which insulates the country from the rest of Arabia. Behind Muscat and the 2,000-mile coastline which faces the Indian Ocean and the Arabian Sea is the famous Hajar range, which cuts off the farouche interior, Oman Proper, from the rest of the eastern world. According to P. S. Allfrey's witty book *Warlords of Oman*, this region 'is well stocked with a people noted among the other Arabs for religious fanaticism and a hatred of their fellow-men'.

Edging right up to the western borders of Oman lies the immensity of the Empty Quarter; huge deserts fill up the central part all the way down to the province of Dhofar, the Ophir of the Bible. From the northernmost tip of the Musandam Peninsula facing Iran, down to Ras al-Hadd at the eastern end, the Hajar raises its savage razor-sharp peaks and sheer, flat-faced slabs of scorching, vertical rocks. Holy Nizwa in the interior is the secret city of the imams, nestling at the foot of the highest peak of Jebel Akhdar. The top of the Green Mountain itself is a large plateau 6,000 feet high, where Mediterranean agriculture flourishes with vineyards, orchards and market gardening. The highest spike of this awesome mountain is 10,194 feet high to be precise, and it can be quite chilly up there in the early morning. The steepest slope, smooth and straight and upright, faces the sea. Split in two gigantic heaps by the wide valley of Wadi Sumayl, this freakish outcrop is made up of two types of rock, limestone in the north and unyielding volcanic lava in the south.

In the north facing the Gulf of Oman, is a vast plain known as the Batinah, literally the flat underbelly. Never more than twenty miles wide, it is blessed with a great number of wadis which trickle down from the rainy heights of the Hajar, and of which Hawasina and Jizzi are the two most important, as they also provide a useful thoroughfare to the other side of the mountains, to Ibri and the famous oasis of Buraimi. This crucial spot, as the centre of the oil dispute of the 1950s, was eventually to trigger off the Jebel War.

As most wadi water evaporates in the infernal heat of summer, innumerable wells have been drilled, whose complicated rope and pulley tackle was formerly operated by blind oxen. Nowadays you can hear the throbbing pulse of the pumps thudding all over the Batinah, sustaining the banana groves and plantations of fig, olive, mango, pomegranate and citrus fruit. The coastline, which is hot and clammy, is lined with gleaming white coral beaches on to which giant turtles heave their ponderous corpulences to lay their eggs in the dunes. Date palms, all 600,000 of them, fringe the shore and shade the fishermen's huts and villages, all of which are covered by a permanent film of white coral dust.

Half-way up this sweeping coastline is the main town of Sohar, the original home of Sindbad the Sailor, and described by historians as 'one of the most splendid cities of the Islamic world'. In days gone by, everybody knew about Sohar. An Arabian author wrote: 'There is no town in the world where merchants are wealthier than here, and all commodities from east, west, south and north are brought to this town, and from there carried to different places.' A prosperous international population of Persians, Syrians, Jews, Chinese and Indians lived in sturdy, handsome houses of brick, mortar and best Malabar teak. Trading in spices and other luxuries from India and the Far East, merchants would take a break on their way to India south of the Straits of Hormuz, loading up in readiness for the long voyage. On the way back, and before confronting the hazards of the Turbulent Straits, they would call in again, and no doubt leave behind a good deal of their accumulated wealth. From East Africa came hides, spices, tortoise shell, ivory, peacocks and slaves, by way of Zanzibar. The Omani merchants, who outnumbered all the rest, traded with Madagascar, Bombay and China. Surrounded by their accumulated treasures, these dazzling princes of commerce dispensed lavish hospitality in their opulent homes. The affluent city was full of mosques of great splendour, whose jewelled domes, sparkling in the sun, could be seen from miles around. The fort, built to protect the town in her golden age and which still stands today, has been many times destroyed and rebuilt, by the Persians and Portuguese and by the Omanis themselves. And after the fall of Muscat and Matrah in the early eighteenth century, the gallant fortress of Sohar was the only one which stood up to the Persian invaders of the time.

South of Muscat come the Plain of Sharqyia, and the Wahiba Sands, a vast arid stretch of desert through which roam Bedu tribes of uncertain loyalties. Umm as-Samim, the Mother of Salt, which lies to the east of the Empty Quarter, is an area of treacherous quicksands, into which herds of goats and stray camels have often disappeared, never to be seen again. The dreaded Duru of the Dhahira desert claim to be the only tribes to know the way through to the other side. Beyond the Qara mountain range in which fierce, independent tribes still live in caves, the province of Dhofar is the only part of Oman which enjoys the benefits of tropical monsoons. From June till September the entire countryside disappears behind an impenetrable fog as dense as any good old-fashioned London pea-souper, and the ocean waves pound the beaches like gigantic battering rams. When all this fury finally abates, the sere brown slopes of the Qara range have turned bright emerald-green, and the tribes and their cattle once more grow sleek and fat. The south-west frontier separates Dhofar from the People's Democratic Republic of Yemen, which kept the Jebel War going for eleven years by terrorizing and arming the mountain tribes of the Qara range.

Because of the rather vague boundaries along the Empty Quarter, it is difficult to estimate the size and population of Oman, but it is thought to be about 82,000 square miles, with 750,000 inhabitants, one-third of whom live on the Batinah Plain.

Not far off the coast of Dhofar are the Kuria Muria Islands which one of the Sultans graciously presented to Queen Victoria and which are not much use to anyone, except for one of them which supports about one hundred souls who, at the time of the previous Sultan, had been condemned to spend their lives in boxes for murdering a British sailor shipwrecked on their shores. The island of Masirah is used as an air force base by the Ministry of Defence and, since time immemorial, by the great sea-turtles of the Indian Ocean as a nursery for their young. This had already come to the notice of the anonymous explorer and author of that incomparable mariner's log-book, *The Peryplus of the Erythrean Sea*. In his day, round about the first century A.D., great banks of oysters were uncovered at low tide, assiduously visited by pearl fishermen. Growing less and less lucrative as time passed, this occupation trickled on until the 1960s, but has now come to a complete end. However, the long ribbons of purple jellyfish which he described still float dangerously on the surface of the sea, burning the skin like acid if they get a chance. And Portuguese men-of-war, descendants of those long-gone first-century ones, continue to arrive in great flotillas after a storm, while at night, glowing with orange phosphorescent plankton, the waves breaking on the shore explode like fireworks, just as they did at the time of that sharp-eyed sailor who never missed a thing.

3 Imams and Invasions

Standing on the balcony at 6 a.m. just before the sun comes out of the eastern sea, looking west towards the dark magenta peaks of the Hajar range, you feel you could reach right back into the dimmest past, to the days when Arabia was a seething cauldron of life, with wave after wave of humanity flooding towards the north in search of living space and fertile acres.

Round about 3500 B.C., owing to a sudden population explosion, the first of these human tidal waves is supposed to have flowed northward towards the Fertile Crescent, splitting off into tribal bands and fanning out, some towards the Nile valley, others heading for the river Jordan, and a third group making for Mesopotamia. From the huge melting-pot of Asian and African tribes who all spoke the same language came the original Semitic race from whom the Arabs and the Jews originally emerged.

The north-western group mixed with the already settled populations of the Nile valley and is thought to have produced the intricate and sophisticated civilization of Ancient Egypt. Semitic Akkad, the oldest language known, probably developed at that time. Then came the second large tidal wave, about a thousand years later, to settle along the banks of the Jordan and become known as the Canaanites. The Amorites annexed what is now Syria and Lebanon, while a splinter group got swallowed up by the emerging Mesopotamian culture, which gradually grew into the Babylonian and Assyrian civilizations. The third movement of population (about 1500 B.C.) became the Phoenicians, the Aramaeans and the Hebrews. In 500 B.C. came the Palmyrans and the Nabateans, all hatching out of the same fertile womb of Arabia. And that pretty well wraps it all up as far as this particular theory goes.

But there is another view. Some historians claim that the Fertile Crescent was already well established at the time, having been colonized long before by a mixed bag of traders, seafarers, pirates and assorted adventurers from the Indus Valley, which appears to have been inhabited even earlier. This most ancient of civilizations would have crept slowly westward, towards northern Oman and Persia, the Gulf States and Dilmun, which we now call Bahrain, and finally drifted towards the land of the Tigris and the Euphrates rivers.

One way or another, they were bound to come through. Blessed with the inborn genius of the Semitic races, success was inevitable. Agriculture was enthusiastically supported by the balmy climate of the Fertile Crescent, and the diligently husbanded land provided bountiful supplies of meat, fruit and vegetables for the great merchant cities of Memphis, Babylon, Nineveh and Ur of the Chaldees. These rich and powerful towns became trading centres for caravans from Asia and Africa, whose untold riches spread all over Europe through the fairs and market towns of the land.

It is only since 1971, when the Historical Society was founded by British residents in Muscat under the guidance of an enlightened and very active Department of Information and Culture, that knowledge about Oman's past began to emerge and be gathered together. This now forms a body of ascertained facts; but these only skim the surface of this secretive country's past, all wrapped up as it is in deliberate mystery since time immemorial. Though friendly on the surface, the people jealously keep their secrets from prying foreign eyes. There are customs, now illegal, which are still practised in the darkest depths of damp and dripping caves in inland Oman, for instance the auctioning of living souls, which used to take place in public in the *souqs*, and is now condemned by law. The auctioneer, standing on a palm log, would knock down a number of souls to the highest bidder. When the buyer's price was accepted, the unhappy owner of the bartered soul, who knew nothing of what was going on, was fetched from his hut and, from that moment on, became the property of his buyer. A rumour recently went round the *souq* of an inland town that a party of these auctioned souls had been redeemed by the Government and brought back from distant Dhofar, and were returning to their homes and families. The entire population turned out and lined the streets to welcome them back.

Certain other freakish customs still linger on among the more primitive tribes. The Jebel people of the southern province of Dhofar, a mysterious non-Semitic race of uncertain ancestry who still live in caves in the mountains, continue to practise female circumcision; this act is perpetrated upon baby girls by their very own mothers at birth. Branding, blood-feuds, witchcraft murders, the killing of unfaithful wives – all these violent customs, and many more, still flourish in spite of unceasing efforts on the part of the Government. It is to be hoped that education, once it begins to seep through, will eradicate a great many of these ills.

Recent finds of copper deposits in northern Oman make it probable that this was the mythical land of Magan mentioned in cuneiform tablets dating from 2000 B.C. and dug up in Babylonian excavations. When Cyrus the Great and his Persian host swept into Oman for the first time in 536 B.C. it was known as Mazun, or Magan. Some say that the people of those days were Cushites, of Hamitic origin, who laid out the intricate web of caravan routes, and built the first seafaring ports. An unknown horde of obscure origin, but supposed to have issued from western Asia in late Pleistocene times, they flocked into Arabia, which was then a lush and fertile valley, well watered by innumerable streams cascading down from the central mountain range. An early poem described it as:

A goodly land,
A land abounding in fields and groves
With pastures and unfailing springs.

But Ptolemy took a different view, depicting it sourly as 'an arid and inhospitable country, a violent and cruel country peopled by inhabitants as violent and cruel as their home'. His visit was obviously not a success.

Right down the centuries plucky, enterprising globe-trotters such as Pliny, Marco Polo, Ibn Battuta and others of their ilk, had landed on the coasts of Oman, pushed inland and reported on what they had seen and heard. In the sixth century B.C. Herodotus quoted the belief of some cultured citizens of the time who thought the Phoenicians had emigrated from the Erythrean Sea to the Mediterranean, where they set up the trading activities which made their name. The tomb of King Erythras, if he ever did exist, is supposed to be on the Island of Hormuz at the entrance to the Gulf, thus giving rise to the name Erythrean (Red) Sea, which in those days included the western part of the Indian Ocean, the Persian Gulf and the Red Sea itself.

Not being of Semitic stock, the tribes of Dhofar look very different from the people of the north, and many of them have Danakil, Somali or Egyptian characteristics. A great number of flints found in the plain south of the Qara range denote an already advanced Stone-Age culture. Dating back to 5000 B.C., the tiny surfaces chipped from the flints show that the workmen of the time already had pretty good mastery over their craft. These stones, collected by Brigadier Colin Maxwell, are now on permanent display in the National Museum of Oman.

When the civilization of North Yemen, having had its rich and glorious day, began to go downhill, the great dam at Marib which had always been maintained in perfect condition gradually began to decay. There were no longer enough public funds to keep it in the condition to which it was accustomed and so the dam silted up, and sluice-gates and overflows became clogged with mud and weeds, and cracks began to appear in the masonry. Instead of these being promptly repaired as in the prosperous past, the cracks were allowed to widen and the faults proliferated. Eventually one terrible day, the fates struck, and the great wall collapsed beneath the enormous weight of accumulated water. Whole towns and villages were washed away, and the golden, thriving civilization of Sheba was annihilated in a few hours.

Made homeless by this catastrophe, many of the surviving tribes, gathering up what they could salvage from the disaster, found their way into Oman and Dhofar. But according to legend, it was a question of honour which drove Sheikh Malik bin Fahm out of his native land of Yemen and brought him into Oman at the head of his tribe. Most people will tell you that the bursting of the great dam dispersed the surviving tribes in all directions, and that Oman got its share of refugees in that way. But that is definitely not how it was with Sheikh Malik. He was a proud man. When one of his nephews was accused of spearing a tribesman's dog to death, the sheikh decided he couldn't go on living in a land where he had been so grievously insulted. Where exactly the insult lay is not easy to make out, but Malik was in no doubt that unbearable loss of face had been incurred. So off he set, followed by a faithful group of friends and sympathizers. On and on they plodded across the desert, until they reached the goodly land of Magan.

When finally they reached Nizwa, at the end of their long trek, they were, not surprisingly, a little put out to find a Persian *marzaban* already installed as governor of the area, which he ruled from its capital city of Sohar. So Malik pressed on to Qalhat with his followers, and from there sent a firm message to the *marzaban*, informing him of his arrival and his decision to settle in the country, adding that he would kindly allow the Persians to remain in the land as long as they behaved themselves and gave no trouble. But should they prove to be a nuisance, then he, Malik, wouldn't hesitate to throw them into the sea.

Outraged by this insolence from an unknown tribal chieftain suddenly emerging from the wilderness, the *marzaban* summoned his trusty warriors, harnessed his elephants and generally prepared for battle. His host set off, 40,000 strong, all gleaming in their armour, with gay pennants fluttering in the breeze and a great clanking of pikes, swords and lances, scrambling helter-skelter along the dry course of Wadi Jizzi, and pitched their camp at Salut outside Nizwa. Quite unimpressed by this glittering array, the rousing warlike figure of

Malik, in scarlet tunic and yellow turban twined around his helmet, led his faithful 6,000 into battle. With their arrows and their spears they made short shrift of the foe, and soon had the panic-stricken Persian elephants stampeding and trampling all over their own side.

The fierce and bloody mêlée lasted for three long days, at the end of which Malik suggested that he and the *marzaban* should fight it out in hand-to-hand single combat. Tired out and a little dazed, the Persian agreed. A space was cleared for the combatants, and they set to, swords flashing, whirring, and striking sparks off each other's blades. Inspired by the consciousness of his own right, Malik whacked his enemy about the head until his brains were exposed for all to see. At the sight of this the Persians lost their heads and sued for peace. Gathering up their dead and wounded, they hobbled back to Sohar to lick their wounds. The Arabs galloped home to Qalhat with glorious tales to tell their wives.

To this day the Yemenis claim descent from Malik, and the rivalry between them and the Nizari, who came later from the north, has never let up. In Izki, one of the oldest towns in Oman, one district is called Yemen and another, Nizar.

After Malik's reign which went on for seventy years, the Yemenis withdrew into the interior, known as Oman Proper, where they proceeded to lead their own independent lives without outside interference.

Legend apart, there is little doubt that early tribal migrations occurred, from both the north and the south. Some hold that Shem, Noah's eldest son, had a couple of descendants named Qahtan and Adnan, and that Qahtan started off the line of true Arabs, or *al-Aribah*, in the south, while Adnan begot the *al-muta-Aribah*, the 'Arabized Arabs', of the north. From these two branches of Arab blood have come all the fighting and feuding and raiding and senseless hatred which has led to all the internal wars until quite recent times. A further rift occurred in the eighteenth century, splitting the tribes into two more rival factions, the Hinawi and the Ghafiri. On the whole, although not invariably, the Hinawi tribes are southern Arabs (Yemeni, Qahtani), while the Ghafiri tend to come from the north (Adnani, Nizari). But all kinds of changes have occurred to complicate the issue. Whole tribes renounce their own side and move over to the opposition, for reasons known only to themselves, so that the confusion is mind-blowing. However, in Oman, every child big enough to understand knows whether he is Ghafiri or Hinawi and knows which tribes are at one another's throats at any given time.

The main Ghafiri tribe in Oman, the Beni Ryiam of Tanuf and Birkat al Mawz, 15,000 strong, are mostly settled on the plateau at the top of Jebel Akhdar and around the foot of the mountain, and many of them are in Nizwa, Izki and Mutti. The latter two towns, together with their capital Tanuf, were flattened by the Sultan's air force in the Jebel rebellion of the 1950s. Bahla, Nizwa, Hamra, all main towns of the interior, are part of the real Oman. Awabi and Rostaq on the ocean side of the Jebel also consider themselves as belonging to this exclusive inner sanctum. Closer to the great mountain are other crucial towns and villages: Ghafat of the Beni Hina tribes, Hamra and Misfah of the Abryin, traditional enemies of the Beni Ryiam from Tanuf and Birkat al Mawz. All these towns and villages, which successfully kept both foreigners and the coastal rulers at bay for so many centuries, and still fiercely independent to this day, also think of themselves as descendants of the true, original, uncorrupted tribes. All of them are Ibadhi, Hinawi or Ghafiri, Yemeni or Nizari. This is the territory where the imams reigned supreme for 900 years.

Since the Prophet had no son, there was a problem of succession at his death. His followers elected his father-in-law, Abu Bakr, as the first caliph. All went well for a time, until a rift occurred. There were those who took the words of Muhammad literally; they were the establishment of Islam, the Sunni. The less fanatical Shi'a, on the other hand, claimed the Prophet's daughter as their own sectarian ancestor. These different ways of looking at the teachings of Muhammad have caused endless religious strife, with each side convinced of being in the right.

When Ali, the fourth caliph, was in power, a sect who called themselves Kharijites, or Seceders, broke away from the main body of Islam. Their complaint was that the true principles of the Faith were being neglected. After a year of troubles, Ali managed to exterminate them in a bloody battle in 658 A.D.. What he didn't realize was that a couple of them had escaped the massacre and found their way to central Oman. There they settled, and within quite a short time the more dominant of the two refugees, named Abdallah al Ibadh, had managed to convert the local tribes to the new Kharijite outlook. This was exactly what the fanatical, inward-looking tribes of Oman Proper needed. They took it up at once with passionate fervour. The new sect insisted on electing their own imams and refused to accept the claim of Muhammad's tribe to go on ruling as a birthright. The imam was elected for his personal qualities alone. If for some reason the tribes no longer approved of him, they withdrew their support and he had to stand down. If no one else was suitable, the post could quite well remain in abeyance until a worthy candidate appeared. There has actually been a period of sixty years going by quite happily without an imam at all; on another occasion there were two, ruling as rivals. Then again, there was an imam of Oman and a Sultan of Muscat and Oman at one and the same time.

The Ibadhis believe in judgement through their own actions. This, but for one saving clause, would be pretty discouraging, particularly as there is no forgiveness for such trespasses as murder, fornication, sodomy, bestiality, perjury, usury, slander, robbing orphans or repudiating old parents. Fortunately when all is said and done, the Ibadhis recognize the fact that it is not really up to men at all to decide who shall and who shall not be saved. It is up to God to choose his own in the end.

Another belief of the Ibadhis is that the Koran and the Hadith should be applied and not interpreted by the imam. The Koran is not just a set of spiritual rules, but a penal code and a guide for the conduct of daily life. Most Arabs follow it scrupulously and, unlike Westerners, actually *want* to be seen practising their religion. So wherever they happen to be, on the back of a truck, in an airport waiting-room or hotel lounge, down on their knees they go, touching their foreheads to the ground, facing what they hope to be Mecca.

The law of the land is based on Ibadhi interpretation of Sharia, the sum total of the rules laid down in the Koran, together with the Sunna (precepts decreed by the Prophet and early caliphs). Jurisdiction is administered by the *qadhi* of a *wilaet* in conjunction with the *wali* (governor) or, in the case of a major criminal offence, or an appeal by one of the parties, the verdict is given by a court of four *qadhis* (judges) of equal rank in Muscat. Final authority rests with the Sultan. A tribal sheikh can give judgement in personal matters but not in legal offences.

Imams have existed since the beginning of Islam. Julanda bin Masud, who was the first to be elected by Ibadhi tribes, was duly massacred during an invasion of Oman launched by the first Abbasid caliph, who called himself the Blood Shedder. So that no one should be in any doubt as to his intentions, he invited his councillors to a feast spread upon the freshly severed heads of his latest prisoners. He was a larger-than-life character who could never resist posturing and showing off, both to himself, and to everybody else. To this end he used every means within his reach, including the most refined forms of torture and cruelty. His successors were no better. Of the nineteen Abbasid caliphs who came after him, nine were murdered, such was their unpopularity. Poor Oman under their régime suffered bitterly from constant invasions. Even the famous Haroun al-Rashid did his best to eliminate the Ibadhis and bring back the orthodox Sunni sect of Islam. Having done their utmost to break the fiercely independent spirit of the tribes by murder and fearful torture and brutality, the invading forces of the great Haroun were finally defeated near Sohar by the Omanis whose frantic resistance was backed by desperation.

Clad from head to foot in the new chain mail which had recently come into fashion, the next invading force was commanded by the governor of Bahrain, well known for his particularly horrifying brand of cruelty. The imam was captured and his head cut off and dispatched to Bahrain for public display. In Nizwa, this monster lopped off the hands and ears and plucked out the eyes of the nobility. In order to torment the rest of the population and cause as much havoc as possible, he wrecked the *falaj* (irrigation) system and burned the holy books.

After all this, the sorrowing land of Oman was subjected

to the tyranny of the Carmathians, a radical sect from lower Iraq, whose weird religious tenets had been eagerly taken up by Bahrain. Their hordes had overrun Syria and Iraq and stormed Mecca, where they massacred 30,000 faithful, leaving the corpses to rot in the streets.

Having gone through several centuries of unremitting adversity, Oman found it impossible to settle down to a humdrum existence again. Their next seven imams turned out to be no good and had to be deposed. This was followed by sixteen more in a row, all elected and dismissed in one year.

It was about the middle of the twelfth century when the Nebhanian kings, a Qahtani tribe supposedly descended from Malik, managed to impose their dynasty and rule the country. Apart from bringing the mango tree over from India, very little is known about them. They appear to have been tyrants, amassing riches for themselves and oppressing the people. Thoroughly disillusioned, the tribes finally rose up against them and managed to overthrow the despots. (It was a descendant of these kings, Suleiman bin Himyar, calling himself Lord of the Green Mountain, who joined the imam's rebellion against the Sultan in 1953, and held the top of the Jebel Akhdar, which became an arsenal for arms and ammunition coming from abroad, to be used for many years against the Sultan's Armed Forces.)

Early in the fifteenth century a new imam was eventually elected after the downfall of the dreaded Beni Nebhan; by confiscating all the belongings of the fallen kings, he did his best to compensate those who had suffered at the hands of the grasping dynasty.

One of the most important things to remember about this remarkable land of Oman is its passionate dedication to self-rule and absolute independence, and its hatred of foreign domination. Therefore, when the caliphate insisted on the people paying the usual tax, and mounted ten invasions over 200 years to enforce it, the tribes, which were usually at loggerheads with one another, drew together to defend both their faith and their freedom. They saw no reason for supporting the distant caliphs, with whom they had nothing whatsoever in common and who only wanted to get at their money. The *zakat* (the official religious tax), is paid on produce grown on land watered by wells to the tune of five per cent and, when watered by *falaj*, ten per cent.

After Oman had become converted to Islam, the Persians who occupied the land were still happily practising their own religion. It was at the fortress of Jemsetjerd, where they had taken refuge from his pursuing forces, that the Prophet's envoy, Amr bin al-As, finally cornered them. He decided that the time had come for these dissenters to give up their pagan beliefs and join Islam like everybody else, but with them he was less lucky. As they had a perfectly satisfactory faith of their own in the Zoroastran persuasion, he had a problem and the only way he could cope with it was to slaughter a great number of them for their stubbornness. Those who got away took refuge in the fortress, where the envoy and his followers besieged them with single-minded determination. Having eventually run out of food and water, they were forced to surrender, and he allowed them to escape with their lives on condition that they left all their gold and silver behind. After this coup, the envoy, 'a man of subtle intellect', pursued his persuasive course to Syria and Egypt, with equal success.

It is difficult to establish any definite historical facts for the years between the reign of Malik and the conversion of the tribes to Islam. Even the Omani epic *Kashf al-Gummah* is rather vague on the subject. But it is generally agreed that, during the period 200–600, the Azdite tribes, Malik's descendants of Qahtan stock, the Nebhan dynasty of Yemeni origin, ruled the interior known as al-Jauf, and the Persians remained on the coast, with Sohar as their capital. Al-Jauf covered the area from Bahla to Izki, taking in the gigantic natural fortress of Jebel Akhdar, the Sumayl valley, and Rostaq on the other side of the mountain.

When the country was finally converted (it didn't all happen in one day), the tribes of the interior, fiercely individualistic as they were, insisted on having their own form of the new faith. Hemmed in on three sides by the sea and a combination of immense deserts and impassable mountains, they were totally unaffected by outside influences. To this day they have remained unchanged, perfectly happy to carry on as they are without interference from anywhere, especially the corrupt world of the coastal areas with its more outward-looking way of life. For this reason, until quite recently, the country was always referred to as Muscat and Oman.

4 Hinawi and Ghafiri

The dark ages of Oman which set in at the beginning of the tenth century, when the kings of Nebhania managed to impose their dynasty, lasted until the first al-Yaarubi imam, Nasim bin Murshid, was elected in Rostaq in 1624. His pedigree ended with 'al-Yaarubi, al-Arabi, al-Himyiari, al-Azdi, al-Yamani, the Upright Ibadhi'. He belonged to one of the oldest tribes which had arrived from Yemen in Malik's wake, 1,500 years earlier.

As a shrewd political and military leader, he saw immediately that Oman's troubles were largely due to the perpetual internal squabbles, and that the only way to unite the touchy tribal chiefs was to give them a common cause. As the curse of Portuguese tyranny was in full spate at the time, he hit on a 'death to the foreigner' theme, and the fulfilment of this purpose became the main object of his life.

Throughout history, the Gulf has fascinated navigators of all the great empires who were drawn to it like a magnet. Sumerians, Akkadians, Babylonians, Greeks, Persians, Portuguese, Dutch, French, Russians, Turks and Britons, all have come on voyages of exploration and discovery along its shores. Already, in 694 B.C., Sennacherib had found it necessary to clear the area of pirates who lay in wait for inquisitive explorers.

The Portuguese who arrived in the sixteenth century did not just come to look around. Settling down in the coastal towns, they instituted a rule of terror, humiliation and systematic torture which was the greatest scourge that Oman has ever known.

When the Ottoman Turks captured Constantinople in A.D. 1453, many of the old trade routes from Europe to India and the East Indies disappeared in the resettling of the vastly expanded Turkish empire, and new routes had to be found. Owing to this disruption, it became necessary for the Portuguese explorers and adventurers to set off in other directions and eventually they found their way to the East African coast and the Gulf of Oman. Pedro Cabal was the first of their navigators to call in at the prosperous Arab colony of Kilwa, one of the richest and most beautiful cities in the world, famous for its silver and gold, its pearls, amber and musk.

After sailing round the Cape, Vasco da Gama arrived next, to terrorize the inhabitants into paying tribute to the king of Portugal. Before they could even protest, he stepped in with his own methods. The sailors he encountered on arrival had their hands, noses and ears cut off, then were piled into boats with their bleeding hands hanging around their necks. Their feet were tied together and, in case they chewed the ropes with their teeth, these were pushed down their throats with pikes and sword hilts. The boats were then fired and driven out to the open sea, a great living, flaming torch. When they saw him coming – his reputation had gone on ahead of him – the inhabitants of the coast of Coromandel came out to meet him. In the hope of saving their lives, they begged to be baptized. After their wish had been granted, they were strangled on the spot and thrown into the sea.

After him came Dom Francisco de Almeida in 1505. He and his vicar-general made a pompous and ostentatious landing, preceded by their Grand Cross and surrounded by a retinue of Franciscan fathers chanting hymns. Then, with pious prayers upon their lips, they got down to the serious business of sacking the city, slaughtering the people and setting fire to their homes. Having dealt with Kilwa to their satisfaction, and proceeding to Mombasa with their fleet, they subjected it to the same treatment. Wholesale looting followed a general massacre of the entire population, down to the smallest child. In despair, the king of Mombasa wrote to his neighbour, the king of Malindi, describing the horrors committed by the Portuguese: 'The stench of the corpses is so great in the town that I dare not go there.' (It was this same conqueror who, two years later as Viceroy of India, blasted his prisoners from the barrels of cannon at Cananor.) And so the great prosperity of Mombasa and Kilwa, founded as trading centres by Oman in the tenth century, was brought to an end in a matter of a few weeks.

In 1507, Alfonso de Albuquerque led his fleet into the bay of Ras al-Hadd, south of Muscat. There he found a great many fishing dhows lying peacefully at anchor. Setting a pattern for a policy of brutality and ruthless barbarity which was to be continued in Oman for the next 150 years, he promptly set the boats on fire. After this, he pushed on to Muscat which he described as 'a very elegant town, with very fine houses'. He dealt with this elegant town in the customary Portuguese manner: the town was burnt down, including all its provisions, the boat repair yard and thirty-four ships which happened to be in harbour at the time. The pillars of the mosque were chopped down, so that the building collapsed into the raging furnace of the burning town. The prisoners he had taken, men, women and children, had their ears and noses cut off and were then set free. This was regarded by the sailors as a signal act of mercy on the part of their leader.

As the first foreign power to attack Muscat, the Portuguese regarded Oman purely as a convenient commercial undertaking and the seat of their very lucrative activities in the Indian Ocean. By the unspeakable tortures which they inflicted on the population, they hoped to subdue the desperate determination of the Omanis to remain free and be rid of their oppressors. Portuguese rule had lasted 150 years when the new imam decided to get rid of them at any cost. His efforts were entirely successful: after a lifetime of unending struggle, he had driven them from the whole country by the time he died. Although they still clung like limpets to their own fortresses of Muscat, Matrah and Sohar, they knew their days were numbered.

The Upright Ibadhi, a strong man in every way, set Oman

on a course of prosperity such as had not been seen for many centuries. After his death, his cousin, Sultan bin Saif I, took over the good work and declared a holy war against the last three enemy garrisons in the land. Mirani was the first to surrender. However, the Omanis had had enough. Only eighteen of its occupants, who accepted circumcision, were spared; the rest were put to the sword. Jalali proved a tougher proposition. However hard the imam tried, he simply couldn't manage to dislodge its residents. In the end it was a shrewd and wily merchant of Muscat named Narutem who thought up a scheme for winkling them out of the fort.

The Portuguese commandant of Jalali had fallen in love with Narutem's daughter and was finally driven by his passion into committing suicidal indiscretions. When the man's frenzy had reached boiling point and the time seemed ripe, Narutem humbly suggested spring-cleaning the fortress in preparation for the coming wedding celebrations. First of all the water tanks, which were filthy, should be emptied and scrubbed out. The rat-infested provisions should be burnt and replaced with fresh victuals, and the gunpowder, soggy from long storage in the dripping cellars, had to be renewed. As the imam's forces were also known to be approaching to set siege to Jalali, the moment seemed propitious for a complete refitting and re-stocking of the stores and the armoury. Dazed and distracted by his infatuation, the commandant happily agreed to all these measures. When the fort stood empty, Narutem informed the imam of the situation, suggesting he should attack on Sunday when the garrison's occupants, having enjoyed a copious lunch liberally reinforced with the heady wines of Portugal, would be basking in a blissful alcoholic haze. Although it all came to pass as wily old Narutem had planned, the garrison put up a surprisingly spirited counter-offensive, considering they had nothing but their side-arms with which to fight back. But they knew they hadn't a chance and, by the end of the day, Jalali was once more in Omani hands. The long, 150–year reign of terror had come to an end; and nothing has ever been as bad as that since then.

Having finally got rid of the Portuguese, Imam Sultan bin Saif's next move was to start rebuilding the country. Nizwa fort, that gigantic pile of masonry which still stands almost untouched by time, took twelve years to finish. The collapsed *falaj* system between Izki and Nizwa was then put back into running order. Horse-breeding, for which Oman became renowned at the time, was encouraged, and horses were exported to India in great numbers. Oman became rich and prosperous. Alas, this state of affairs soon came to an end after the Imam's death, when his son Bilarab, who succeeded him, was set upon by his brother Saif bin Sultan, who considered he ought to be imam himself. The usual inter-tribal feuds followed with all their accustomed savagery. During these fearful succession wars, Saif became known as the Scourge, and Bilarab as the Butcher. A great number of innocent people were drawn into the bloodbath, and the newly restored *falaj* system suffered another setback.

It is amazing to think that such a bloodthirsty brigand as Bilarab could have had the delicacy of feeling and the artistic talent essential for conceiving and building a lovely edifice like Jabrin Castle. Although powerful and imposing and quite able to defend itself, Jabrin nevertheless has, with its mullioned windows, its turrets and its trellised balconies, the unmistakable look of a Renaissance palace. It was here, in despair, that Bilarab sought refuge when he realized that his brother was going to succeed. Finally defeated in his own fort, he prayed for death and his wish was speedily granted. To this day he lies there, peacefully mouldering away in his grave.

When Mombasa asked Oman for help against the Portuguese who, though evicted from Muscat, still held sway on the East African coast, Saif bin Sultan sent a fleet of dhows and warships to lay siege to Fort Jesus. Saif had nominated himself imam after his brother's most convenient death.

The beleaguered garrison of Fort Jesus, decimated by the plague, nevertheless held out doggedly for another thirty-three months. When it finally surrendered, only a handful of the original 2,300 were left. From then on, Saif proceeded to make amends for all the misery he had caused while engaged in appropriating power and hunting down his brother. Trade and business received substantial help. Once more the *falaj* network, the lifeblood of the land, was restored, giving an immediate shot in the arm to agriculture which came into its own for the first time. The great houses of the new merchant class proved an avid market. Along the coast of the Batinah, Saif planted extensive gardens of date and coconut palms, which have been kept going to this day. Consequently, his own private fortune prospered, and when he died in Rostaq in 1711, he owned 700 slaves, twenty-eight ships and one-third of the date plantations of the country.

Now that the principle of hereditary succession was firmly established by the new dynasty, Saif's son Sultan inherited the imamate. With his strong navy which had to be kept occupied, he roamed the seas, captured Bahrain and raided the Portuguese settlements on the Indian coast; and his fleet gradually acquired a reputation for lawless piracy. With the plunder from all these activities he built the great fort at Hazm, in which he chose to die. His son, aged twelve, and naturally called Saif bin Sultan (since Arabs always alternate the names of father and son) was his obvious successor, now that the hereditary principle had been established. Things which had been going so well until then now went back to normal. The usual anarchy and tribal wars promptly started up again, this time in the shape of a savage Hinawi–Ghafiri civil war, which was to bring the Yaariba dynasty and the age of prosperity to an end.

The civil war of Oman, with its endless Grand Guignol interludes, ranks as one of the major melodramas in the history of the Middle East. The great rift between the Hinawi and the Ghafiri tribes occurred in the early eighteenth century. Very roughly, the division was Yemeni-Ibadhi-Hinawi, the descendants of Malik, of Qahtan stock, and Nizari-Sunni-Ghafiri, of Adnan descent. According to legend, a certain Mohammed bin Nasir al-Ghafiri, from Bahla, who had set forth to pay homage to the newly elected Hinawi Imam, was badly treated on arrival and retired in a huff, determined to wipe out the insult received at the hands of the Hinawi. The actual truth is probably that Mohammed bin Nasir had set his heart on the imamate himself, only to find his move had been anticipated by his Hinawi rival. Getting his Beni Ghafir tribes together, Mohammed declared war on the new imam's tribal forces; this was the beginning of the great civil war of

1722, which has split the tribes into two rival factions ever since.

It was obvious that a boy aged twelve couldn't possibly rule over Oman. But for some reason the tribes had taken a fancy to him, and foolishly wanted to see him set up as imam. The *Ulema* (the Elders), who wisely wanted to see their own candidate, Muhanna, nominated, smuggled him into the fort at Rostaq, and there they proclaimed him imam. Muhanna was obviously a good choice and he got down to work, helping trade and fostering exports. The country was beginning to pick up again. But behind the scenes lurked the discontented son of Bilarab, who had died of a broken heart at Jabrin after being defeated by Muhanna's father, Imam Sultan. This resentful young man, Yarub bin Bilarab, couldn't abide the sight of his cousin ruling as imam, so basely murdered him and somehow managed to get himself elected instead. Having achieved this, he went off to Nizwa, taking young Saif, now deposed, with him.

Enter the Beni Hina tribe. Convinced that the boy Imam Saif had been dispossessed, they attacked and captured Rostaq – one wonders why not Nizwa, which was at the time harbouring the two heroes of the drama. Again for reasons which I fail to understand, the new Imam Yarub had to resign, and the boy Saif was elected for the second time. Unbelievably, Yarub then became his regent. The Beni Hina tribes, having engineered this coup, were happy with the outcome. Not so the Ghafiri faction, who now assumed that the Hinawi would henceforth be unduly favoured and promptly rose up in arms. The Ghafiri marched on Nizwa, finally catching up with Yarub at Firq, where they attacked him. Not wishing to make too much of it, he graciously withdrew, and the boy Saif was proclaimed imam once more, this time with the blessings of the Ghafiri.

You would be justified in thinking that everybody would be satisfied by now. In fact, this was far from the case. All the scrapping and feuding had had its effect; the tribes, having sniffed the heady smell of gunpowder, were thoroughly roused and not at all prepared to give up so easily. The Hinawi, now considering the imam to have been kidnapped by the Ghafiri, captured Muscat and Barka. In reply, the Ghafiri attacked

41

Barka, with a horde of some 15,000, while the Hinawi wheeled towards the coast and captured Rostaq and Sohar. The Ghafiri now gained control of the Sharqyia province south of Muscat, and from there they pushed on to the Batinah coast.

When eventually the leader of the Ghafiri, Mohammed bin Nasir al-Ghafiri, decided he had had enough and wanted to resign his post as the imam's new regent, the *Ulema* not only turned down his resignation, but promptly proclaimed him imam. At this point Mohammed suffered a character change: from a normal man, no better or worse than anybody else, he suddenly turned into a savage beast. Young Saif was taken hostage, and Yarub was put in irons and forced to hand over the keys of all his forts. At Rostaq, Mohammed's warriors behaved like fiends, inflicting unspeakable tortures on the women and children trying to escape from them.

Mohammed established his headquarters at Jabrin and ruled Oman from there. He took part in all the raids and imposed terrible sufferings on all those who dared to oppose him, chopping off ears, noses, limbs, and burning out eyeballs for the slightest reason, and sometimes for his own sadistic pleasure alone. For five years he carried on in this atrocious manner until, to everybody's relief, he was killed by a bullet outside Sohar, where his enemy, the Hinawi leader, also lost his life. At one stroke the country was delivered from the two abominable despots.

Young Saif, who had been the cause of all this terrible blood-letting, was not worth the candle after all and his feeble rule enraged the tribes, who rose up against him. In self-protection, the young imam called in the help of the Persians. Delighted, they made straight for Muscat which they had always coveted anyway. Using Hannibal's old trick, they tied lighted faggots to the horns of goats, which they then let loose on the heights surrounding the town. The inhabitants, thinking this was the foe, rushed out to meet them. Meanwhile the Persians, swarming in from behind, easily overran the empty and undefended town. However, led by a useless and incompetent officer, they failed to capture the key points of Mirani and Jalali. Eventually they retired to Sohar, which they also ignominiously had to abandon.

A great many of the solid achievements of the Yaariba

dynasty were destroyed by both sides in this senseless war. The *falaj* system was wrecked once more, so that agriculture inevitably declined and, as is usual in times of war, it was the poor and the humble people who bore the brunt of it all.

5 The Isle of Zanj

Lush, exotic, exuberant and a blaze of flamboyant colour, the roots of Zanzibar were laboriously put down over a period of millions of years by untold generations of the tiny coral worm which breeds in the warm tropical waters of the Indian Ocean.

As the largest coral island off the east coast of Africa, it is also one of the most attractive, with its miles of white sandy beaches edged with coconut plantations easing their way down to the shore, and groves of banana trees lazily flapping their heavy gleaming fronds in the sea breezes. Although the island lies in a very hot zone, a constant wind blowing off the sea keeps its temperature just bearably off the boil. Visitors from the West sometimes describe it as humid and sluggish, but the local population find it very much to their taste. Nobody in this kind of climate can be expected to work too hard, and life is conducted at a gentle, leisurely pace.

In Zanzibar (from Zanj, a Persian word for Negro, and bar, a coast) the people, though dark of skin, can hardly be described as true Negroes. Waves of immigration and invasions have each added their influence: Persians from Shiraz, a restless lot always on the move (you find them on top of Jebel Akhdar as well), Omani Arabs, the Bantus from Africa. As the latter have certain Hamitic features in their make-up,

Negro blood is far from being the main ingredient in the mixture. Of the original inhabitants, the Watumbatu, the Wapemba and the Wahadim, very few specimens remain on the island.

Nobody quite knows why the first attempt at growing cloves in 1801 failed – it just did. But when Said the Great arrived from Oman in 1828 with his powerful war-fleet to put down a rebellion, in spite of unexpected local resistance he had the crop growing and flourishing in no time. Also, by ordering every landowner to plant three clove trees for every coconut palm which died, he set the foundation for Zanzibar's future success and prosperity. He himself owned forty-five plantations of the valuable spice. Having taken a great liking to the island's seductive environment and balmy climate, he built himself a pleasure dome by the sea for weekends and carefree dalliance with his harem, while his headquarters for business and state occasions were in the centre of the town.

Having set up his thirteen-year-old son as governor of his East African possessions, he immediately clapped a five per cent duty on all goods landing there, thereby increasing his takings tenfold in one artful move. Sultan Said fondly described himself as 'nothing but a tradesman'.

From then on the little island grew in wealth and fame. The harbour was continually bobbing with merchantmen from the East India Company and all the great European ports, as well as the most prosperous trading centres of the Mediterranean, Syria, the Lebanon, Egypt and the Gulf. In 1839 it was the Americans who controlled trade by dumping great quantities of the traditional glass beads, and firearms, in exchange for ivory and tortoiseshell. It was they who built the first consulate on the island and after them, in descending order of popularity, came the British, the traders from Hamburg and the French.

Exports included copal, coconuts, ivory, hides, red pepper, ambergris, beeswax, hippo teeth, rhino horn (for aphrodisiacs), and blackamoors' teeth which were actually cowrie shells. But at that time the greatest profit by far came from the sale of human flesh. The streets teemed with a motley crowd of Negroes, Arabs, Indians, Persians, Swahilis, and all the various mixtures in between. The only difference between

Zanj as it was then and Zanzibar as it is now, and for that matter any other Eastern port at the present time, was the large number of slaves running wild in the streets like packs of famished wolves. They attacked, robbed and murdered anybody foolish enough to be out after dark. As for the domesticated ones who knew all the tricks, according to Alan Moorhead 'they were the laziest, the dirtiest, the most dishonest of servants'.

Five thousand of this motley crew were Arabs. Together with the Indian merchants they owned fleets of trading ships, ran the money-lending rackets, and the very profitable ivory trade. But business didn't take up all their time – in fact there was a great deal left over with which they didn't know what to do, and boredom lay heavy on their hands. So they gathered larger and more exotic harems, and they had to pep themselves up with stimulants in order to cope with the challenge. And they complained perpetually about the growing of jasmine on the island, claiming that its voluptuous scent undermined their virility, while it seemed unduly to excite the ladies. For the Europeans, it was an indolent and tedious life. Most of the men took to drink and acquired black mistresses, while their bored wives appropriated all the best Negro lovers. Living conditions were terrible. Drinking-water was polluted beyond recall, cholera was rampant and malaria flourished. V.D. was endemic and medical services unknown. Instead of being buried, the bodies of dead slaves were cast on the beaches for the dogs to feast upon, and so it is a wonder that plague didn't break out on the island. The stench everywhere was appalling. You had to be tough, both physically and mentally, to survive.

At that time Zanzibar was the greatest slave-trading centre in the world. Here, the most notorious market in the East held its gruesome daily sessions. Of the overall population of 200,000 beating hearts, 150,000 throbbed with despair in captive Negro breasts. Slavery has never borne the same obloquy in Arabia as in the West. The Eastern way of life has been based on it since time immemorial. And so were the great civilizations of Greece and Rome. The Old Testament regards it as an accepted fact. In antiquity slaves featured in every well-to-do household as a matter of course. The

Prophet, on the other hand, appears to have disapproved of the institution. Although he didn't actually forbid it, he declared that anyone who ill-treated his slave would be refused entry into Paradise, and if a man had committed a murder he could wipe out the crime by setting one of his slaves free.

Backed and encouraged by long-standing historical need, slave hunters would march inland through the Sahara into Africa from the north, along the Fezzan–Kawar route. In the east, the Arabs from Zanzibar would trek from the coast into the interior to round up carefree, unsuspecting men, women and children. Driven by spears, trapped in nets, flushed out with flaming torches, they were herded and shackled before they could realize what had happened. Under the slaver's whip and yoked by the neck, chained to one another and covered with sores, wounds and vermin and riddled with dysentery, many of them died on their feet on the long agonizing march to the coast. In 1863 David Livingstone, who was in the Lake Nyasa district, came across fearful traces of this abominable commerce, in the shape of the crumpled skeletons of those who had died, huddled under trees or crouched in their huts. The stench of death lingering in the humid tropical atmosphere was overwhelming. But to the traders this meant nothing. They knew that most of their victims would die on the way (four out of every five, according to Livingstone's guess), and so they rounded up thousands more than they needed, to cover the losses.

After this terrible trek to the coast was over, came the even worse hell of the voyage across the sea to Zanzibar. Packed in layers in the holds of the ships, many more would perish on the way for lack of air and water. The voyage, under normal circumstances, lasted fifty-eight hours, but in bad weather it could drag on for anything up to ten days. In such cases, only a handful of the poor brutes would make it, out of a consignment of perhaps four hundred.

The survivors who finally reached the market place were in a pitiful condition. Haggard, starved, diseased, half-crazed with fear, anguish and despair, they were rubbed all over with coconut oil to make them gleam with an enticing glow of bogus health. Then silver bells and jewellery were hung around their necks, wrists and ankles, to be snatched away as soon as a sale was effected. Finally, to hide the horrors beneath, the miserable wretches were painted all over in broad red and white zebra stripes.

Business would start in the late afternoon, as soon as the town roused itself from its siesta. Ringing a bell and marching at the head of his shackled human herd, each merchant would call out his wares, drawing attention to their good points. A customer would insist on putting his prospective buy through his paces: with whatever strength he had left, the slave had to run, jump, flex his muscles and bare his teeth. Snoring was considered a serious drawback, and was subject to rebate. A young man in good health would cost about £8, but girls could fetch up to £21 if well endowed and comely. Circassians, who were worth their weight in gold, never came on the market at all, but were dispatched instead to the various sultans' harems straight from the source. A rich man might easily own up to 1,000 slaves.

The Zanzibar market saw a turnover of 40,000 to 45,000 'heads' a year, on which Government tax was one dollar per slave. By the time they reached the markets of Muscat, India and Persia, the price, and the tax, had risen considerably.

After all the horrors of capture, shipping and the slave market, those who made it to Muscat could consider themselves lucky. It is very rare for a slave to be ill-treated in Oman. Lt Wellstead, exploring the country in the 1830s, reported that if a slave was not happy with his master, he could appeal to the *qadhi* and ask for a public re-sale which would always be granted. On the death of his master he would automatically be set free anyway. Remarking on the considerable humanity with which slaves were treated in Oman, Wellstead added, 'They receive a degree of consideration and kindness which is not always extended to servants in Europe.' In the past, several well-known slaves had risen to surprisingly elevated positions, such as the famous Suleiman bin Suwaylin, a trusted slave of the then sultan, who sent him to Dhofar as *wali*, after he had been a councillor and commander of the army. Suleiman had his own slaves whose devotion to their master equalled the *wali*'s loyalty to the sultan.

As slaves automatically follow in their master's religious footsteps, they are all Muslims. They may, if they so wish, dress exactly like their boss, and eat from the same plate. In Oman they say, 'A slave is the slave of his master, but otherwise as free as you are.' He may own slaves of his own and marry a free woman, in which case his children are born free. Where he does come off worse, however, is in only being allowed two wives, whereas his master can have four.

Any slave who decides to abscond, and appeals to the sultan, is allowed his freedom on the spot. And of course he is freed if he can reach the famous flagpole in the British Embassy grounds in time. Colonel Smiley, while Commander of the army, once received an escaped slave from a perplexed ambassador. Voluntarily enrolling in the ranks of the army the man, who may have been a compulsive bolter, ran away once more.

There is no longer any traffic in slaves in Oman. Those who remain were born into their estate and deliberately chose to stay in their master's household, where they are treated like sons of the family. But the practice still continues in other parts of Arabia, where plane-loads of shackled children are sometimes to be seen in pathetic huddles on desert landing-strips. Parents are usually to blame for this, in the wilder parts of Iran and Baluchistan, where they thankfully hand over an unwanted daughter in exchange for a few rupees.

Small boys are usually castrated and sold as eunuchs for the rich men's harems. The invention of this barbarous custom has been put down to Queen Semiramis who reigned in Assyria in the ninth century B.C. But this seems unlikely, as the tradition is surely as old as history. Condemned by the Prophet as an evil, the practice was horrible beyond belief: after the crude and brutal operation, the little victims were buried in the sand up to their necks, in the belief that total immobility would hasten healing. The result in most cases was septicaemia, and a slow agonizing death in the scorching heat of the sun. Out of 35,000 children thus tortured every year in a 'eunuch factory' in the Sudan, less than 4,000 survived their martyrdom. This business, which had been going on for thousands of years, only came to light, or rather to the top of humanity's conscience, in the nineteenth century.

There is nothing new in man's inhumanity to man; it is a recurring, perennial, suppurating sore. Similar atrocities are being perpetrated by some African dictators upon their own countrymen and tribesmen at this very moment.

The measures taken to abolish the vile traffic of the slave trade are too well-known to need repetition, and the name of Wilberforce in this connection brings to mind all the dedicated work he put into it. As a result of his indefatigable efforts, an Act of Parliament of 1807 made it illegal to collect or disembark slaves in any British colonies or dominions. However, before this Act, Great Britain had exported four million 'heads' a year to slave-hungry America – so let us remember the beam in our own eye before we start reviling other cultures.

After this, badgered and bullied by the British Government, full of its own new-found virtue, Sultan Said eventually agreed to stop all export of slaves to Christian countries. Sir Robert Burton remarked that 'his friendship with us cost him dear'. Although the sultan himself lost a great deal of money, as well as prestige in Oman, the trade continued to flourish, under the counter as it were, for a long time afterwards with the merchants, not the ruler, continuing to grow rich on it. The task of policing the jungles and the east coast of Africa was beyond anybody's capabilities. So, for the time being, the only tangible results were considerable loss of face for the sultan among the tribes of Oman, who took the view that he had been cleverly manipulated by the British for sinister reasons of their own, and a serious cutback in revenue, from which the country didn't recover until oil began to show its capricious head. The tragedy of Oman's collapsed economy did nothing to alleviate the hardships suffered by the wretched Africans, who were still caught by the thousand as before. The Arabs, who saw no harm in the practice, had no intention of giving up so lucrative a business and, if anything, they did better out of the restrictions, as prices inevitably went up. To make up for the diminished numbers caught, more slaves were packed into the ships than before, and five were crammed in where only two were loaded before.

When Livingstone's report on the horrors he had seen in central Africa were published, the British Government was determined to stamp out slavery at the source by making it illegal in Zanzibar itself. The new sultan, who had seen what had happened in Oman at the time of his grandfather Said the Great, was dead against the scheme. It was with the greatest difficulty, and the presence of a gunboat hovering off the coast, that he was at last persuaded to sign the abolition agreement. The slave market in Zanzibar was officially closed in June 1873, and a Christian church built upon its site.

This did not of course put an end to the evil, which continued to flourish for a considerable time, with human shiploads being landed at night, to be picked up later for transport across the Indian Ocean to their final destination.

Tippu Tib, an immensely rich merchant whose fortunes came mostly from the sale of slaves, was a cultured and very sophisticated man who owned a palatial mansion in Zanzibar. It was here that all the caravans, returning from central Africa, finally ended up. Some brought ivory, monkey skins and leopard hides, but most profitable of all were the chained gangs of suffering humanity, for whom this brutal brigand had no mercy whatever. Barbarous though he was, this schizoid monster was also a consummate host whose invitations were much sought after on the island. It was not until after his death that the slave trade began to lose its impetus in Zanzibar.

6 'I am nothing but a tradesman'
— Said the Great

The Yaarubi dynasty came to an end when Imam Saif bin Sultan II, who had been the cause of the civil war, called in a mercenary Persian force to put down his own people. And it was Ahmed bid Said, the *wali* of Sohar, who finally managed to save the situation by getting rid of them.

Ahmed was an ordinary merchant of humble origin. But his ambition was great, and his ability and personal qualities were equal to those required of a ruler. He was in fact the founder of the dynasty which is still in power today.

His first claim to fame was as Governor of Sohar, the last important town not yet in the hands of the Persian occupier. When eventually they did besiege Sohar, Ahmed gave himself up without making trouble, on condition that he should be confirmed as *wali* of Sohar and Barqa. In exchange, he undertook to pay regular tribute to the overlords in Muscat. Cunningly he let this fall into arrears, on the grounds that there was no safe way of sending the money over to the capital. The Persians, growing short of cash, soon lost many of their troops through their inability to pay their wages.

It was then, in their weakened and depleted state, that Ahmed laid on a great feast in their honour in Barqa. When his unsuspecting guests, bloated with food, were relaxing comfortably, Ahmed gave the signal, and his men fell upon the assembled company, slaughtering as many as they could. A couple of hundred survivors who escaped the bloodbath begged for mercy, and were packed into a ship bound for Persia. Catching fire by chance, the ship was burnt to a cinder and, wondrous to relate, all the Persians were roasted alive, while the Governor's guard alone survived. Nobody mourned the victims, as they had behaved little better than the Portuguese, slaughtering the inhabitants, throwing their children over cliffs, and selling their women on the slave-market at Shiraz. Having got rid of the last of the Persians, the delighted population elected Ahmed as imam. To show there was no ill-feeling, he married a daughter of the defeated foe, who bore him four lusty sons. And it was one of his grandsons, Said bin Sultan, or Said the Great, who was to rule Oman for half a century, and become the founder of Zanzibar.

Young Said was seventeen when he learned that his murder was being planned. His cousin, who was Regent at the time, was very unpopular all round on account of his sympathy with Wahhabism which was then very strong in the land. Wahhabism, which has caused Oman so many headaches, is a movement started by one Mohammed ibn Abd al-Wahhab, who was shocked to the core by the Saudis' relaxed approach to their faith in the 1740s. His tightening of the reins spread like wildfire in the fanatic Arabian breast and, by the end of the eighteenth century, it had extended over most of the peninsula. The people of Ras al-Khaima, who were overrun by the Wahhabis and embraced their tenets in 1800, regarded them more as a military power than a religious sect, which was a perfectly accurate assessment, as the movement is nothing if not a theocracy.

The difference of opinion lies between the right wing or 'high church' side of Islam, the purist element, and a more relaxed outlook, represented by the Shi'a on the other side. From these differences many of the troubles have sprung over the last 250 years.

Throughout history, Wahhabi raids from desert tribes have plagued central Oman. These periods were the only times when Omanis, who were usually scrapping furiously among themselves, clubbed together to fend off the invader. During the early part of his reign, Said was plagued by incessant incursions of this kind. Aided and abetted by the treacherous internal backing from dissident elements among the Ghafiri tribes, and encouraged to attack their enemies the Hinawi, the raiders sacked Sohar and stormed through the Sharqyia, where they managed to win over the Beni bu Ali tribes to their side. On frequent occasions the sultan had to pay them off to clear them out of the land. After a profitable raid of this kind, they would retreat to their haunts in the heart of the Nejd desert, where they roosted until ready for another sally. For many years they remained a recurrent menace.

But to return to young Said, struggling to establish his rule: when he heard that his cousin the Regent was plotting to murder him, he decided to pounce before any undesirable damage was done. In Western eyes, the story is pure bloody murder, but remains entirely justifiable to the Arabian way of thinking. 'The sovereign has a right to govern until another and stronger shall oust him from power, and rule in his stead,' is a well-known saying. No limitations are placed on the manner in which the ousting is carried out.

The Regent's country house near Barqa was the scene of the crime. They were all chatting amicably together, when Said suddenly pulled out his *khanjar* and plunged it into his cousin's breast. Badly wounded, the terrified man leapt out of the window and landed on a pile of dung, on which he broke his leg. Dragging himself along, he scrambled on to a horse and galloped away to the open country. Considering a wounded political opponent to be twice as dangerous as a hale and hearty one, Said set off at once in pursuit, followed by his accomplice. Exhausted by pain and loss of blood, the injured man was resting under a tree when they caught up with him. Between the two of them they made short work of their victim: one hacked away at him with his sword, while the other drove a lance through his heart – and that was the end of the would-be murderer of young Said. Political assassination being perfectly normal in Arabian ruling families, Said was immediately acclaimed by the populace as the liberator of his country from foreign interference. The Regent, who had encouraged the hated Wahhabis, was less than popular in his lifetime, so that nobody mourned his death.

As the first ruler to use the word 'sultan' (which means

power or authority), Said was to govern with prudence, sagacity and moderation for the following fifty-two years. Under his rule, prosperity in Oman reached its highest peak. Although very strict in his own religious observance, this broad-minded monarch tolerated all forms of faith in Muscat in the interests of trade. His infallible instinct for business led him to encourage foreign merchants from every land to settle in his capital.

Although by nature a tradesman rather than a warrior, Said was none the less frequently drawn into tiresome and inevitable wars to protect his country. At this time Muscat was first and foremost a transit port between Europe and India, and an enormous amount of shipping sailed through the Gulf. One of his main concerns had been to build up a reliable merchant navy. The fleet included dhows, dinghies and a great number of square-rigged boats. Although the sailors were an intrepid and fearless lot, their stamina and endurance were continually and severely put to the test by the Qasimi fleet of Ras al-Khaima. Their sheikh had decreed that all ships sailing through Gulf waters, either to or from India, owed him a passage tax, or toll. When the captains of trading ships indignantly refused to pay up, the Qawasim sailed out in vast numbers, attacked the ships, massacred the crews and took whatever loot was available. As it was unlawful, according to their religious beliefs, to rob living men, the victims had to be slain before the plundering could start. These ruthless pirates were helped along in their raids by the half-hearted attitude and the feeble, irresolute policy of the East India Company which forbade force being used by their captains until they were attacked, by which time it was generally too late.

It soon became obvious to all that the new Sheikh of Ras al-Khaima, who had signed an undertaking not to attack British ships and to give three months' notice if unduly pressurized by the Wahhabis to do so, was deliberately trying to keep down piracy in the Gulf. As this didn't suit the Wahhabis in the least, they soon threw him out, putting the Sheikh of Rams in his place and setting him up as vice-Regent over the entire Trucial Coast. Under this pitiless, rapacious brigand, the raids became more savage than ever. The Qasimi fleet was now a formidable armada manned by 19,000 sailors in all. These doughty warriors could not have been very different from the huge brawny lads who take part in the annual boat races in Abu Dhabi, with their shaven heads and massive chests, the shiny brown skin stretched over their mighty rippling muscles.

Twenty per cent of all the loot captured by these murderous hordes had to be dispatched to the Wahhabi command in the Nejd, from where the well-organized raids were planned against Oman. As all this aggression was going unchecked, escalation mounted merrily and, in 1804, nine British cruisers were attacked. The brig *Shannon* was captured in 1805 and its entire crew massacred. The captain, who had his arm chopped off, would undoubtedly have bled to death, had he not dipped the stump into a convenient pot of boiling ghee. By 1809 the East India Company saw they would have to change their policy and decided to send a punitive expedition to Ras al-Khaima with the help of Sultan Said. The town was shelled, and fifty-three ships of the fleet riding in the bay went up in flames, as did the E.I.C. ship *Minerva*, which had been captured the year before when it ran into a veritable Qasimi armada manned by 5,000 stalwart buccaneers. After a battle lasting two days, the indomitable *Minerva* had been eventually overcome and its heroic crew massacred to a man under the eyes of its captain, whose fate was sealed later when he was hacked to pieces on deck. In 1814, Sultan Said himself only just escaped capture when his flagship *Caroline* was attacked on its way to Bahrain.

In 1819, another expedition was launched against the troublesome State. The Sultan dispatched three warships and 4,000 men, while the British contributed an enormous fleet under the command of Major-General Sir William Grant Keir. For six terrible days of fire, blood, dust and the booming of cannon, the British fleet bombarded the enemy stronghold, while Said was laying siege to it on the landward side. At night, when the assault subsided, the people of Ras al-Khaima crept out to collect British cannonballs to fire from their guns next day. In the end the Sheikh and his 1,000 henchmen capitulated; in 1820 a treaty was signed by the powers of the Trucial coast and Bahrain. This guaranteed that there should be 'a cessation of plunder and piracy by land and sea on the part of the Arabs, who are parties to this contract forever'. This undertaking was observed to the letter for one blissfully peaceful year. One can only guess at the self-control exercised by the lusty crews of the war fleet during that year, considering they had nothing else to do, and precious little to think about. War at sea was their métier, their sport and their livelihood. At the end of the year, unable to bear idleness any longer, they attacked (just a little) merchant ship, roped its crew to the anchor, severed the chain and dropped the pathetic bundle overboard.

In 1853 the Treaty of Peace in Perpetuity was finally signed. This was a real achievement, for the problem was very much more complicated than was understood at the time. The ruling clan of the Qawasim are the Hawala, of Adnani origin, who have lived on the shores of the Gulf for as long as they can remember. When trading started in an organized way between Persia, Mesopotamia and the East India Company, the Qasimi reaction to increased activity in their own waters was swift and merciless. Settled on both sides of the Strait of Hormuz, they considered they had a right to control foreign influence off their own shores. Bereft of this, they lost their chance of remaining the main power in the region. The attacks launched against passing ships in their territorial waters were regarded by the Qawasim of the area as perfectly legitimate, and any booty acquired during the raids as well-earned and justified loot.

The teachings of Wahhabsim, which the Qawasim had taken up in 1800, proclaimed their right to it, as any booty plundered during attacks on foreign ships was decreed *halaal* or lawful. But these warriors, in spite of their ferocity in warfare at sea, never molested women, and their courage and unswerving devotion to their sheikh was invariably reported by the rare English captains who survived the bloody encounters.

After the treaty of 1853, the Qasimi sheikhs honourably kept their word as best they could. But intermittent attacks on shipping in the Gulf nevertheless continued, until steam finally took over from sailing ships. This was not, however, the end of Sultan Said's troubles from the Wahhabi camp.

The Beni bu Ali, the fierce warlike tribe who had been seduced a few years earlier by the Wahhabis, eked out a discontented existence at their headquarters, Bilad Beni bu Ali, in the Sharqyia province. What they were pleased to call their port, Al-Ashkhara, was a convenient stretch of beach where boats could land without actually keeling over in the surf. The Beni bu Ali, as new converts to Wahhabism, regarded themselves as enemies of the Sultan and, as such, were always on the look-out for a chance to ravage, raid and pillage the surrounding countryside or any ship which might be temptingly sailing by. In 1820, they attacked an Indian merchantman which was pursuing its lawful way along the coast without bothering anybody. The Political Agent for the Lower Gulf, a Captain Thompson, sent an indignant letter of protest to the Beni bu Ali. Wholly unrepentant, the irrepressible tribe answered by murdering the representative and his colleagues on the spot, as soon as they landed at Al-Ashkhara with the letter. Outraged, Thompson agreed to join the Sultan in an expedition against the rebel tribe. Landing at Sur, rather than chance the treacherous beach, they scrambled up the Wadi Falaij as far as Bilad Beni bu Hasan, the camp of a tribe whose loyalty to the Sultan could be relied upon. Then on 9 November, the punitive force fell on the Beni bu Ali, hoping to take them by surprise. The outcome was disastrous. The savage resistance put up by the tribe was entirely unexpected: fighting like demons, they threw themselves into the ranks of the advancing soldiery, wrenching their firearms out of the troops' grasp, hacking through them with swords and *khanjars*, 'even with the bayonet sticking in their body'. With a frenzy never before seen by the bewildered troops, they defended their fort to the death. With such savage determination and armed only with their swords, they won the day. Three hundred and seventeen of Thompson's men were killed, as well as 400 of Said's. The Sultan himself showed great courage on the battlefield, dragging to safety a British casualty, although he had already been wounded himself. As his men were fleeing, he was heard to remark, 'Let those who wish to do so leave me to my fate.' The carnage was terrible to behold, and defeat was total for Captain Thompson and the Sultan. Bombay, appalled by the nature of the disaster, announced that reprisals would have to be taken. Those proud, indomitable tribesmen would have to be subdued at any cost.

Major-General Lionel Smith took charge of the next expeditionary force the following March, sailing from Bombay with fifteen warships and eleven more for horses. Battle was joined on the very spot where the first had been fought the previous year. Once more the rebellious tribesmen went into combat with savage desperation. Even the women did their bit, seizing guns out of the hands of the dead to shoot at the enemy, after dragging away their fallen menfolk. But this time, only twenty-eight men were killed and 165 wounded on the British–Omani side, and a large number of tribesmen were dispatched to Bombay, where they spent a couple of years cooling their heels in relative comfort. After this they were sent home again with generous grants with which to rebuild their ruined village. The wisdom of this policy became apparent when Lieutenant Wellstead, who was the first European to visit them since their defeat, called on them one day without warning. To his considerable surprise, this intrepid young man was welcomed by the defeated tribe with a 'tumult of acclamation'. Grabbing his tent, they pitched it for him just outside the ruins of their fort destroyed by the last British victory, on the very spot where their tribe was almost wiped out, and reduced 'to their present petty state', after being the most powerful in Oman. Delighted to see an Englishman, these astonishing people, showing absolutely no rancour for all their sufferings at the hands of the British soldiery, fired questions at him about some of the quainter customs of Great Britain. Of course, religion was their major interest, the next burning inquiries being about women. Was it true that in England they could be seen shamelessly dancing and disporting themselves with men in public?

Referring to the last battle, so disastrous for their own side, they discussed our fighting methods, our equipment, and the extraordinary amount of kit carried by our troops on to the battlefield. Why for instance, they wanted to know, did we burden ourselves with barrels of liquor for the soldiers?

Wellstead was equally astonished by the attitude of the women. As their sheikh was away on a pilgrimage to Mecca, his wife and sister ruled the tribe, and received the lieutenant in the master's absence. Veiled from head to foot – 'not a finger was showing' – they grilled him mercilessly. For a frugal, plain-living people like the Bedu, the number of possessions we move around with is incomprehensible. The need for two glasses on the table for each person astounded them. Why not just fill one as often as necessary and do away with the other? On the subject of the war they were as forgiving as the men. 'We have fought, you have made us every compensation for those who fell, and we should now be friends,' they declared. What they needed was the help and protection of Great Britain. And to this end they would gladly hand over a port (the beach of Al-Ashkhara?) to foster trade between the two countries. But, as Wahhabis, their hostility to the Sultan was fanatical, and they wanted nothing whatever to do with him.

The prosperity of Oman under the wise and sober rule of Said was beginning to decline. The main reasons for this were the abolition of the slave trade, which had brought a comfortable revenue to Oman, and the suppression of the arms traffic. This infuriated the tribes of the interior, who were convinced that this had been engineered by the British for their own dark reasons.

Said the Great was next plagued by a terrible epidemic of cholera in which 10,000 of his people perished. After this, a serious rebellion erupted in Zanzibar. Assembling his war fleet, he hastened to the island to subdue the rebels. At the sight of the great ships bristling with guns, the troubles soon subsided; and at this time Said decided to settle down and improve the lot of the islanders. Having achieved this with his cloves, he next cast a predatory eye on Mombasa, which was so well protected by Fort Jesus that not even the powerful Omani fleet could intimidate the coveted town.

In Qanbalu (Madagascar) reigned a formidable queen who had recently lost her husband. The Sultan, who had designs on her army and was trying to get her help over Mombasa, sent an embassy laden with precious gifts, together with an offer of marriage, and a request for 2,000 men. Queen Ranavalona graciously accepted the gifts and asked for a coral necklace to be sent as well. As for marriage, however, she much regretted that the customs of her island did not permit her to marry a foreign ruler. As she was reputed to slaughter her subjects by the hundred to pass the time of day and to boil missionaries and foreign envoys alive, Sultan Said may have been well out of it.

Having been jilted by the bloodthirsty queen, he next turned to Britain for help, but Palmerston, who was then Prime Minister, had no wish to get involved so far afield. Perhaps to console the disappointed Sultan, Queen Victoria sent him a flurry of gifts, which included her portrait, a four-poster bed, a state carriage which couldn't be used as there were no roads on the island, a tea-service and a snuff-box. In exchange for all this royal bounty, he presented her with the Kuria Muria Islands.

In 1854 Said the Great visited Muscat for the last time. On the way back he died of dysentery on board his ship. Of his two sons, Thwaini received Muscat as his lot and Majid got Zanzibar. In order to seal the separation, the Canning Award of 1861 stipulated that Zanzibar, which was considered the better inheritance, should hand over 40,000 rupees a year to Muscat. This 'final and permanent arrangement' was supposed to make up to Thwaini for giving up all claims to the beautiful island of Zanj.

7   Instant Oman

'Green trees, sweet water and a kind face' —
An Arab dream

The history of a country is all very well, but I am craving for
the present, to see what Oman looks like now, in all its nooks
and crannies. Last year, when I was shuffling about in the
hot sand of the Al-Ain desert, the moonscape of the Omani
mountains in the east drew me like a magnet. The longing to
look over the top, and poke about in the remotest corners of
that withdrawn, closed-in, forbidden land, was overpowering.
Before I left England, people who had never been here in
their lives said to me, 'It hasn't changed for a thousand years.'
For obvious reasons I can't say what it was like a thousand
years ago, but there is one thing certain: I would not have
flown out *then* in the Sultan's private VC–10, a comfortable
and elegant little flying boudoir, all done up inside in scarlet
and white – red for the Sultan's flag, white for holiness.

Having made known my great longing to explore, the very
first Friday which comes along is set aside for the purpose by
my kind host. With a picnic in the boot, we drive off early
under the vigorous leadership of our Brigadier, his friends
Dim and Patrick, and Rosie my chaperone. The road, smooth
as a race track, swings between piles of rock sticking straight

out of the ground like canines. Quite separate from one another, they increase in height and girth as we go deeper into the mountains. Little tufts of tender green (it is still March), like fuzzy fluff, sprout here and there on the smooth purple rock-face, food for goats.

'This is where we always bring visitors,' announces the Brigadier as an oasis suddenly appears behind a corner consisting of an even larger clump of bare craggy sugarloaf peaks. 'In half a day we can show them a selection of every feature in the country, all packed into one spot. I call it Instant Oman,' he adds for our information.

A couple of hours north of Muscat, the oasis of Fanja dominates the entrance to the wide valley of Wadi Sumayl which cuts the great mountain range of Oman in half. This gap is the main route from the coast to the closed and secret recesses of the interior. There are others, less wide and shallow, such as Wadi Jizzi (leading from Sohar to Buraimi), Wadi Hawasina (Khaboura to Ibri) and Wadi Falaij between Sur, south of Muscat, and Kamil.

The great split between the limestone range of Jebel Akhdar and the southern volcanic rocks starts at Fanja, rising slowly to a couple of thousand feet. At its inner end is Izki, that restless and turbulent city of great antiquity. Starting among the wild oleanders of the wadi banks with a few desultory shacks and spindly date palms, Fanja covers the whole side of the hill, right up to the top where an ancient fort presides in all its crumbling glory. Here indeed you can find everything. It could almost be a Hollywood set but the fact is, like Topsy, it just growed of its own accord. With all its sprawling picturesque untidiness, it is a typical Omani village. Overlooked by its fort, and a watch-tower on every surrounding height, the oasis shelters clusters of mud and *barasti* huts. A vast, complicated irrigation system in perfect running order, with its mud-banked canals filled to the brim, swirls along in the shade of the palm trees. To my amazement, this water which runs as clear as a mountain stream is almost too hot to touch. But in spite of the temperature, shoals of little *falaj* fish wriggle along with the current, rushing up like a pack of wolves as soon as you put a finger in. Old men, straight-backed with white whiskers floating gently in the breeze, squat as still as lizards under the palm trees, a rifle sticking up between their knees, pointing at the sky. Women with friendly unveiled faces and all a-flutter with green, purple and orange veils potter about among the huts or stroll along the canals with enormous bundles on their heads.

Under the palms, in the steaming green twilight of the oasis, a small girl, sitting on her heels beside the running hot water of a *falaj*, is doing her washing in a yellow plastic bucket. Unable to resist the temptation and thinking nothing of it, I take a quick photograph on the way. Happening to look up just then, she leaps to her feet with a yell of terror and sprints off through the trees, howling and baying like a hunted animal.

'Whatever is the matter with her?' I ask, dismayed by the shattering display.

'I probably smiled at her,' says Dim to comfort me. 'Anyway, between the two of us we've made her day.'

The appalling racket is the signal for all the children of the oasis to come rushing up to meet us. Down the hill and through the trees they come, cantering with leaps and bounds, the boys in their white calf-length *dishdashas* and little lace prayer caps on top of their tight black curls, their brown faces split from ear to ear by half-moon grins filled with large gleaming white piano-keys. The girls trip along, flapping their brightly coloured veils and proudly showing off the silver flowers screwed into their nostrils. Some have gold coins dangling between the eyebrows, and small silver barrels, like the kind worn by St Bernard mountain dogs. Hanging on a chain and bouncing on their little flat chests, these tiny containers hold sayings of the Prophet to protect them from the evil eye. Most of them, boys and girls alike, brandish one single foam-rubber sandal (made in Hong Kong), just to show they own one – or perhaps a pair is shared between friends. A kind of Brotherhood of the Sandal.

Followed by this merry crew, all gaily chattering and pointing out objects of interest, we climb into the heart of the oasis. Strolling along a brimming hot-water *falaj* under the date palms at least gives an *impression* of coolness after the scorching heat of the roadside where we have left the landcruiser. Peacock-blue roller birds flash through the undergrowth, criss-crossing the path like bright-feathered arrows. Sugar-birds cluster around hibiscus flowers. And up in the trees the deafening uproar of the cicadas screeching their little heads off almost drowns the raucous squawks of the magpies.

Suddenly a curious-looking creature on stork legs, with a hen's head and vulture neck, scuttles across our bows and leaps over the *falaj* with demented cackles. Surprisingly, the wing feathers are tied up with dainty little strips of blue ribbon. An identical specimen follows, decked out in scarlet bows, then a whole flock hurries past, all in different liveries, screeching like banshees at our approach.

'What kind of birds are those?' I ask, unable to make out the breed.

'Plain straightforward Omani hens,' Rosie informs me. 'The bows are how you tell them apart.' Like race-horses in the West, each bird is wearing its owner's colours. With their ribbons fluttering like pennants, some taking to the air, others streaking along on their spindly legs, they all disappear into the graveyard, as if only there will they find sanctuary, like so many fugitives of the Middle Ages dashing into the first church when pursued by the law.

The graveyard, bleak, barren and dry as the dust of the dead, is tucked up beneath a great rock topped by a sand-coloured watch-tower. Judging by the incredible number of headstones sticking out of the ground, it looks packed to the brim as if, with the best will in the world, you couldn't possibly fit another bone in. And yet it is still in use, we are told. Beside it stands a tiny mosque, and a mud tank filled to the top, with scalding *falaj* water running in at one end and a little waterfall splashing out at the other. Waltzing gaily in the middle, a plastic bag and various other bits of flotsam revolve in an eddy in the midst of a swirling green scum.

'This is where they wash the dead before popping them into their final resting place next door,' the Brigadier informs us. This water, which is used for washing purposes of every kind, for both the living and the dead, and for household linen and pots and pans, is every bit as potable as London Thames water. I have drunk it myself, quite raw and unboiled, without ever feeling the slightest twinge of discomfort. When I asked a Government official how cholera and typhoid epidemics were avoided, he said that the *falaj* water was constantly filtered and purified, just as London's best tap-water is.

Behind the mosque a glass-clear spring oozes out of the rock, splashing into a little pool surrounded by lush, spongy mosses and ferns, all of which seem to thrive on the near-boiling temperature of the brook.

'Is it volcanic?' I inquire. But no, it appears to be due to solar heating of the rocks which absorb the sun's burning rays, warming up the pools and streams which lurk beneath the surface.

Fanja has the best water network of all Arabian oases I have come across. The *falaj* canalization, the oldest in the Middle East if not in the whole world, originated in Persia where it was known as *qanat*, and where there were over 100,000 miles of channels, some going all the way down to a thousand feet below ground. Canals of this type occur from north-west China to the Western Desert. Sargon of Assyria described some of these in 714 B.C.; and the Greek historian Polybius said they were already ancient in Parthia in his own time.

Brought across the Gulf by the early conquerors, the system probably reached Oman in the tenth century, if not before. Specific tribes in ancient Persia, known as Muqani, specialists of the *qanats*, have been dedicated since earliest times to this art, handing down the precious secrets of water-divining from father to son until the eighteenth century, when the last of the tribes, through a quirk of fate, all died off together and were buried with their secrets.

Though expensive to maintain, the system is a blessing in the searing temperatures of Arabia, as the cool underground canals, sheltered from the furnace of the sun, are protected from the fierce evaporation of daylight hours. For a couple of hundred years the *aflaj*, unattended for lack of expert know-ledge, crumbled or silted up and generally fell into disrepair. It was not until modern times, when technology took over from perception and the esoteric arts, that Sheikh Zaid, ex-Governor of Al-Ain and now President of the U.A.E., brought the system back into working order in his own Union. Here in Oman, due to the Sultan's efforts and determination, this effective ancient irrigation system is earning its keep once more.

The early *qanat* diggers, who had this special talent for smelling out water through thick solid rock, sometimes as much as a hundred feet down, would trail along the base of a mountain range until they hit the spot, and then they would start digging. Using only pick and shovel and their own fingernails, they moiled and they toiled until they reached the blessed water. And sure enough, it was always there, lying in lovely fresh pools, trapped between two layers of impervious rocks, deep down among the very roots of the mountain. From the mother pool they scooped out underground canals high enough for a man to stand up in, every so often sinking a shaft from the top through which they could get some light and air, and hoist the loose soil through. Seen from above, an underground canal can be followed by the piles of rubble heaped along its course like giant mole-hills at regular intervals, all the way down to the end of its run. When the stream, flowing along a gentle slope, eventually breaks surface, it is led away into a complicated system of irrigation rivulets, to water the various date gardens, alfalfa fields and little patches of private gardens of the oasis. Based on the principle that water seeks its own level, wherever a *falaj* crosses the path of a wadi the *qanateers* would dig below the bed of the stream, leading their own sweet water in a U-shaped tube beneath, then up again on the other side, through the medium of an inverted syphon.

It is the *wali*'s job to control water distribution: its flow and the irrigation time of each date plantation, alfalfa field, or small private garden is his responsibility alone. An exacting task which must become quite a headache in times of drought and local water disputes or inheritance laws.

The story is told in Oman of a rich and beautiful princess with an amazing pair of eyes which could see very much further than the common run of mortals. One fine day, as she was idly gazing around the countryside from the highest tower of her castle, she spied in the far distance, working in a garden in Sohar, a man drawing water from a *falaj*. With her unusual sight, the princess clearly saw the entire course of this canal which happened to be above ground, running from the bottom of her tower to the very feet of the handsome gardener in Sohar. Plucking a lime from a nearby tree, she thrust one of her rings through the rind, driving it deep into the flesh of the fruit. This she tossed into the *falaj*, setting it off on its way towards the man who had caught her roving eye and her fancy. On and on rolled the lime until, borne along by the flowing water, it reached its destination. Realizing when he had picked up the fruit that such a gem could only come from the palace, the young gardener duly returned it forthwith. But alas, it was the prince, not his wife, who was there to receive it back. To punish her for her intended infidelity, the irate prince had her beautiful, far-seeing eyes burnt out of her head.

Apart from the splendid irrigation system of Fanja, the most remarkable feature of the oasis (to me, anyway) is the number of expensive cars dotted about, parked at all sorts of curious angles under the date trees.

'How on earth can these people afford such cars?' I ask, truly puzzled.

'One member of the family goes off to work in Matrah or Muscat or Ruwi, and earns enough money to keep all his relatives going,' explains the Brigadier. 'And of course, for the sake of face and to prove that he is now a rich man, he has to have an expensive car.' Rather surprisingly, these are kept in perfect shape, prinked and polished to a gleam. Unlike the Arabs of some other States I know, Omanis are careful, courteous drivers. Never once along the highways did I see the rusty carcass of some once-expensive car, abandoned by the roadside. Accidents, too, are rare.

Having 'done' Fanja, we push on along Wadi Sumayl. Past Bidbid we branch off the road on to a dirt track leading towards the watercourse and the military base, where our Brigadier was formerly posted as Colonel of the Muscat Regiment. As a veteran of the Dhofar War, in which he was wounded, Patrick has been invited to lunch by his ex-brother officers in the Bidbid Mess, so he and Rosie go off and leave us at this point. Here the wadi is as wide as a multi-lane motorway. *Aflaj* leading away from it take water into the fertile valley beyond. Heading straight for the wadi, we plough down into the gravel bed, surging slowly through the first shallow streamlet and emerging safely on the other side into the dry gravel centre of the wadi. Well-used to this kind of lark, the landcruiser takes it in its stride and, expertly piloted by the Brigadier, swings easily in and out among great boulders, huge clumps of reeds and bulrushes, and dessicated carcasses of long-dead trees carted down by the winter floods, the whole decorated with tattered plastic bags and bits of old washed-out rags. The bank on the far side is a solid mass of pink oleanders, and the fertile valley behind is bright apple-green as far as the foot of the purple mountain range of the Hajar in the distance. Swaying slightly we cruise on, crossing several shallow streams of Alp-clear water.

'When are we going to stop?' asks Dim, presumably beginning to feel peckish and wanting his lunch.

'Over there on the little beach beyond the pool,' answers our leader, swinging the wheel to point the vehicle straight at the water. Down the slope we crunch, churning noisily into the surprisingly fast-flowing current, right into the centre of the stream. And there, with a great shudder of its whole frame, the landcruiser grinds to a full stop, settling firmly into the loose gravel of the river bed. Revving up merely ploughs us in deeper. Water soon oozes through the floor and floods in with a great rush as we open the doors.

'Bugger,' remarks the Brigadier mildly, 'I didn't realize it was so deep.' With great restraint, Dim forebears to comment. This is, after all, *his* vehicle, borrowed for the day's excursion. We get out and push. We might as well try to shift the Green Mountain. A couple of young Omanis sunbathing on the little beach we were making for get up to add their slender weight to ours. But the old girl is well dug in, and there is no moving her. 'I will have to get some help,' announces the Brigadier.

'Take our car,' offers one of the young men without hesitation, and he hands over the keys.

A good hour later, a great Army recovery vehicle comes panting and puffing up the wadi bed. Inside are the Brigadier, Patrick and another officer, to help with rescue operations.

'We will have her out in no time,' says the latter confidently. 'But we must get to the other side first so we can pull her out,' and down the slope he plunges with his own truck. Splashing into the water and grinding a few feet forward, he comes to rest beside our own barouche – and there he firmly sticks. Pushing a monster of that size is out of the question; subtler means will have to be employed.

As this is men's work, and there seems to be nothing much for me to contribute, I set off on a little stroll to explore the surroundings. With magnifying glass at the ready and armed with a prodding-stick, I pick my way along the stream, poking cautiously about among the stones and disturbing enormous quantities of colourful low-life: beetles, with eyes on circling stalks like radar, centipedes with toes curling up towards heaven, and lizards with blue-spotted necks, all come scurrying out before my stick. Huge dragonflies, with heavily-veined see-through wings, zoom about over the water, where shoals of wadi fish lie in the shade of the overhanging rocks. This is where officers of the Bidbid Mess take their daily dip. As it was also the favourite swimming pool of a large tribe of water snakes, a few hand grenades tossed into their midst had cleared the area a couple of years earlier. But since then the fish have returned. So, as I say to myself, why not the snakes as well? They may well be lurking, curled up in those nooks and crannies underneath the large overhanging boulders and lying in wait to seek revenge for the outrage perpetrated upon their forebears. As I trudge along the gurgling stream, with roller birds and colourful bee-eaters streaking across my path, I try to identify the vegetation which lines the wadi's edge. Wild oleanders are everywhere; tall grasses with a bump on top which makes them look like knobkerries sway ponderously in the breeze. Bulrushes and sedges grow in clumps, and the *sawga* plant, with scented orange flowers. Here also flourish the *samarra* and the *sunt*, a kind of acacia with mimosa-like flowers. A few feathery *tarfa* (tamarisks) grow on an island in the middle of the wadi, safe from camels' greedy teeth, whose favourite delicacy it is. *Succul*, a kind of aloe, also sprouts along the edge, and everywhere are great clumps of jasmine with large powerfully scented blooms, a good deal more spectacular than our less showy European varieties. Among the humbler wild flowers are celandine and speedwell, and a tiny kind of dandelion which I also spotted on the banks of the Jabrin *falaj*. In wadi Beni Kharus beyond the mountain, among the wild oleander, the *samarra*, the *sunt* and the flaming orange *sawga*, there would be apricot, peach and almond blossom as well at this time of year.

When I get back to the seat of trouble, both trucks are miraculously out of the water. Somehow or other these clever men have done the trick and, after all this labour, they thoroughly deserve their swim. So into the lovely warm wadi water we plunge at last. Following local custom, and well aware of the horror with which all Arabs regard the smallest square inch of bare female flesh, I always go in fully clothed in shirt and jeans. And I am not alone. A hundred yards downstream, a merry group of Omani ladies are doing the very same thing, wading into the water with their many-coloured veils floating around like the fins of some exotic tropical fish. There are advantages to this habit; within seconds the Brigadier, lying on his back in the water, is twitching and cursing at the constant bites of the mini pirhanas of the pool. My denim armour is proof against the little brutes, as well as offering much less temptation to the possible water-snake population and the over-familiar embraces of local leeches.

These wadis, an important feature of Oman, are used as roads into the interior where no highways exist. Now that there is no longer an embargo on moving about the country (the previous sultan insisted on people staying where they were) there is constant coming and going in the interests of trade, barter, shopping or simply feeding animals which, for some obscure reason, are frequently kept at a considerable distance from their source of food, so that little donkeys, loaded with great bundles of alfalfa, are frequently seen toiling along the beds of dry wadis.

But these waterways are not just useful trade routes. They also act as sources of constant entertainment and enormous enjoyment. At the weekend, which is Friday here, entire families from the towns set off in taxis for a day's spree along these bumpy highways and byways.

One fine day the Brigadier decides to lead an expedition to Wadi Daika, the widest and most spectacular of all these rivers; along its course are scattered deep viridian pools beneath the overhanging rocks of the gorge through which flows the torrent when in spate. So off we set, with Rob and Audrey, in whose lucky Landrover we are riding this time.

'They've built a road since I was last here,' remarks the Brigadier appreciatively as we skim along smoothly on the best possible British-made road surface.

Every so often Rob, who is driving his own vehicle, stops, leaps out and takes a quick snap of yet another gingerbread-coloured peak of extravagant shape.

'There goes an Egyptian vulture,' he remarks, pointing out a great straggly bird swooping down, with feathers sticking out untidily all over the place like an old scarecrow in a high wind. Landing heavily on top of a lizard's carcass it makes a great to-do of getting all its wayward bits and pieces folded together about its person.

One of the nice things about Daika is that it is not redolent of gruesome war memories. Like any other self-respecting Omani wadi, no doubt, it has its own bloody tribal history, but this is decently contained within the ancient folklore of local tribes.

Suddenly the beautiful highway comes abruptly to an end and dissolves shamefacedly into a field of gravel. A dirt track leading off to the right is the obvious course to follow from now on. Reducing our cruising speed, we bump along fields of alfalfa, date gardens, banana plantations. Here are coconut trees too, as we have reached the very northern limit of the tropical, monsoon-swept territory of South Oman.

'This landscape reminds me of Malaya,' remarks Rob, driving through a typically reminiscent coconut grove dotted with leaf huts, stray hens and bare-bottomed toddlers.

'Yes!' we all chorus, struck by the similarity ourselves.

'Aren't we well-travelled!' exclaims Audrey, who seems surprised.

The mud villages through which we cruise are just wide enough for the Landrover to squeeze through. Finally, after an hour or so, the track comes to an end and we hit the wadi. Mostly wide expanses of dry gravel, it has one or two narrow streams of water snaking along like shoelaces. The fine gravel soon changes to stone, the stone to rock, and finally to great boulders lying about like a herd of slumbering elephants.

'Last time I lent this vehicle to someone who drove it over

these stones, the gear-box went,' remarks Rob sorrowfully, as the wheels buckle under our weight.

'I should engage all four wheels if I were you,' counsels the Brigadier helpfully, as we plunge into a deep trough then start clambering about in a field of sizeable boulders which take us shuddering round the first bend.

The wadi narrows between the rocks of the two mountains on either side. From time to time the stream takes a short-cut across our bows, and we have to drive down into it and up again on the other side. I try not to think of Bidbid. If we stick here nobody will bail us out. There is certainly no military outpost anywhere near, nor a village, not even a leaf hut or *fareeg*, however humble. As the gorge narrows, deep-green pools begin to form beneath the overhanging cliff. We are hot, we are dusty and, above all, we are thirsty. We long for that promised swim in the turquoise pool we are making for.

'Can't we stop now? Isn't that it yet?' pants Audrey every time we skirt round one of these smooth gleaming sheets of water like plastic lakes in an architect's model.

'Not yet, the water's not deep enough. You couldn't possibly dive here.' Nobody really wants to dive. It's just the idea.

Painfully the Landrover grinds on at two miles an hour. First we try one side of the wadi, then the other. The car shakes and shudders and moans in protest. 'No wonder that gear-box went,' groans Rob, who is suffering as much as his machine.

'With *you* driving, it could never happen,' I reassure him as convincingly as I can. Suddenly the gorge, which had narrowed like the neck of an adder, widens out into a huge open circular space. We are there at last. On the right is the large deep-green lake, with a dark-blue one opposite, and a huge noble-looking willow tree bang in the middle of a field of white stones. Within seconds we are in water which is the same temperature as the air. I never get used to this lack of transition between the two elements – the only difference being that one is usually wetter than the other. Sometimes more, sometimes less.

'Are there any leeches?' asks Audrey, up to her neck in the bottle-green liquid.

'Don't even think about it,' advises the Brigadier, who is soon twitching and revolving violently, trying to shake off the battalion of *falaj* fish which have obviously homed in on him already. I walk in fully clothed as usual, and nobody bothers me in the least. Neither fish nor leech can sink a tooth into me.

'When the wadi is in spate,' our leader informs us, 'water reaches half-way up the gorge. It happens within minutes,' he adds reassuringly, 'and nobody has time to get away.'

After a long refreshing soak we lie on the blistering stones to dry off, and Michael's delicious curry puffs are produced, washed down with loomey, limes boiled in water with sugar, then iced.

As we munch our way through these delicacies, the sun slowly swivels round the craggy peaks. Soon it will be out of sight; it is time to go. The journey home somehow seems less bumpy. The Landrover, like a horse bolting back to its stable, takes the obstacles in its stride with far less huffing and puffing. As it is Friday, the weekend of Islam, the wadi is full of homing traffic, once we leave the depths of the gorge. Entire families, who have been picnicking on the dry gravel, pile into their waiting taxis, twelve, thirteen, fifteen to one vehicle, and make for home. Not surprisingly, some of these overloaded arks bog down when crossing a stream. It is already getting dark as we stop to rescue one of these casualties. Up to our knees in water, we gather behind and PUSH. Nothing happens. Another taxi arrives, sails through successfully, and stops on the other side. All its twenty occupants disembark and the male element comes to the aid of our already substantial party. Still nothing happens. A smart cream Mercedes sweeps through and stops, disgorging its sole occupant, an elegant gentleman in dazzling white robes and bougainvillaea turban who steps unconcernedly into the water in all his finery and inquires into the cause of the trouble. As he returns to his car for the necessary kit, Audrey suddenly spies a large group of ladies huddled together on the dry bank.

'Come and help,' she urges, 'come and push.' But the ladies have no intention of doing anything so foolish.

'No, no,' they say, '*you* help;' meaning, of course, if you are crazy enough to take on men's jobs. At this point the taxi shoots forward, and I fall flat on my face in the middle of the stream. The elegant gentleman had produced the jack which lifted the car out of its rut. His beautiful robes are soaked, his fine calfskin sandals are ruined, but nobody, least of all himself, thinks anything of it. This is just ordinary wadi weekend routine.

8   The Green Mountain

As the helicopter bends sideways to avoid slicing up the mountain with its spinning blades, its shadow looks like some huge monstrous spider crawling up the rock-face several hundred feet below. Sitting in front beside the pilot is like floating along in a fishbowl. Entirely made of perspex, even the floor is see-through, so that jagged peaks below rear their greenish heads at us like the back-teeth of some ancient crocodile.

The extraordinary mountains of Oman, once seen, are never forgotten. Sharp, stark and entirely bare, they rise to a height of 10,000 feet, and are visible 100 miles out at sea. Piles of totally, relentlessly denuded rock march along for hundreds of miles, forming the central range which divides the flat eastern plain of the Batinah from Oman Proper. Here, in its craggy recesses live the most cliqueish, fanatic, and fiercely independent people on earth.

Al-Hajar, the great limestone range which gets its name from the colour of the rock, is formed from ophiolite, which was dredged up from the bowels of the earth during some fearful planetary upheaval in the dawn of cosmic history. Some hold the view that the name of Jebel Akhdar is misleading, unless you understand the true significance of the word 'green', in the sense of young and alive. It means simply that the mountain is made up of living limestone, as opposed to the dead volcanic outcrop of the rest of the range.

Starting in the northernmost tip of the Musandam Peninsula, at the entrance of the Arabian Gulf, Al-Hajar, the Stone, runs along the Gulf of Oman to Ras al-Hadd, at its easternmost point. About half-way down its total length the wide gap of the Sumayl valley splits it in half.

It is the actual make-up of the rock itself which geologists find so intriguing. For fossilized sea-shells to appear one mile up in the sky is unusual, to say the least. Even more disconcerting for these scientific gentlemen is the rock formation of Jebel Kaur which sticks out at right angles from the main range, and about which they can't make up their minds at all. Some claim it was cast up by the sea in a moment of wrath, then flung across the spot it now occupies. Others are convinced that it was regurgitated by the earth at the same time as the rest of the range. One way or another, the result is the same – and quite startling when you are flying along the deep narrow ravines, peering into all those holes and caverns, with the bare, green-tinged wall of rock rising sheer on either side and sometimes in front as well. Huge rolls of cloud billow and tear ahead, sucked along by the powerful draughts howling through the canyons. Swinging in and out, skirting the jutting crags, we rise higher and higher, sometimes diving through the racing clouds, until we finally reach the top. Coming up from below and peering over the edge, level with the sharp rim of the plateau, is a curious sensation. We have to climb still further before we can land on the helipad at the Sultan's Armed Forces (S.A.F.) station, which was built at the end of the Jebel War. A road is planned, and may well have been started, which will lead part-way up the mountain, but at the moment there is no other way to the summit.

Jumping out of the helicopter into our self-raised cloud of dust, we are met by the colonel in charge of the military base at Saiq. An enormous breakfast awaits us in the Officers' Mess with eggs, bacon, sausages, baked beans, toast, fruit juice and coffee. The Brigadier orders the lot. 'They were bloody beef sausages. I *hate* beef sausages,' he grumbles afterwards, his mind no doubt flashing back to the grisly wartime so-called sausages of his prep-school days.

Strengthened by this gargantuan feast, we set off to view the sights, and pile into a Landrover expertly piloted by a brisk young Omani corporal. First we have to call in and admire the station's pride and joy, the new army shop. And there, on top of the enormous breakfast we have just put down, we must swallow a tin of fruit juice apiece. This little ceremony is decreed by the immemorial laws of hospitality.

Back in the Landrover once more, Rosie Loyd and I cram ourselves into the passenger seat. We leap from rock to rock, bucking wildly. 'I'm glad they've improved this track,' remarks the Brigadier. 'It was really awful last time I was here.' At this point a particularly vicious jolt hurls Rosie and myself to the roof. 'Hang on to each other, girls, you might get a bit knocked about,' he adds, as he nearly shoots out of the vehicle himself.

The village of Saiq was the stronghold of the rebels, the collecting point for guns and ammunition and the terrible mines which plagued the lives of the Sultan's forces for so many years. We walk along narrow dusty tracks between several rows of mud huts. Children, goats, hens, all play about together in these peaceful lanes.

In a field beneath an almond tree, the *wali* is holding his *majlis*. A large handsome carpet, eked out with a few plastic mats from Bombay, has been spread in the dusty field. Elbow to elbow all round the edge, the noble-looking elders of the village, in Kashmir turbans and belted robes, sit on their heels. (The soles of the feet should always be decently concealed from sight. To stick them out at anyone, as inevitably happens when you cross your legs, is an unspeakable insult.)

With *khanjars* stuck in their belts, rifles and camel-sticks neatly lined up in front and sandals laid out on the outer edge, they are ready for the business of the day. The Brigadier, stepping briskly up to the *wali*, shakes hands, as everybody stands up to greet him. Rapid Arabic rattles away between them, incessantly sprinkled with heartfelt *al-Hamdal-lillahs* (thanks be to God). Rosie and I, knowing our place in the Arab world, hang back, prepared to wait in the background until the men have finished their business. But to my surprise, they wave us into the magic circle, and every one of them shakes hands with us in turn. I begin to realize that in Oman women are tolerated around the place far more than in the rest of Arabia. *Never* before have I heard of women invited into the *majlis,* that most exclusive of men's clubs, where communal and private affairs are discussed in all their aspects.

Beneath the spreading almond tree, plastic thermos flasks stand about, filled with coffee. A bunch of rifles is leaning against the trunk of the tree. Taking our place among the men, we kneel on the edge of the carpet. Across the field comes a young man bearing a large tray filled with tinned pineapple cubes. This is dumped on the carpet before the *wali,* who propels it towards Rosie. 'Right hand only,' hisses the Brigadier into her left ear. After this has gone all the way round, the same young man comes up with a mess-tin full of water. To my horror he comes straight to me and holds it under my nose. Utterly panicked, I cast around frantically for inspiration. All eyes are glued on me. Do I drink it? Wash my hands in it? Pour a libation? With a wild guess, I dip my fingers and waggle them around briefly in the water. *Al-Hamdallillah,* it was the right thing to do! The mess-tin moves on to Rosie, who does the same, then they all follow suit. After this comes coffee, a tiny drop at the bottom of the cup, flavoured with the usual cardamom. Politeness dictates you should have at least a second helping. After this I waggle my cup, which means 'No more thank you, lovely stuff, but I've had enough'. My waggle is obviously not authoritative enough as I am firmly given a third and then a fourth drop. Then it is Rosie's turn. Everybody drinks out of the same cup. As the young man on my right is afflicted with a heavy cold, I am thankful to have been served first. *Another* departure from usual Arabian customs. A WOMAN served first . . . Unheard of!

The day's business then begins. The *wali* shuffles bits of paper around the in-tray, picks one up, squints at it and puts it back. After he has done the same with two or three more, an old man comes striding across the field with his rifle in one hand and a large brown envelope in the other. Its contents have to be examined next, and discussed around the carpet.

The day's work is done. It is time to take our leave. Everybody stands up and shakes hands. Then, to the sound of many blessings and *Hamdallillahs*, we set off towards Sharaija. A sky-van appears over the edge of the plateau, flying in supplies. This service is practically non-stop, as almost everything has to be brought from below. This particular load consists of cement bags. Coming up the steep track from Sharaija, a mud village glued to the side of the precipice, a young man in a cream-coloured *dishdasha* and turban to match is leading a donkey towards the cement dump. Speaking in fluent English, he explains that he is rebuilding his house, which got a bit knocked about during the Jebel War. This smooth, princely figure, speaking with an Oxford accent and straight out of the *Arabian Nights*, humping sacks of cement on to his donkey, is a scene worth recording. And what's more, he has no objection to having his picture taken.

Sharaija, a corruption of Shiraz, was originally a Persian village. A thousand years before the Special Air Services stormed Jebel Akhdar to subdue the rebels, the Persians had already achieved this extraordinary feat, scaling the perpendicular 10,000-foot-high cliff-face by cutting steps into the rock. Defying the hefty boulders hurled at them from above by the desperate inhabitants of the plateau, the invaders, unused to the climate of Oman, were amazed to witness the precious stones dropping from their helmets and feathers coming unstuck from their arrows in the blazing heat of the fiery mountain furnace. Although their line in glue obviously left something to be desired, these ingenious Persians must have had trained technicians who mastered the art of mountain engineering at an early stage. Cutting a perpendicular staircase 10,000 feet high out of the living rock is no task for amateurs at the best of times, and least of all under a continuous shower of rocks and boulders raining down from above.

Having eventually reached the summit and subdued the terrorized local people, the new masters, who were certainly no soft overlords, at once got down to an impressive terracing job, probably using the villagers to dig and delve. Curving in and out, following the wavy contour of the rock, they cut huge shelves out of the green stone which they then filled with soil scraped up from the plateau above, or more probably heaved up from the valley below. This they then proceeded to plant and sow with cuttings and seeds which they had thoughtfully brought with them. Vineyards began to grow in neat rows on the new terraces. Apricot, fig, peach and almond orchards flourished. Vegetables, with garlic and onion the most successful, soon sprouted. And the plateau, one mile up in the sky, became a delightful little paradise. At that altitude, the weather was never too hot for the crops, and there was enough rainfall to keep all the greenery going.

This massive limestone block, only twenty miles across and surrounded by its bodyguard of perpendicular slabs, is pockmarked with holes and caves, inhabited by a unique goat-like creature (which occurs nowhere else) known as the tahr, or Hermitragus Jayakari, for those who want the scientific name. Almost extinct at one time, it is now protected and, encouraged by all this touching care, is increasing enthusiastically. A nimble-footed, sandy-brown little beast, it proudly sprouts a black dorsal mane sticking straight up along its spine, and wears dark splodges all over its face and legs. A cute little black muzzle and long, thin, curving horns curling backwards complete the picture. It is a shy creature, but if ever you come across one by chance you will know it at once. There is no mistaking a tahr. Other rare gazelles, such as the marica, or rhim, both the Goitred and the Dorcas kind, which also occur, are equally in danger of extinction.

Other denizens of this remarkable mountain are foxes, leopards, wild cats and panthers. Wolves grow larger here than anywhere else, and there are striped hyenas and porcupines. The list goes on for ever: the Arabian hare, the hyrax and the coney, exotic black rats and their flying cousins, the large bare-bellied tomb-bat, and the Egyptian fruit bat. Eagles continually swoop down on all this wild life, followed at a respectful distance by fleets of Egyptian vultures. The plateau is full of bird song, from golden orioles to bulbuls and bee-eaters, hoopoes, bright-blue sunbirds and rollers. In the spring, as wild flowers begin to cover the ground, a multitude of butterflies and insects hatch out of all their eggs and cocoons, and crawl out of their hideouts. Huge dragonflies glide in circles over every bit of exposed water, including the officers' home-made swimming pool at the military base.

But time was, not long ago, when this little paradise high up in the sky was a formidable fortress bristling with lethal arms and great caches of mines and ammunition. Through the fields of lucerne and under the pomegranate trees in bloom, guerrilla forces, armed to the teeth with the most modern weaponry, scuttled about like murderous soldier ants on the warpath.

Furthermore, interior Oman, never very well-disposed towards Muscat and the coastal areas at the best of times, had become incensed a hundred years before when Great Britain managed to prevail upon the sultan to give up the slave trade. This was the immediate, undeniable beginning of the collapse of Oman's fortunes. From a prosperous land with many cities of great splendour and vast agricultural areas watered by a well-kept *falaj* network, they sank into an even deeper trough after the loss of Zanzibar in 1861. The tribes from Oman Proper withdrew their support from the sultan, and this eventually led to the return of the imam, and all the troubles which followed in its wake.

By the Treaty of Seeb, drawn up in 1920, it was hoped to unite Muscat and Oman, and to put an end to the continual hostilities between the two. 'The people of Oman' (meaning the inhabitants of the interior) undertook to remain at peace with the sultan and to forgo attacking the coastal towns in the future. When visiting the coast on lawful business, they were to have 'full rights of movement and security'. Moreover, any claims against them in trade or other matters were to be settled by Sharia Law, and no longer by bloody massacres. On his side, the sultan undertook not to interfere in tribal matters; and it was further agreed that coastal townspeople could enter Oman on peaceful business missions without the danger of being set upon at first sight.

Suleiman bin Himyiar, self-styled Lord of the Green Mountain who claimed to be last of the descendants of the kings of Nebhania, was not much loved by his subjects on top of Jebel Akhdar. But they had a healthy respect for him and a fierce kind of loyalty. When he and the imam were finally defeated in the late 1950s, at the end of the Jebel War, it was with their help that he managed to escape. Not one of them would ever give away his hiding place. As a merciless tyrant and feudal ruler who owned large gardens and orchards on top of the fertile mountain, he didn't hesitate to appropriate all the available water for his own needs, not giving a thought to the parched, dried-up little gardens of his subjects. A bit of a megalomaniac, his pet ambition was to be totally independent of both the sultan and the imam, running his own mini-State within a State. This he then planned to place under the protection of one of the Great Powers. Much to his surprise, both Great Britain and the United States turned down the honour. Enraged at being thus spurned, he dug in his toes and decided to get his independence at any cost. When the new Imam of Oman rebelled against the Sultan in 1954, Suleiman jumped on the bandwagon for his own dark purposes. A man of questionable repute, Ghalib bin Ali of the Beni Hina tribe had set himself up as imam in 1953 without bothering with the usual elections in case they went against him. Ghalib had a very competent brother, Talib, who was *wali* at Rostaq. This vigorous and effective man took command of the rebellious forces; from then on the 'Dreadful Trio', Suleiman, Ghalib and Talib, were in business. To back their nefarious cause, money came in in plenty from abroad, as well as all the arms and ammunition needed. Truculent factions among disaffected tribes were trained in up-to-date methods of guerrilla warfare. So expertly was all this done that several years were to pass, and a great many lives were lost, before peace could be restored in Oman. To this day, neither Suleiman nor either of his cronies has ever been caught. Already backed by Talib and Suleiman bin Himyiar, Ghalib was now joined by Salih bin Isah, Sheikh of the Sharqyia province and leader of the Hinawi tribes. The four of them together, surrounded by their wild rangy warriors, were a formidable crew to reckon with.

To add one more complication to the already hideously tangled skein, a section of the Iraq Petroleum Company was eyeing a hump of rock sticking out of the sand in the plain, east of the great mountain range. This spot, Fahud, the Mount of Leopards, gave every outward indication of standing on top of a rich and prolific oil deposit. The Sultan, who was all for coming to terms with the oil company, declared that the matter came within his own jurisdiction according to that clause in the Seeb agreement which gave him the power to deal with matters concerning the whole country as well as its external policy. The imam claimed it was an internal matter, and therefore entirely his own affair. It was deadlock.

With the backing of Great Britain, and on behalf of the Sultan and the oil company, the little private army known as the Muscat and Oman Field Force was detailed to annex Fahud. With this success under its belt, the Field Force then charged around triumphantly and captured the towns of Nizwa, Ibri and other centres in the Interior. All these were, of course, part of the imam's territory. This jolly escapade, which was entirely bloodless, became known as the One Shot War. As the imam wasn't really one, since he hadn't been properly elected and had therefore never been recognized as such by the Sultan, the situation was confused and without precedent.

Soon after this the Sultan arrived on a royal progress, to celebrate and confirm the glorious victory by taking possession of Nizwa, the holy of holies and, of all cities of Oman, the most ingrown, xenophobic and jealous of its own secrecy and independence. In his book *Sultan in Oman*, James Morris paints an endearing picture of the very dignified Sultan Said bin Taimur hurtling full pelt across the desert from Salalah to the interior (or Oman, as it was then called). Leading a convoy of trucks filled with slaves and camping equipment, he was on his way to receive homage from the defeated sheikhs.

After spending several days roaring through a self-raised dust-storm at breakneck speed, he arrived in Nizwa and was greeted along the streets by a wild rabble of ancient warriors, eager to show their undying loyalty by firing their blunderbusses in the air. Women cackled and cheered, truck horns hooted, children waved the red flag of the Sultan. From the fort, where ancient Portuguese cannon banged away a noisy salute, blowing bits of the fort away in the process, a cloud of white smoke arose, through which figures with ramrods could faintly be seen, like a faded nineteenth-century battle-scene etching. And there, sitting in his tent outside Nizwa in total silence and with a great air of authority and hauteur, the Sultan allowed the ex-rebels to come in and sit with him on the floor in wordless submission. For hours on end nobody spoke. But all knew what each was thinking.

After a couple of days, all but one of the tribal chiefs of the interior had turned up: Suleiman bin Himyiar, Lord of the Green Mountain, the most infamous and the most dangerous of the lot. When on the third day Suleiman bin Himyiar, Lord of the Green Mountain, finally did appear to pay mock homage to the Sultan, it was in the most unexpected and eccentric fashion he could devise. In contrast with all the stately camel caravans shambling along in the last two days, Suleiman actually pelted down the mountainside in a cloud of dust, ensconced in the back of a large American car. Brandishing a rifle, a Negro slave sat on the boot with his legs dangling inside through the back window. In this manner, the Lord of the Green Mountain, flanked by a couple of chinless young men who were probably his sons, arrived to surrender to the Sultan. In fact it was only a gesture: he was playing for time, feigning submission to give himself a chance to collect more arms and plot a whole lot more mischief. Anyway, as soon as his bogus gesture was made, up the mountain he bolted again.

Having thus retaken the whole country under his wing in his lightning tour, the Sultan united Muscat and Oman in a way which hadn't happened since the death of Said the Great in 1856. Meanwhile the Field Force, busily cruising around the interior territory and setting up garrisons here and there, eventually began to notice a chilly note creeping into their daily rapport with the local inhabitants. The two-faced Suleiman was polite enough whenever they ran into him in the streets of his capital Tanuf at the foot of Jebel Akhdar but, on the whole, things were turning sour.

The rebellion, hatched abroad by Talib and Salih, was scheduled to erupt in two different places at the same time, under Talib in central Oman, and under Salih's brother Ibrahim in the Sharqyia. But the tribesmen, on whose fiery response they were counting, only produced a very lukewarm reaction, and the whole thing went off like a damp squib. Talib's dhow, which was expected with himself on board as well as a whole shipload of arms and ammunition, broke down somewhere on the way and arrived too late. Ibrahim, losing his nerve, rushed off to Muscat to throw himself on the Sultan's mercy. There he was invited forthwith to become a guest of His Majesty in the fortress of Jalali, in the company of an inveterate alcoholic, an amiable but unpredictable lunatic, and a general assortment of political prisoners and dangerous criminals.

When Talib eventually arrived on his temperamental dhow, landing on the Batinah coast north of Muscat, he made straight for his home-town of Balad Sait. There he straightway proclaimed the restoration of the imamate in open defiance of the Sultan.

Suleiman, who was under house-arrest in Muscat, got the news by bush telegraph. Slipping past his guards, he made straight for his lofty kingdom, and began rallying his tribes at once. This meant that the whole of Jebel Akhdar and its foot-hill towns and villages were in a state of war against the intrepid Field Force. The position was a nightmare one: caught in the narrow gorge at Balad Sait, the Field Force were cut off from their camp beyond Nizwa and trapped between the fort and the village. The Abryins of Al-Hamra, who had promised to protect the heights, never turned up; terrorized by Talib's threats, they prudently kept away.

In a temperature of 120° in the shade, the heroic retreat began through the mine-infested gorge and the trucks went up like fireworks. Battling their way through twenty miles of concentrated hell, the betrayed Force fought hand to hand, with enemies in every house, and guns at every window and poking out of the trees and over garden walls. The heroic retreat is in many ways reminiscent of the epic withdrawal from Spain of Charlemagne's nephew Roland through the Pass of Roncevaux in the Pyrenees, where he and his knights were cut to pieces by the Moors and Saracens of the time. The retreat from Balad Sait was a fearful, appalling massacre. Those who escaped the mines and the bullets crawled off into the mountains to have their throats cut or to die of thirst among the sizzling rocks. Not many, apart from the British officers, made it back to camp.

At the end of this carnage, the odious imam returned to

holy Nizwa and took up his bogus appointment once more, and so the fighting had to continue. Gradually a new force began to come together, consisting mostly of the Muscat Regiment and an assorted collection of newly trained recruits at Bait al-Falaj.

In his witty book *Warlords of Oman*, P. S. Allfrey describes the making of soldiers out of raw, free-ranging desert Arabs. Admittedly he was writing of his experiences in the Trucial States and not in Oman, but 'breaking in' an Arab tribesman is probably much the same, whether it is on the eastern or western side of the Hajar range. Their total inability to cope with parade-ground discipline, where they all set off in opposite directions and 'broke into little knots and discussed their impressions', makes endearing reading. The sergeants would then 'demonstrate a drill movement; the recruits would chat about what they had just seen, applauding or criticizing'. Another of these apprentice soldiers' problems was footwear. Unused to anything coming between the horny pads of their feet and the scorching sand, they simply couldn't get used to being shod. 'An about-turn was accomplished by a shower of shoes shied into the air by their happy foot-stamping', as Allfrey so felicitously puts it.

The Muscat soldiery, 100-strong and soon to become known as Haughcol, after its new leader's name, set off along the narrow lethal passes snaking into the interior. As most of the vehicles had been blown sky-high at Balad Sait, new transport had to be procured. In the event, this turned out to be a fleet of ramshackle old fish lorries which plied its odoriferous trade between the coast and Muscat. New, hideously expensive Landrovers had also been acquired. Off they all set along Wadi Sumayl, that glorious valley filled with date palms, small picturesque mud villages and, wherever the slightest rise occurs, forts, turrets and castles dominating the scene. Allfrey, who took part in this jaunt, and describes the operation in his usual witty style, writes of the surprise he got on their first night stop in Wadi Sumayl. There, packed into a dozen or more stinking fish lorries, was a wild horde of 'loyal tribesmen' under the command of the then Sultan's half-brother, Sayid Tariq. These trusty warriors' enviable job was to overrun the liberated villages and keep the rebel population under control, all of which was immensely appealing to this loot-happy mob.

From their camp in Wadi Sumayl the little army settled down to harass the enemy as much as they possibly could. Allfrey set off on patrol with a platoon of the Muscat Regiment, a couple of mortar sections, and an R.A.F. officer equipped with a radio for calling up fighters out of the blue whenever necessity demanded. It wasn't long before this little detachment attracted fire over its head. After setting up the mortars on top of a hill, everybody prepared for battle. At this point the patrol leader decided on a show of force. Summoned by the radio, the Venoms were there in no time, swooping down over the rebels with an ear-splitting screech of sirens. But the enemy had seen it all before. To the patrol's astonishment, they simply leapt to their feet, waved their rifles in the air and loudly cheered the fighters' splendid performance. As the object of the exercise had not been to offer them a free show, the next swoop meant business and there was no more derisive cheering after that.

While patrols went on nosing their way into the foot-hills of the Akhdar monster, Brigadier Maxwell was stationed on the other side with a company of Cameronians, a collection of Trucial Oman Scouts and the gallant remains of the Sultan's Armed Forces. A handful of seconded Scottish troops were preparing the main attack; night and day they hammered enemy outposts, tucked away among the rocks above the Nizwa road. The R.A.F., who were lending a hand, bombed castles and forts occupied by Talib's warriors and dropped leaflets inviting the population to give themselves up. As few of the tribesmen were blessed with any reading ability, this particular side of the operation must have fallen on somewhat stony ground.

Mutti, at the entrance of a deep narrow wadi near Nizwa, is the starting point of another bolt-hole up the mountain, and was another of the Beni Ryiam towns to make a lot of trouble for the Sultan's forces. But it did this once too often for its own good: the men of Mutti laid an ambush in broad daylight for a patrol and a Royal Marine sergeant was killed. Sayid Tariq's revenge was total annihilation of the village. He and Colonel Smiley's men poured paraffin on to every house in the village and set them on fire, so that no more mine-layers would lie low within its precincts or prepare ambushes again.

Suddenly, to everybody's surprise, the rebels all caved in together and organized resistance came to an end. Nizwa, holy Nizwa, was once more in the hands of the Sultan; but the dreaded trio who had started all the trouble had disappeared. In the general chaos which followed, they had scuttled up the mountain once more, there to brood and hatch another of their poisonous plots.

Jebel Akhdar, surrounded by its circle of gigantic slabs, each ending in a sharp prong, was pretty well unassailable. A great deal of time, blood, sweat and tears were to pass before it was eventually subdued.

It was not until Colonel David Smiley had arrived to take charge of the impossible operation that things began to look up for the first time. This brave, intrepid soldier had spent most of his army career frolicking with Irregulars. 1941 found him behind the Italian lines with a pack of commandos. Volunteering for Special Operations Executive in 1943, he had parachuted into Greece. Trekking over the Albanian frontier, he had organized resistance against the Italians, then the Germans. He had worked with guerrillas of every kind and all political colours. Then, running out of possibilities in Europe once the war was over, he set off for the Far East, where he parachuted into the north-eastern jungles of Thailand to help with the resistance against the Japanese. With all this experience behind him, there was obviously no better man to cope with Jebel Akhdar, and if it hadn't been for him, the three leading rebels would probably have continued to sit in their eyrie, plotting endless mischief and festering like a permanently running sore, until the end of their days.

For the first two years, the new Army Commander had to cope with non-stop road-mining. Mines were brought down from the arsenal at the top of the mountain and laid along the roads by specially trained guerrillas, usually under the benevolent eye of the *askars* who were supposed to prevent the operation. To begin with, small five-pound American army mines were used. If properly sandbagged, a vehicle running over one of these might lose a wheel, but nothing more dramatic than that. When the heavy U.S. landmines were introduced a year later, casualties, sometimes fatal, began to occur. This menace was organized efficiently abroad; the bombs came over the mountains or by dhow to the Batinah coast. It was impossible to control the smuggling and laying of those deadly eggs. Talib was said to pay 1,000 Maria Theresa dollars for each successful explosion. The only reprisals were short prison spells for the offenders but, as they were never caught anyway, even the death sentence would have been a piffling deterrent.

One very galling incident, which rankles to this day, was Salih bin Isah's lorryload of weaponry. Into this vehicle he packed forty or so of his best-trained warriors from his own province of the Sharqyia equipped with ample supplies of bombs, mortars, anti-aircraft machine-guns, hundreds of mines and a radio set. All this stuff, which came from friends and sympathizers abroad who wanted to see the downfall of the Sultan, was smuggled into Oman on small donkeys led by cherubic little boys and innocent-looking white-beards. An empty truck was then driven across the frontier post to a given spot, where it ostensibly broke down. After all the deadly material had been assembled and the detachment of young warriors had foregathered, the truck was duly loaded and set off for the mountains. Challenged at Rostaq, it sped on regardless. At Awabi, at the foot of the mountain, it was challenged, then shot at, but the driver pressed on at top speed and got away. Eventually this lethal hoard was loaded on to Jebel donkeys and, when it finally reached the top, came as a powerful shot in the arm for the defence of Suleiman's fortress, and for the sowing of the deadly seeds along the roads at night. By 1958 this had become a serious plague: two or three trucks were habitually blown up in one day and something had to be done. Colonel Smiley was the man who did it.

After he became convinced that no ordinary soldiers would ever succeed in storming the lofty fortress, he got in touch with his numerous influential friends. Through their good offices he managed to get a couple of squadrons of S.A.S., on their way home to England on leave from Malaya, deflected to Oman.

Meanwhile useful reinforcements arrived, in the shape of a squadron of Life Guards, who were sent off to look after Nizwa, Izki and Awabi. Throughout the campaign these stalwart soldiers proved unfailingly invaluable. Colonel Smiley gives them a first-class write-up. 'We never ceased to bless the authorities for giving us these Life Guards,' he writes. 'They really entered into the spirit of our war, and when not engaged in a protective role with their Ferrets, were happy to turn themselves into Infantry and carry out arduous and dangerous duties up the mountain.'

The Jebel was entirely surrounded when a company of the Northern Frontier Regiment at Tanuf and a squadron of Trucial Oman Scouts at Yankil blocked off the last approaches. After that, the rebels on the top were completely cut off and supplies could only reach them by humping them over very steep and nasty rocks.

In October, the Commander of the 22nd Special Air Services Regiment came out on a flying visit to see for himself if the job was really worthy of his men. After prowling around the foot of the monster for a day or two, and a few low flights over the top, he was perfectly satisfied that their talents would not be wasted on this particular operation.

In November, an enterprising Contract officer, by dint of probing and poking into the ravines and gorges of the Jebel, had hit upon an unguarded way up to the top. Starting from the village of Hijar just above the military station at Awabi, he had scaled the Persian steps, cut into the rock all that time ago, on the north side of the mountain. This was the first time the plateau had been reached, and proved a tremendous boost to general morale. Soon after that, D Squadron arrived, numbering eighty of the toughest and most determined men on earth, armed to the teeth and with a morale of tempered steel and muscles of hickory wood. In spite of all these qualities, one of their non-commissioned officers was tragically killed during one of the early patrols. On another occasion a couple of troops climbed the famous steps and strolled unchallenged across the plateau as far as Aqabat al-Dhafar. There, a bunch of rebels who were holed up in one of the caves pounced on them, and a stiff battle ensued. Fortunately, damage occurred on the rebel side only. After that, a platoon of the Muscat Regiment settled down firmly at the top of the Persian steps, and stayed there to harass the rebels and draw their fire and attention away from other parts of the mountain.

It was a funny kind of war. Fierce and fought without quarter though it was, scribbled little messages fluttered up and down the mountain between the assailing forces and the besieged, conveyed by the women who took their rations up to the look-out posts on top. On one occasion, the rebels sent down word that the loudspeaker attached to one of the aircraft, through which the S.A.F. counselled immediate surrender, was making a funny noise and the message was garbled and unintelligible. Furthermore, all aggression on both sides stopped during the afternoon, so that everybody could have a nap during the torrid months of summer. At night, when bivouac fires were lit, giving away one another's positions, nobody ever shot at them.

And then, one day there came a request for a truce. For two weeks there were no more air-strikes, no more bombing and, at night, the roads were free of mines. The rebels wanted a breathing-space to take stock of the situation. After that it was back to all-out hostilities again.

Soon it became apparent that, in order to subdue once and for all the plague on the plateau, reinforcements would have to be called for. Consequently in January, A Squadron arrived from Malaya, and went straight into the fray, while D Squadron returned to the questionable delights of Bait al-Falaj for a well-earned rest. Fresh from the steaming jungles of Malaya, A squadron was feeling the cold on the frosty heights of the Jebel which got quite nippy during the long winter nights under the stars.

D-Day was planned for 25 January, but because of bad weather it was put off until the following night. In order to confuse the rebels, several attacks were made at various points during the preceding weeks. A masterly stroke, which completely put them off the scent, was to warn the donkey men – in the strictest possible secrecy – to get ready for a midnight scramble up the mountain from Tanuf. This, as expected, was reported to Talib within a few hours. So, although the donkeys themselves proved quite useless as pack animals in the very tough conditions of the assault, their drivers, by their treachery, unknowingly played a major part in the final victory.

Sayid Tariq's loyal tribesmen, all 250 of them, were to lend a hand and join the assault. In the south, some fifty or so Beni Ruaha were to go up with the S.A.S. Squadrons and, in the north, about 200 of the unreliable Abryin, who had been the cause of the disaster at Balad Sait, would join a platoon of the Muscat Regiment and start the climb at Awabi. All decked out in their robes, *khanjars* and colourful turbans, the only mark by which they could be distinguished from the rebels, once on top, was a red arm-band. Venoms would flatten out any resistance, and other aircraft from Sharja would drop supplies. A couple of helicopters were standing by at Nizwa to take any wounded away at once.

Duly alerted by the donkey men, the rebels were all huddled up at Tanuf and Aqabat al-Dhafar, where they were meant to be. One outpost with a couple of sleepy sentries turned out to be the sole opposition met with on the chosen trail. Both were swiftly dispatched with a hand grenade.

Nine and a half hours after the beginning of the rope climb, the S.A.S. reached the top according to plan. The hideous ascent had taken place during the night. In the half-light of dawn, the supply planes duly dropped their loads, 30,000 pounds in weight, an impressive drop of essential equipment. Seeing all these parachutes floating out of the morning sky, the rebels immediately assumed this to be an air invasion. In wild panic, they took to their heels without waiting for more. Only a small group of Beni Ryiam, taken by surprise, found it more prudent to surrender than to fight it out. They were detailed to go and round up the rest of the rebels and persuade them to return to their homes. When they realized that their own normal practices were not being followed and no reprisals were being taken, they cautiously began to creep back to their villages. Cleverly pinpointed, a bomb had been dropped right on top of Suleiman's own residence without touching any of the surrounding village huts. Topped with the Sultan's victorious flag, the rubble was left exactly as the bomb had arranged it, 'pour encourager les autres', as the Brigadier succinctly put it. That was as far as official punitive retaliation was to go.

The Terrible Three had once more vanished off the face of the plateau, evading capture again. And even though Suleiman's own tribes now complained about them bitterly, nobody was prepared to give them away. Shortly afterwards, Colonel Smiley heard they were in hiding in the Sharqyia. Before he had time to trap them, an interfering officer who had no business meddling with such matters rushed to the spot to try and bag them himself. Far too fly for him, they fled once more, and have been out of the country ever since.

The loyal tribesmen who had made it to the top (many of them, finding the whole business too exhausting and tedious for words, had melted away in the heat of the climb) at once got down to the serious business of looting. After loading up entire caravans of donkeys with stolen rifles, they trekked off down the mountain with their enormous haul.

When I met Colonel Smiley in London, he told me that he was taken to Suleiman's hideout by one of the rebels. Like Ali Baba's cave, every corner was stuffed with treasures of every kind, including enormous quantities of arms. In the main part of the cave he found a huge pile of documents and letters, giving the fullest information about the rebel organization, and a great number of supporters' names in Oman. It turned out, as expected, that the mine-layers and arms smugglers were operating under the benevolent eye of the *askars* who were supposed to suppress them. And one of these gentlemen, who had been entrusted with a very special stretch of road, had been doing the dirty work himself. His treachery had been well disguised beneath a convincingly deceptive outward show of loyalty.

Crawling on hands and knees into the innumerable labyrinths of the cave, Smiley had lost his way, coming up against blank rock every time he turned a corner; it was a long time before he saw the light of day at the end of a tunnel. As a reminder of this unnerving experience, and as a souvenir of the protracted and unorthodox campaign, he took with him a brass tray on which he still serves coffee to his guests at home.

And that was the end of the Jebel War. Now that it was all over, reconstruction started up at once. At Government expense, emergency provisions and building materials were flown up from the plain in a non-stop airlift; dwellings were patched up, wells dredged out, and the *falaj* system laboriously restored to full working order.

Brigadier Maxwell was appointed Military Governor of the mountain kingdom, and no one better could have been found to carry out the ticklish problem of winning the rebels' friendship and confidence than that gentle, kindly officer.

9 Coral Sands of the Batinah

'Honour the date palm, for she is your mother' —
The Koran

The usual funerary stones, or triliths, are sticking straight out of a dusty field as we drive past the shanty town outside Matrah on our way through the mountains towards Bustan. Audrey is taking me on a beachcombing expedition.

Since at death the Bedu of the desert are simply popped into a hole in the sand wherever they happen to drop, without so much as a stick to mark the spot, I never cease to be amazed at the close-packed crop of raw natural stones of these graveyards. There are seventeen of them in Muscat alone, each one consecrated ground, and never to be used for anything else until Kingdom come, which is hard luck on the development and construction boys, but it is nice to think that the poor bones will be left to lie in peace for evermore. As for mosques, there are only thirty-six in Muscat, whereas in Matrah there are forty-five.

'Where do the women pray?' I once asked an Arab friend.

'At home, I suppose,' he answered vaguely, and with supreme lack of interest. The Prophet, I know, did not exclude them from the mosque. He just thought they were better off at home.

'So it's the men who won't let them into the mosque?' I persisted.

'That's right,' answered my friend smugly. To him this was perfectly normal. There is, I am told, a mosque for women only in Oman, but this I have not seen and have no idea where it is, if in fact it exists at all.

All round the graveyard grow suburban residences made of palm-leaves and oil cans (*burmails*). Although the area looks rather like Misery Corner, the people who come out of these hovels are clean, clear-eyed and healthy-looking. The children playing around in the dust have plump little behinds, mostly wagging bare in the sun. The women, supple and sinuous, move about among the crawling babies, the dogs and the piles of rubbish.

We drive on through the newly-cut cleft blasted out of the mountain. Still quite raw from the recent dynamiting, it glitters in the sun. This is March and Oman still enjoys the blessings bestowed upon her by the little rain which fell last winter. Looking closely at the mountain, I can see tiny sprigs of green bravely pushing their way through the rock; this is, for a brief period, what mountain goats feed on; after that, their diet is a mystery. For the rest of the year, those Omani crags are as bare as the face of the moon. There is no soil, no water, no vegetable life of any kind. Poised, chamois-like, all their hooves bunched up together on the very top of one of these needle-pointed crags, some of these quaint creatures stare down at us with mild interest.

'Much too hairy for this climate,' remarks Audrey disapprovingly. 'You would think a short light coat would be more suitable.'

With their long brown fluffy fur flapping around their ankles, they look like medieval war-horses robed for battle, just waiting to rush into the fray.

Kicking off our sandals, we shuffle barefoot along the edge of the water in the coarse coral sand. The shell situation is disappointing, as the last tide has only brought up the broken bits lying about at the bottom of the sea. But it is a treat just to stroll along on the edge where the tiny waves break, and nowhere a soul in sight. Nothing but the hot blue sky overhead and the immense Indian Ocean stretching all the way to Bombay without a break.

Our next port of call, below Qurm Heights, is a better bet from the shell-gathering point of view. Leaving the car on the track for the very good reason that it can go no further, we hitch up our skirts and wade knee-deep through the shallow lagoons on the way to the beach. As soon as we set foot on it, the beach rises up in a body and begins to roll down towards the sea like a moving staircase. Thoroughly alarmed at our approach, the crab population has jumped on to its toes and taken off, making for the safety of the surf as fast as the little wretches can go. For make no mistake: there is nothing lovable about these creatures. We come across a dolphin, washed up by the last tide, stone dead, surrounded by a congress of these crabs who, their greed being stronger than their fear, continue busily to nibble at the dead eyes despite our presence. A little further on, a turtle lies on its back, its leathery arms and legs hanging limp from the shell like empty sleeves, with all flesh scooped out; crawling out, a scuffle of sand-coloured claws clacking together in alarm. One of the curious things about these ghost crabs is that their young skim along every bit as fast as the parents. Sprinkled about among the big horny adults with their great white claws pounding the sand like pistons in their panic flight, whole clouds of minute specks flow along among them on invisible hair legs, like puffs of sand blown along by the wind. A short distance from their holes, they build curious little mounds of sand shaped like the tall chimneys of the Potteries. When you kick one of these turrets, the occupant of the hole next door clambers out of his house, carefully arranges his heaviest and thickest claws together, and begins to drum on his doorstep, in the hope of striking terror into your heart. And there he will remain, endlessly twiddling his thumbs, as long as you stay around the vicinity of his hole. But only in the safety of the water will he actually come up and start nibbling your living flesh.

His cousins, the hermit crabs which scuttle in their millions on the Batinah coast, swap shells every time they grow out of their home. This is a delicate operation needing careful timing. Bereft of their armour, they are as vulnerable as shelled peas, ready for picking up by any predator around. When a hermit begins to feel cramped and bursting at the seams, he sets off at once in search of an empty shell of the right fit. This is not easy, as his brothers and sisters and contemporaries, all thousands of them, have reached a similar pass at exactly the same time. And they too are on the lookout for a home of the same size. When the right thing has eventually been run down, speed is of the essence. I once watched a couple of crabs coming from opposite directions making for the same shell. Not having spotted each other they met, to their horror, on the doorstep. An ugly scuffle ensued, and while their claws were locked in combat, a third party quietly slipped into the shell behind their backs. A dirty trick of course. But it's sink or swim in the crab world, as everywhere else. On another occasion I came across a poor brute with an acute housing problem. The best he had been able to find was half a clam shell with which to cover his nakedness. Every time he took a dip, the wretched thing slipped off his back. Diving about among the waves and scrabbling around for his elusive home, I've never seen such a worried crab.

Qurm beach goes on for ever, all the way up the Batinah coast as far as the very north of Oman, about 200 miles along to the Musandam Peninsula. Thousands of shells lie about on the sand and long ribbon-like ridges of broken fragments snake along, marking the limit of the last high tide. There, like milestones dotted the length of the beach, great lumps of brain coral lie about among the shells with the disconcerting aspect of outsize human brains. As these lumps are riddled with tiny holes they are used as bricks for building private houses in the Gulf, and I have seen some desirable residences in Sharjah made entirely of this type of coral, forming intricate lacework patterns all over the walls. Owing to the infinitude of these minute cavities, the slightest breath of air filters through, keeping the temperature inside deliciously cool.

The Indian Ocean contains all the right ingredients, not to speak of the balmy environment, necessary to nurture the most intricate and extravagant shapes in the world of cowries, volutes, cones and bivalves. The most astonishing among these creatures is the giant clam, Tridacna Gigas, which lurks in the shallow coral waters of the coast, and grows to the imposing size of a couple of metres long. They are what is known as suspension feeders, which really means a kind of roving dustbin, sucking up whatever delicacies may be floating around. But should they come upon lean times, the crafty creatures have developed a second string by manufacturing food in their very own tissues. This is known as zooxanthellae, unicellular algae living right inside the viridian mantel lobes (the vast bright-green lips of the creature). This cunning alternative forms a kind of home-grown vegetable patch which is cropped whenever required and dispatched down to the digestive system to be dealt with in the usual manner.

Another variety of this ingenious breed, a kind of bivalve with smooth round pink cheeks called Intrari Intraria, grows to a mere six inches in width, and hides his shame by digging deep down in the sea bed, over 100 feet into the soft ooze before he can feel secure. Having reached this secluded spot, he ventures out a hairy arm through which he breathes and sucks up any left-overs which come drifting down from the richer layers above. He is a humble fellow, and not choosy about his food – which is just as well in that neighbourhood.

The melon shell, about the same size as its fruit namesake, has a smooth pink shiny doorway, reaching from end to end for the monstrous head and foot all-in-one which creeps out to seek its food and meet its friends on the ocean floor. A conchologist friend of mine who collects this particular mollusc tells me she has to shoot it to bits with a revolver before it will lie down and keep still. When they can get hold of these shells, the fishermen use them for bailing out their boats in bad weather. The spider conch, or Lambis Lambis to use its Latin name, is regarded as a very tasty morsel, roasted in its shell on the beach and consumed on the spot. The money cowries are as thick as thieves everywhere and come in all sizes. In order to keep their shine, they have to be caught alive, and persuaded to leave home by hook or by crook. If allowed to die in their beds, the shells grow quite dull, and no amount of polishing with face cream or olive oil will bring the glow back into their cheeks. Top shells, whose lustrous iridescent inner lining was used for making mother-of-pearl buttons, were saved from extinction through over-fishing in the nick of time by the break-through of the plastic button.

now tops are said to be happily on the increase once more. Walking along the beach I collect a great hoard of pink snail-like shells of minute size, which I thought would make an exotic necklace for my six-year-old grand-daughter. Instead of this they ended up, alas, in the alimentary tract of my *one*-year-old grand-daughter.

As we plod along the edge of the rising tide, gulls swoop down over the shallow water, spotting prey. A reef heron in his 'dark phase' steps daintily along on thin green legs, fastidiously shaking the drops off his yellow toes before putting them back into the water again. From time to time his long thin orange beak stabs the waves and comes up with a fish skewered on the end. This he tosses into the air, snaps it up half-way, and down his long neck it goes in a flash. Further out at sea, an old wreck half out of the water serves as a love-nest to a couple of herons. The passionate couplings in which they frequently indulge are accompanied by deafening screeches, which Pliny assumed to be cries of agony. Breaking off from time to time, they come gliding over and, using us as bait, plunge into the water at our feet, as shoals of man-eating fish begin to nibble our toes. In the wake of the greedy little fellows come the murderous mackerel, pounding after them, followed by bigger fish still. It is the food chain in action under our very noses.

Oman is a great place for fish – and I don't just mean in the sea. They crop up in the caked mud of dry wadis, waiting for the floods to come and float them free again. Once back in their element, their appetites sharpened by months of fasting, it is no wonder they pounce on everything that comes their way, and tender human flesh is high up on the list of their favourite diet. Not content with sea and wadi water as their playground, they seem to grow out of the very heart of the mountain as well. The *falaj* irrigation system, tapping underground lakes in the depths of the rock among the very roots of the mountain, comes rushing out, squirming with famished small fry. The only place I didn't see any of these ferocious *fleisch-fressers* was in the hot pool at Rostaq, where the copper-blue water bubbles up from the depths of the rock, all pitted and pock-marked as if fiery raindrops the size of golf balls had once cascaded on to it.

The Indian Ocean, frothing with life, is said to be the most under-fished sea in the world. Whales, all kinds of sharks, swordfish, marlin, tuna, grouper, dorado, barracuda, can be clearly seen just below the surface. And Colonel Smiley describes giant rays, thirty feet across, leaping out of the sea and flopping down again with a smack like a thunderclap. Fishermen constantly bring out new varieties which have never been seen before. Whether polka-dotted, or covered with stripes, spikes or whiskers, they are all invariably good to eat. In the underwater coral forests, parrot and porcupine fish waltz sedately in and out among the sea-anemones and the ponderous lobsters. Skimming along and frisking about in the froth of the waves, flying fish pursue their wayward path. In the early summer, moray eels and sea snakes are on the prowl, hunting for wives. Portuguese men-of-war, feared and loathed by bathers and fishermen alike but happy to go wherever the wind will take them, arrive in great flotillas.

This enormous 200-mile-long coast of gleaming white sand sweeps up from Qurm to the very top, with only one interruption. A slice of the Musandam Peninsula had to be handed over to Ras al-Khaima, the old pirate State of the Persian Gulf, during one of the Wahhabi invasions, in exchange for getting rid of the enemy. This is more of a theoretical nuisance than a real one; there is still a great deal of shoreline for fishing purposes. Of really crucial strategic importance is the fact that Oman owns the tip of the peninsula which controls the entrance to the Gulf.

The wadis breaking up the long coastline end in *khors* (inlets) of brackish water, often edged with mangrove swamps. Otherwise, the entire length of the shore is lined with a green agricultural belt. There are schemes afoot, planned on a national scale, for turning this lush and fertile area into an immense market garden, which will eventually feed the entire Arabian Peninsula. The whole of the Gulf and Saudi Arabia will clamour for its produce. Water will be dammed and piped into huge reservoirs instead of being allowed to run wastefully into the sea. The coast is lined with small settlements of thatched huts, mostly housing members of the Hawasina and Yal-Saad tribes, as well as vast colonies of scorpions and camel spiders. The skeleton of each hut is constructed out of split palm logs lashed together at the corners. The splitting is ingeniously achieved with a minimum of trouble and equipment by inserting iron wedges in judicious places, so that long rents run the length of the bole in a flash. Plaited palm fronds line the walls, and leaf mats cover the sandy floor. These cool, desirable residences are known as *bait zur*. In other parts of Arabia, where air-conditioned estates have been put up in an effort to anchor the desert tribes to more sedentary lives, these *barasti* huts are usually preferred by the Bedu.

The more important villages of the Batinah all have their forts, sometimes in good order, but more often picturesquely crumbling away on top of a rock on the skyline. The sheikhs and their families live in tall houses, beautifully shaped out of mud. So far, the most important products of this fertile coast consist of huge crops of limes. Grown in enormous quantities, they come in two kinds: those which turn yellow when dried and come from the interior, and a far superior breed, cultivated on the coast, which go black and can be stored for a couple of years. These are worth a third more than the canary variety, and mostly go to Iraq, where they are used for flavouring rice. Other crops include olives, mangoes and pomegranates, figs, vines, bananas and citrus.

'Honour the date tree,' enjoined the Prophet; and this instruction has been followed with conscientious love and care by the Arabs of the Batinah, who compare the date palm to a human being. Like him, it dies when its head is cut off; a severed frond (or arm) will not grow again; and its topknot is covered with a dense, compact mop, like hair on a human head.

Phoenix Dactylefera is the best variety of all the 650,000 date palms which grow on the Batinah plain. Along with camels, these noble trees often form a large part of a girl's marriage dowry. Each one is registered, and may even have a name of its own, for all I know. A fine upstanding male palm in the pink of condition will be able to keep a hundred females going with the greatest of ease, and a good stud soon acquires a reputation for miles around. Artificial insemination, which has been practised since ancient times, as is shown on Assyrian carvings, helps matters along by hastening natural processes.

Admittedly P. Dactylefera is the Rolls-Royce of the palm tree, but there are over one hundred other kinds as well, each with special virtues of its own. Good soft dates run into at least a dozen first-class varieties, of which the favourites are Fardh, Khalas and Khanaizi. Al-Batinah umm-Silah, which turn bright red when ripe, are boiled down in enormous cauldrons and used as cattle fodder. Pliny claimed he could list forty-nine different varieties if only he could remember all their outlandish names. A good housewife, using different kinds in turn, should be able to serve tasty date meals in as many different ways as there are days in the month. There are said to be twenty-two different kinds on the Batinah, and in the interior, where they are better, there are sixty-two.

Fish, the other profitable activity of this promising coast, is also exported by the boatful. Sardines, which you can smell miles away, are dried in the sun and fed to animals. The pigmy cows of the Dhofar mountains subsist on these all through the winter, until the coming of the monsoon which turns their pastures green again. Sharks, also hung up to dry on washing lines, are dispatched into central Oman, where they are considered a delicacy. Personally I would prefer to feed the sharks to the beasts of the field and eat the sardines – but it is all a matter of what you are used to.

Sohar, the capital of the Batinah and traditional home of Sindbad the Sailor, was for 1,500 years renowned as the most scintillating town of the Middle East. An Arab writer of the tenth century said: 'The rest of Islam hardly knows that a town such as Sohar with its wealth and development exists on the Persian sea.' It must have been a gay and lively place, with its cosmopolitan *souq* reeking of spices, camel dung and frankincense, jingling with harness-bells and the tinkling of women's jewellery. The harbour would have been packed with dhows loaded with precious carpets from Persia, silks from India, gold and frankincense from Dhofar, myrrh from Somalia, ivory, monkey skins and peacocks from East Africa and Zanzibar. All of which is probably not very different from a prosperous Middle East port nowadays.

Built at the end of Wadi Jizzi, Sohar was protected by a

massive fortress said to need 1,000 souls to man it. When the infamous Portuguese admiral Albuquerque had captured Muscat, he insisted on the surrender of Sohar, which he knew quite well would otherwise have been a thorn in his flesh. In 1645, the prosperous city offered trading facilities to Great Britain, and a treaty was duly signed the following year. From then on, Christians could be seen mixing with the jolly crowds of Muslims and Jews milling around the town, living proof of the religious tolerance which prevailed at the time.

When Said the Great eventually took Sohar back under his wing, the once glittering capital lost its independence and prosperity and its cosmopolitan brilliance. Nowadays the fort is little more than a picturesque tumbledown old ruin which couldn't possibly be defended by any number of valiant men, let alone 1,000.

Right down at the other end of the Batinah, where the mountains reach down to the sea at Qurm Heights, lies the fount of the new prosperity which has hit Oman in the last few years. At the foot of the rocks a wide sandy plain is studded with the installations of P.D.O., including half-a-dozen sparkling tanks for storing the crude before it is piped into the tankers queueing up on the skyline out at sea. On the heights above the great containers is Ras al-Hamra, the new development which houses the oil-station personnel. Up the road is Ruwi, just outside Matrah, all brand-new shops and supermarkets. And a little further up the road is Bait al-Falaj, now the headquarters of the Sultan's Armed Forces who are housed in a fort originally built 150 years ago as a weekend palace for the Sultans. The old airport also was there with its narrow, dusty landing-strip. Many are the tales told by veterans of the Jebel War, hardened leather-souled old toughs who quaked and quivered as their aircraft came wobbling down to earth with wingtips scraping the rock-face on either side. This desirable spot is now used as a helicopter landing stage and general parking lot.

10   Khaboura

A hideous creature of dragon-like aspect with horns and scales and a heavy tail suddenly scuttles across the track.

'Very good, very good,' says the driver, smacking his lips and pointing at the disappearing monster. It seems that some of these ungainly desert lizards, which can reach five feet in length, are regarded as particularly delicate fare by the Bedu. P.S. Allfrey mentions a meal of this kind which he once consumed, having been told it was rabbit. Gristly, I seem to remember, was how he described it.

We are on our way to visit 'the Durham University project ad al-Khaboura.' This admirable venture, established a few years ago in the oasis of Khaboura on the Batinah coast, is one of those noble, idealistic, non-profit-making undertakings which the British still go in for in underdeveloped countries. Its object is to help the local people, by teaching and example, to make the best of local resources and expertise with as little cash as possible. All the staff at this establishment are, of course, graduates. Even the goatherd is a college man.

Jo Butler, who looks after the infant-welfare side of the undertaking, meets us as we swoop into the yard in a cloud of dust. Totally unconcerned by this sudden sandstorm she says, 'Come in and have coffee, and I will tell you all about it.' Tall, blonde and elegant in her sage-green *dishdasha*, she leads the way to a prefabricated bungalow all draped in jasmine and bougainvillaea.

In Muscat I had heard that she did a marvellous, dedicated job in the most terrible surroundings and appalling living conditions. So I am speechless with astonishment when invited to park myself on a modern sofa, in the gayest, most attractive, coolest open-plan room I have seen in Oman.

'Are you an artist?' I can't help asking, as I stare at the *art nouveau* prints, the bright cushions, the jolly lamps, the marvellous combinations of colours. This could easily be one of the more attractive artists' studios in Chelsea.

'No no,' she says firmly. 'Nothing like that at all.'

Lapping my Nescafé and goat's milk, I begin to ask questions.

'We are linked with P.D.O., who sponsor us,' she informs me, taking no notice of my goggling. 'They give us transport and look after our generator, and magic things like that.' Magnificent power stations have been built all along the Batinah coast. Through the window I can see one of these space-age constructions gleaming in the distance, in the middle of a field of dust.

'Why don't you use local electricity?' I ask, surprised.

The answer is that the resplendent monsters are still waiting to be connected: all along the Batinah coast, just sitting there looking beautiful in their aluminium glory, but totally useless until somebody remembers to do something about it. This may happen at any minute now.

Thanks to P.D.O. who run the generator which powers the pumps, there is plenty of water, so European vegetables can be grown in the short winter season. This was part of the plan to teach the local women how to raise and cook these (to them) strange-looking weeds.

But it is the goats which are the main pride and achievement of the settlement. Grown from nothing to a herd of eighty, they were developed to their present standard by the last goatherd, a young Reading University graduate. Obviously knowing his stuff, he sent to England for a few Anglo-Nubian studs, which he then crossed with local she-goats. This produced a hardy new breed, bigger, stronger and yielding more milk as well as much better meat.

107

At the festival of Id, after Ramadan, and at weddings and other ceremonies, local families slaughter their animals, particularly the males. After the feast is over, they are invariably surprised to have no sires left for the females. One of the problems of the project is to make the village people understand this point. My guess is, they know perfectly well what they are up to: they just want to have their goat and eat it – which is exactly what happens. In desperation, the graduates of Khaboura have instituted a kind of rent-a-husband system. The females are brought to the station, where their owners pay a few *baizas* a day for their keep, and they have a marvellous time consorting with the great, lusty, resident he-goats of noble Anglo-Nubian descent. After a three-months' visit to this delectable holiday camp, they regretfully return to their dusty villages and their one meal of lucerne a day (if they're lucky) and frequent snacks of brown paper bags and disintegrating foam-rubber flip-flops. In due course they proudly bring forth their aristocratic progeny, which people come from miles around to admire.

Weaving is another venture which had a good run for its money at Khaboura, but wasn't able to put down enough roots to survive. And this in spite of the fact that a fully qualified English weaver came out to see if something could be done about starting up a lucrative cottage-industry on the spot. 'The Omanis spin and they weave,' says Jo. 'This high-powered weaver-girl, she was called Gigi, brought out some fairly simple spinning-wheels to see if the local ladies would like to try them out.'

The local ladies, who are paid a couple of *ryals* for a kilo of spun yarn, are delighted to do so. The fruit of their labours is packed ceiling-high and goes on growing, patiently waiting to be woven into useful mats and camel-bags. The wool is mostly the natural cream or brown, though some of it gets treated to a dip in a red dye called mahaleb. This is made from a special kind of leaf in Ibri. Here in Khaboura they sometimes use madder, but as it fades in the sun it is less popular.

Jo steps across to a corner of the room and roots around among a lot of plastic bags. 'This strip was woven by an old man sitting in a hole in the ground working an old-fashioned loom up in Sohar,' she says holding up a thick tobacco-brown length of fabric for my inspection. Even I can see that it is a very fine piece of weaving. But it is a dying art, and there are very few original old Omani weavers left.

Poor Gigi's task was overwhelming. 'To get things going as a viable concern was a bit slow. And then you've got to find a market for your wares,' says Jo sadly. It takes a long time to produce one article, let alone dozens, 'and as soon as you announce you are going commercial, the delighted hotels quickly put in for a couple of hundred.' To meet such orders (Habitat in London also clamoured for several gross) you would need to have the entire population of the Batinah weaving away day and night without stop. Poor Gigi, quite distracted, sat at her loom like Penelope unable to churn out the stuff fast enough, so in the end they all lost interest, and her mats and camel-bags were eventually sold at auction by P.D.O. Mercifully, the goats are only shorn once or twice a year, so there is a limit to the quantity of spun yarn that the local ladies can produce.

Then bee-keeping was tried out, and of course a highly-qualified apiculturist was appointed to try his luck. The first pedigree swarm which arrived from England broke out of its travelling coop, creating pandemonium at Abu Dhabi airport, where no bee had ever been seen before. The second consignment, which made it to Khaboura, perished from lack of local nectar. There are no blooms and precious few flowering plants and shrubs around the oasis.

One great success is the combine harvester, which chugs around the villages hiring out its services for one *ryal* an hour. In fact, it is in such constant demand that more of its kind have been ordered. Some wheat is grown and crops of pulses like lentils and chick peas.

But the basic diet of the local inhabitants consists of rice and sea-food.

Quantities of flat and white fish are caught along these shores, as well as plenty of shark. Tuna is a great luxury, and also very expensive. 'Fish is their protein,' says Jo. 'They also eat dahl and chick peas. And they make a fine sort of Arab-type bread which is very thin. The dough is made out of brown flour and water, which they roll around a very hot skillet. Unlike chapattis, it is wafer thin.' At about 9 a.m. they eat a thicker version of this which they call *gurth*, spread with a smear of honey or jam, or sprinkled with a little sugar. With this they drink tea. Or they mix milk with cinnamon. 'That's rather nice,' says Jo reminiscently. Dates are also on the local diet, though gritty and not of a very good quality; also onions, and tomato paste. Sometimes tamarind goes in with the fish. The seed is soaked, and the flavoured water is then used for cooking. As for the rest, it depends on what the nearest little Indian store may have. A few cheese portions, and sometimes biscuits. Except at Ids and weddings, meat is never eaten. But they have hens, and some adventurous souls even go so far as to eat eggs, in spite of the bad odour in which these are held. 'In fact there's not as much malnutrition as you might think. Not as much as I expected when I first came to this country,' adds Jo.

'How do the local ladies react to you? Are they in awe of you?' I ask.

'No, in fact we are very good friends. We discuss all sorts of things. They are very curious.' Every day they want to know what Jo is wearing under her *dishdasha*.

'Well, pants, you know,' she informs them.

'Oh,' they invariably squeak, 'she's got pants on.' And this goes round the circle of delighted ladies for a few minutes. Eventually the husbands will be informed that the Inglesi was wearing pants under her *dishdasha* today.

'They can't make me out at all,' Jo continues. 'You see, I'm not married, and I've got no children, and this is completely outside their experience.'

'Are you *sure* you've never been married?' they often ask in great puzzlement.

'No, no, never.'

'But why?' This can't sink in at all.

'Well you see,' explains Jo, 'if I had a husband, I couldn't come round and see you and look after your children.'

Ah, that's a point. And they all mutter about it for a while. But still they come back to the burning question.

'Are you *quite* sure you've never had a husband at all?' In Arabian society this is completely unthinkable.

I ask Jo about her relations with the husbands.

'I get on just as well with the men as with the women except, of course, when visitors arrive, and I get pushed off to the women's quarters.' Often, if she has trouble being understood by a Bedu lady, she asks if the husband is at home. When he appears, everything is sorted out as he explains to his wife the point that Jo is trying to make. For men have a language of their own which is quite different from the one spoken by the women, who go in for a lot of grunts. These are in fact a kind of vocal short-hand and can mean all sorts of different things, according to the tone of voice used at the time.

Jo looks after the children and general welfare work of the surrounding villages. Every morning she sets out in her Land-rover with a box full of medicines and baby foods. I ask if she has the sole responsibility for the area.

'In fact I don't treat sick children,' she says. There is a free Government dispensary in Khaboura for the purpose. But some of the villages are miles away, and the mothers can't walk in the terrible heat carrying their sick infants all the way there and back. Taxis are expensive, and not everybody has a donkey. If it weren't for Jo, many babies and small children would get no attention at all. What will happen when she leaves? Jo shrugs her shoulders. Expensive mobile clinics are not necessary. A medical orderly equipped with a Landrover could carry on her work perfectly adequately. With a fleet of such vehicles, the everyday health problems of the entire population could be looked after at minimal expense.

This morning we are going south, to a fishing village planted on the beach just above the high-water mark. 'One of my dirtier villages. There is a lot of trachoma there.' Jo herself caught the dread disease while tending her afflicted friends. It took her six months of treatment in London to get rid of it.

She sees ante-natal mothers, although she doesn't run classes for them. They have to go to Saham for that. One can't help wondering how many have the time, or take the trouble, or even can afford to get there. Her concern is mainly with feeding problems, of which there are quite a few. She sells baby foods at wholesale prices, and gives away to the really needy the multivite supplements which are handed out to her free of charge.

Most of the time it is simply a question of ignorance. Even mothers who have had six or seven children still don't understand the basic needs of a baby, once her milk has gone dry.

'Perhaps they can't get hold of the proper food to give them anyway?' I suggest.

'That is sometimes the case. And then, of course, it's superstition you're often up against.'

'Really? Such as what, for instance?'

'If you give a small child eggs, it will never talk. And this is tragic. For they do have hens, and they do have eggs.' Jo's face gets tense and set. 'They still go in for branding, though not quite so much, because I get very angry about it.' This is perpetrated by some old crone in the village. 'They also have a thing called a *zaah*, a kind of seance.' The patient, even the tiniest of babies, is confined inside a *barasti* hut with the entire family for two or three days and starved for that period. There are special magic words and chants; incense is burned; the drums beat. Jo, who strongly disapproves, explains that this kind of treatment will almost certainly kill off the patient. The answer always is that if he is weak, he will die. As he wouldn't be subjected to this in the first place if he *weren't* in a bad way already, the result is nearly always fatal. It may well be a built-in system for preserving only the more robust members of the tribe.

But Jo doesn't see it that way. 'I get quite furious about it,' she says.

'How do they take it?'

'It all depends. I tell them, ten years ago they didn't have a hospital. Now they do. They *must* take their troubles there.' But there is always someone in the background to shoot down modern methods: either granny, or mother-in-law, or some other old crone who won't lightly give up her authority. 'It is very difficult with young mothers. In a powerful matriarchal society like this, grandma has more of a say in the handling of the new baby than the mother has . . . particularly if she is only fifteen.' But Jo has found a way round: she takes mother and child inside whenever she can, leaving the outraged mother-in-law on the doorstep. At first this went down very badly, but now it is gradually becoming accepted custom and no longer so bitterly resented. Jo's cheerful and friendly ways eventually bring round even the most reluctant hearts. Nobody bears her a grudge for very long.

And then I ask the burning question. Do they know about the pill? Are they ever interested in it?

'Oh yes,' says Jo. 'In fact, I've got two of my ladies on it.'

'Do the husbands know about it?'

'Yes. In this case one of them is a schoolteacher who was in England for a couple of years. And the other is a Jordanian.'

Some of the others beg her for it. 'We will give you money if you get it for us,' they say. But this is not the point. First they must talk about it to their husbands. And if *they* agree, Jo will send them to the hospital. There, all sorts of tests will be made to ensure that it is quite safe in each individual case. And then, after all this rigmarole is over, and if they are still keen, Jo will get it for them.

'But it is a very difficult problem,' she says. 'The husbands want a lot of children, like they want a lot of goats or camels, for prestige. Also it is a kind of insurance against old age.' If you have a large family in Arabia, the chances are one or two of them will look after you in your old age. And besides all this, it is Government policy to encourage an increase in the birth rate.

One argument that the husbands understand and accept is that, if you space them out, you get bigger and better babies, instead of a tiny sickly one every year, as so often happens when the mother is exhausted by childbearing. And some of the women, who don't even like their husbands, tend to neglect the children, and simply don't feed them. 'There is a case of this kind in the village we are going to visit this morning,' says Jo sadly. 'It is very distressing.'

I ask about multiple wives. There are seldom more than two, and it works better if one is quite a bit older than the other. When both of them are young there is inevitable jealousy, even though each wife usually has her own room. In ideal circumstances, they look after each other's children, even breast-feeding the rival's baby. But any man who can afford it tries his hardest to have two homes, one for each family.

We have finished our coffee, and visiting time is upon us. We leave Jo's cool and cheerful bungalow and set off on the clinic round. Equipped with medicine-chest and supplies of baby food, we climb into her Landrover.

As we leave the compound a roller bird with lapis-blue underwings darts out of the banana trees. On the other side of the track, the superior Khaboura goats graze placidly in their long stretches of roped-off, high-quality grass, a strip for each animal. It is all very scientifically worked out.

'It's rough driving along the beach,' says Jo. 'We will go inland down the main road. Ten miles of struggling over the dunes would take half the morning.' As it is, we are there in half an hour. Slowly we plough into the loose grey sand. A flock of crows rise heavily from a rubbish dump. All round, empty Pepsi tins are lying about. The usual ragged plastic bags flap from the knib and sumr trees. We stop outside a brightly painted tin door which opens on to a courtyard of coarse sand. The house at the end, made of raw breeze-blocks, is one of the cleaner residences. Most of the rubbish has been carefully stowed away into a couple of plastic dustbins. As far as I can see, this is a waste of time and effort. A scraggy sheep, poking the lids off with his long pointed nose, deftly scatters the contents about on the sand.

We kick off our sandals and climb the steps on to the verandah where a couple of women, squatting on a plastic mat, watch us coming. The younger of the two is holding the baby. A man, who has spotted the Landrover, strolls up and crouches beside me. 'He's a bit loopy,' says one of the women. 'Take no notice of him.' The man grins, as if this was a compliment.

The baby card is produced, neat and clean in a plastic folder. On this are scrupulously noted at each visit the baby's weight and general state of health. You can always tell by the care taken of the baby card the sort of household you are dealing with. 'It is a matter of pride with the better families,' says Jo. We are obviously in quite a superior home. The loopy one begins to tell us about himself. On leave from Abu

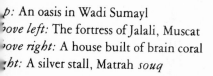

p: An oasis in Wadi Sumayl
ove left: The fortress of Jalali, Muscat
ove right: A house built of brain coral
ht: A silver stall, Matrah *souq*

Top: A fort in Wadi Sumayl
Above left: Falaj in Fanja oasis
Above right: Stranded in Wadi Bidbid
Right: Storm clouds over Wadi Bidbid

Above: There were few places which couldn't be reached by truck

Below: Early morning chores in camp

Top: Dawn ambush on Jebel Akhdar
Left: Exchanging 'the news', soldiers of
S.A.F., Jebel Akhdar
Above: The rebel leader's house after t
bombardment, Jebel Akhdar

Above: An oasis in the heart of the Hajar Range

Below: The peaks of Jebel Akhdar which were scaled by the S.A.S. during the tribal rebellion

Above: Sharaija, Jebel Akhdar, built by the
Persians in the ninth century

Below: Persian terracing on Jebel
Akhdar – the coral reef effect is a reminc
that the Green Mountain was once unde
the sea

bove left: An old man on the Green
ountain

bove right: Repairing the *falaj* system
ter the tribal war

Below: The water is flowing again on the
Green Mountain

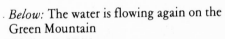

Above: The town of Hazm seen from the fort

Above: 'Washing-line' in sumr tree, near Rostaq

Below: Falaj in the oasis of Rostaq

Below: The great fort of Rostaq

Young Omani setting off on a jaunt

Top: The ancient city of Sumurham, centre of the frankincense trade

Left: Nizwa *souq*, silversmith at work

Above: It took forty Maria Theresa dollars, melted down, to make Captain Bennett's coffee pot in Nizwa

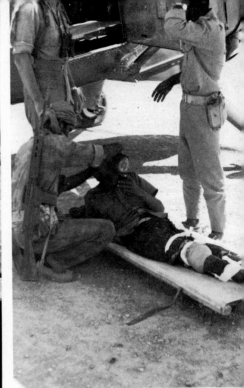

Top left: Captain Bennett in his sangar during the Dhofar War – monsoon clouds are rolling in from the sea

Top right: A wounded Adoo is being given a drink of water by S.A.F. soldiers during the Dhofar War

Left: Manned sangars on the Qara during the Dhofar War

Bottom left: Midway Road. An armed convoy of the Sultan's Armed Forces has been ambushed

Above: The Sultan's palace on the beach in Salalah faces the Indian Ocean

Left: The late Sultan Said bin Taimur in his palace in Salalah, with the then Colonel Thwaites

Above: The ladies of Dhofar, descended from East African slaves, are suspicious of the camera

Left: Ex-rebels of the Qàra, cave-dwellers and cattle-owners

The denuded shores of Dhofar turn brilliant green during the monsoon

The Flying Doctor is waiting for the women
of the tribe to appear at his clinic in the
Qara Mountains

Fishing boats off the Batinah Coast

The Sultan's horse

Dhabi, he is a policeman in the Union Force, where he makes a lot of money.

But we have come to see the baby, and Jo picks it up. 'This is a nice breast-fed little number,' she remarks appreciatively. She should know, she is a connoisseur. From a plastic cover she whips out a contraption that looks like a kitchen clock. 'This does for the goats as well as the babies,' she says, whisking out a pair of plastic pants into which the tiny creature is inserted. The pants are hooked on to the weighing machine and Jo stands up, holding the whole thing aloft with both hands to read the dial. I have never seen it done that way before.

The baby, dangling in its blue plastic knickers, its legs poking through the holes, begins to sway and spin giddily. As I grab it by one foot to steady it, the arrangement lurches to one side. 'I've had them tip out of these before,' Jo remarks calmly. 'It does them no harm when they drop on the sand.' The mother gets an appreciative little speech of encouragement for looking after her offspring so well, and we push off to our next port of call.

This is a *barasti* hut with a plastic mat on the sand and a welcome patch of blue sky overhead. Nobody has bothered to build the roof. A dozen women and children, dressed in bright blue, scarlet, purple and viridian bits of cloth, are packed into this small space. The children, squatting among the women, splutter and sneeze with dreadful colds and coughs. Many already have trachoma. Dead-still and solemn, they watch in silence. Even the tiniest tots look on, quiet and perfectly composed. There is no shoving or whining or clinging to mother.

'Are they always so good?' I ask.

'Yes, this is the way they are brought up.'

'But how is it done?' I ask, thinking of our own rampaging little emancipated dears at home in the West.

'They are just *told*. And they behave. If not, they are put outside. They are never beaten. You can't say they look terrorized, can you?'

Indeed not. Quite the reverse, in fact. Calm and serious, but certainly not terrified. It has always been like that with the Bedu: bad behaviour just doesn't exist. And as I look more carefully at these brightly dressed little things with runny noses, rheumy eyes, terrible coughs, some with huge abscesses, others with open sores, I notice the almost adult patience and fortitude in their faces and eyes.

The baby here, dressed in bright orange trousers and purple tunic, all made by hand with huge stitches, is very small. There is a lively argument about its age, with all the women offering a different opinion. 'The mother says it is twenty-five weeks old, but the others all seem to know better.' Its chief trouble is constant crying. Jo pulls off the tiny drawers. No nappies are ever worn in these parts. The belly is as round as a watermelon, and just as hard. Already the unhappy little creature has been branded four times. Jo is very angry. In no uncertain terms she scolds the ladies, whose mulish looks show no repentance.

An old crone, swaying on her heels, defiantly claims to have ordered the branding herself. 'It is the right thing to do. It is the only way to stop the crying,' she croaks belligerently.

Jo picks up the baby and holds it over her shoulder where, after a couple of hearty belches, it falls asleep at once. The instant silence is dramatic. The women are awe-struck by Jo's powerful magic. She tries to explain about wind. 'There's nothing else wrong with the baby,' she tells them, 'just wind.' And to me, shaking her head, 'They just won't accept the obvious.'

The next patient's problem is that he simply won't grow. At one year, he is no bigger than a four-month-old. The mother, a stunning beauty of classical looks, aged about twenty, is expecting her seventh next month. Her entire family, all six of them, are lined up against the wall, as still and quiet as a row of plaster-casts. The baby card is produced, badly stained and half chewed away. 'This is the one the goat got, if you see what I mean,' Jo says, holding it up and squinting at it to try and make out the last entry.

Withdrawn and silent, the mother refuses to answer any questions. 'She's given up, she's had enough, she just can't cope any more,' Jo explains. 'She's not feeding the child; that's why he doesn't grow. She knows it perfectly well, and that's why she won't look us in the eye.'

116

A man who has just come in keeps prodding her. 'Listen to the lady,' he says, 'do as she says.'

'Is it her husband?' I ask.

'No, probably a brother. All the men of the family assume responsibility if they are around.'

After this distressing interlude we call at a prosperous, harmonious two-wife family, where the husband is a sailor in the Sultan's navy. The house, made of breeze-blocks, has a staircase going up to the roof terrace. Inside, the only item of furniture is a brand-new television set beneath its plastic cover. Cockroaches scuttle about the floor undisturbed, and we step carefully out of their way in our bare feet. An enormous aerial mast leans across the wall, poking right through the open ceiling to the terrace above, its complicated network of spiky bits of wire hanging over the outside of the house. A small boy of about eight is rigging it up most expertly with lengths of rope. In one corner a small girl is nursing a baby.

'Do the children always do all the work?' I ask.

'Yes. As soon as they can walk. Specially the girls, which is unfortunate, as they are taken out of school when an older sister gets married.'

This is the house of the two wives that Jo has already told me about. The young plain one is the mother of the three children. The older woman, who is childless, has a face like an early-Christian mosaic. When Jo has finished her inspection of the chubby, cheerful infant, the older wife follows us outside to find out what I am doing on the clinic run. Rather than embark on a lengthy rigmarole about my ploy, Jo tells her I am a visiting doctor from England. After peering at me closely, Senior Wife shakes her head. 'Memsahib is no doctor. Memsahib is on holiday,' she declares stoutly.

This is the end of the morning's work, and we make for a house where we have been invited to coffee. The little room is already full. Apart from the usual plastic mats on the floor there is no furniture. In one corner, and out of reach of rats and scorpions and camel spiders, a cradle hangs from a hook on the ceiling. It is a shallow wooden box, whose base has been replaced by a criss-cross of string, a kind of cat's cradle. A rag, which serves as a mattress, is spread over the string. And round it all is wrapped a small blanket to keep the

117

mosquitoes out. Snug inside this little swinging tent, the baby of the house is fast asleep.

Squeezing into the ranks of the coughing, sneezing throng on the floor, we take our place among the guests, tidily folding our feet underneath our crossed legs. A tin plate filled with canned peach slices is brought in and placed in front of us, together with a saucepan of water. As the guests, we are invited to help ourselves first. Having washed my right hand in the saucepan, I plunge it into the slimy syrup, feeling around for a slice of peach, under the unblinking gaze of our friends. The bits slither away as I chase them around the plate. After I have finally managed to capture a portion I pop it, dripping, into my mouth and, thinking this is my lot, I wash my fingers once more. But my hostess has different views and informs me that I don't have to wash every time; and it transpires that I have to consume another two morsels for manners' sake. This, under the eyes of all those solemn, hungry children, is almost more than I can bring myself to do.

Cardamom coffee comes next, in the usual minute cups (made in Hong Kong), and the rest of the company finish up what is left of the peaches.

As we step outside, the day's catch is coming up from the fishermen's boats. The housewives of the village come out of their huts to buy the family lunch. Little gangs of children, bearing huge bundles of driftwood on their heads, come trotting sedately down the beach. This is the high note of the day. Fires are lit, rice is boiled, fish is roasted in the embers, and all along the coral sands of the Batinah shore, families are squatting around their crackling twigs, coping somehow or other with the bones in their fish with a well-washed right hand only.

11 Of Forts and *Askars*

'The Arabs keep pledges more religiously than almost any people' — Herodotus

'The place is crawling with snakes,' says my Muscat host in whose house I am dining. 'I wouldn't go near it if I were you.'

We are talking about Jabrin, reputedly the largest fortress in Oman which was built in the seventeenth century by the Yaariba imam, Bilarab bin Sultan, who died of a broken heart and still lies, one hopes at peace, in his sleepy crumbling castle, watched over by his guardians, the famous snakes.

In spite of the warning, I am determined to see Jabrin as soon as an opportunity presents itself. In the end, in fact, I saw it twice. Built more as a country residence than a fighting fortress, it is the most graceful and delightful of all these great massive piles in Oman. Seen from a distance, driving along the track which leaves the Nizwa–Ibri road, you think you have come upon the Sleeping Beauty's castle, as the huge honey-coloured crenellated battlements suddenly appear above the palm trees of the oasis. The nearer you get to it, the stronger the fairy-tale feeling grows. A gigantic tamarind tree, already mentioned by nineteenth-century explorers, still stands there in all its glory, casting heavy shadows over the gateway. Underneath its dense foliage, the *askar* and his cronies pass the time of day where Colonel Miles camped for the night, on one of his tours of the country when he was Consul-General of Oman.

As we approach, a bearded *askar* leaps out of the shadows and posts himself in front of the main gate, his rifle across his chest. Politely we ask if we might visit his fort, as we have come all the way from Muscat for the purpose. On no account, he replies, can we go inside as the place is unsafe, and anyway there are the snakes. Ignoring this, we inform him that we have permission from the Minister of Culture to visit the place. Haughtily, he tells us that the Minister himself, were he to materialize in front of our eyes now, would be powerless to get us in. Not a soul would cross his threshold until he got the O.K. from his *wali* in Bahla. In the end, after a good deal of arguing, he concedes that we may walk round the fort, skirting the outside walls. And with this we have to be content.

The Sultan, concerned for the future of this delightful castle, had asked the Muscat Historical Society to carry out a survey of the crumbling fort and to report on its general condition. As a result, the repairs have been entrusted to an Italian expert who has already achieved a good deal of the restoration and expects to be at it for another four years. There is still an awful lot of work to be done before the castle is in proper working order again.

As we walk round the corner, a crude kind of scaffolding rises out of the surrounding chaos and clambers giddily up to the battlements on the eastern and western sides. Climbing over huge piles of rubble and great teak and sandalwood timbers lying about in unconcerned disarray, we eventually reach the *falaj* which streams, clear and cool, out of the depths of the castle. A few yards further down, the water swarms with the usual *falaj* fish, frolicking about in their accustomed hordes. What this small fry feeds on is a mystery. Nobody ever seems to know.

Having completed a full circle, which gives us an idea of the size of the enormous building, we eventually end up outside a small gate in the wall. Obediently standing well away from it, I peer inside. 'Shall we sneak in for a second?' I foolishly ask.

'It would be the best way to get a bullet into your head,' answers wise Captain Andrew Bruce, who is my guide for the day. At this precise moment, our friend the *askar* suddenly appears round the corner, pointing his rifle straight at us. 'A good moment *not* to be found inside,' remarks the Captain drily.

In fluent, emphatic Arabic, the enraged *askar* addresses us with furious indignation, convinced that we have been inside the castle courtyard despite his orders. Hotly denying his accusations, we do our best to appease and reassure him. But with every word we speak, he grows perceptibly more angry. Herding us along with his gun, he announces that he is marching us off to see his *wali*.

With spirits at a low ebb and considerably sobered by his unreasonable, impassioned attitude, we hurry along, wondering if we will make it to the car without being shot in the back first. These men from Bahla are tricky customers, of uncertain temperament, and notoriously trigger-happy. And what's more, they are well known for their intense dislike of foreigners.

A week later, still undefeated, we turn up once more, this time by air, having flown over Jebel Akhdar in a skyvan. The same Cerberus is at the castle gate. But this time, to my considerable astonishment, wreathed in smiles, he steps aside and waves us through. Perplexed but delighted, we hastily shuffle into the courtyard. This is Oman, I reflect to myself, and it is futile to question its mysterious ways.

A young Indian who is in charge of the restoration work appears. No, he says, nobody has telephoned from the Ministry to say we are coming. But of course he is very happy to show us round. No trouble at all, just step this way.

As the great castle gate, with its domed, painted ceiling has collapsed, another, smaller entrance is now in use. Hastily plunging into the gloom before our friend has time to change his mind again, we climb some steep and very dark stairs. Through the intricate maze of erratic scaffolding made out of odd planks, old trees, steel girders and rope ladders, the whole tied together with bits of wire and string, you can see the

huge wooden buttresses which seem to be the inner walls'
only support. Several of the rafters are lying on the ground
in the dust, splintering where they have come to rest in their
decay.

Gingerly picking our way through the gloom, we emerge
into a large room with a high ceiling and latticed windows,
covered with a complicated plasterwork pattern. Deep arched
cavities scooped out of the walls originally served, our guide
informs us, as shelves and store cupboards. I can imagine
great jars, which they still make in Bahla, filled with pulped
dates, sesame oil, grain or just plain water, tucked away into
these alcoves. All round the room, at floor level, are gun slits,
slanted in such an ingenious way that all the approaches are
covered from every angle. The draughts, howling through the
slits during a storm, must be pretty horrific. Everywhere the
walls are propped up by eccentric wooden scaffolding. Many
of the main supporting beams are crumbling and sagging
under the weight of the ceiling above. As the period when the
castle was built was one of great prosperity and good taste,
and no expense was spared, the sandalwood ceilings were
painted with delicate flower patterns. Like the Sumerians
4,000 years earlier, Bilarab used sissoo wood for the heavy
doors, the powerful beams and the supporting posts of his
dream palace. Some of the domes, already restored, are covered with intricate plasterwork, made up of a close pattern of
brilliant stylized flowers. The woodwork is carved with flower-
and leaf-designs. Some of these rooms seem to come straight
out of the Italian Renaissance, with their frescoed ceilings,
and stone-mullioned and latticed windows. The view from
the large top-floor room, with windows looking out on all
sides, is staggering. The breeze, coming in through the gun
slits at floor level, blows little puffs of dust around our feet.
Our guide tells us that this was the mosque of the castle, but
every book I have read on the subject firmly states that it was
a school founded by Bilarab for his own progeny and the
children of the palace retainers, with all teachers' fees paid
out of his own privy purse. The pupils, who were taught
mathematics and the Koran, were fed on bananas as an aid
to concentration. From this seat of learning many scholars
sprouted; they then spread out all over the Gulf where they

became the wise men at various rulers' courts. Skeet mentions a gallery round an inner courtyard, through which flowed the open *falaj* waters. Here, with the help of a golden bucket and chain, the ladies of the harem drew water for the making of saffron. With this useful and enthralling occupation they beguiled the long hours of enforced inactivity.

Built on no obvious plan, the rooms, sleeping ledges, private praying corners, snug cosy chambers, huge halls, intimate alcoves, small steep stairs leading up to exiguous guardrooms, follow one another in extraordinarily random fashion. It all looks as if bits had been added here and there at odd times, on the spur of the moment or as an afterthought. At no time in the building of the enormous castle does there seem to have been any coherent planning, yet the whole is enchantingly spontaneous, carefree and harmonious. It is a wonder that such hefty masonry can look so elegant and weightless. But in spite of this enticing and appealing aspect, Jabrin was nevertheless able to defend itself. From its two crenellated towers it overlooks the forbidding range of Jebel Akhdar, the vast uninterrupted plain which melts into the Empty Quarter and the great central desert of Oman in the south.

The *majlis* or courtroom of the imam (who took no chances) is furnished with bolt-holes in the floor, one at each corner, leading into an escape tunnel in the bowels of the fort. This we refrain from inspecting, as it is here that the snakes I was warned about lead their secret, secluded lives and it is considered wiser to leave them undisturbed. Instead, our Indian friend offers to show us the dungeon, where prisoners were kept at the imam's pleasure. Following him down a dark stone spiral staircase into the innermost recesses of the fortress, we grope along tunnels and endless cellars. The deeper we go, the warmer and darker it gets. Soft felty things flit by, presumably bats, and the stale taste of dusty cobwebs seals our lips. At last, the end of the road: we have reached the black heart of the castle, a huge domed cell with a sandy floor. Without light or air and in total darkness, the prisoners were left here to rot in despair, sometimes for years on end, until the end of their days. And, quite possibly, the snakes living in the escape tunnel next door crawled in from time to time to inspect the latest recruits. It is the most sinister and horrific prison I have seen in Oman: grimmer by far than the fortress of Jalali, where the inmates may have been shackled and chained, but at least they could see the sky through the bars of their cells, and they got all the light and air that everybody else enjoyed, as well as the smell and the sound of the sea.

On the way out of this spooky hell-hole, our friendly guide invites us once more, as a last gesture of hospitality, to visit the tunnel. After peering briefly into the entrance of this snake-pit, we decide to call it a day. We have seen all we wanted. Jabrin was well worth a second visit.

Nizwa, holy Nizwa, the spiritual heart of Oman and stronghold of the imams, is our next port of call. The town is decked out with flags and gay bunting in honour of the Queen's visit. 'Civilization is the beam of light in the path of future generations', claims a banner stretched across the entrance of the *souq*. This hopeful message is repeated with many variations, hanging about among the date palms and the private gardens of the town. By the main gate beside the great tower, the ancient tamarind tree spreads its shade over the gathering cattle market. Camels stand about, aloof and resigned to the dreadful life which is the fate of all camels. Ancient broken-down trucks and Landrovers swarm like a great herd of buffalo, raising blinding dust-storms all round. A few thin, spindly, long-legged sheep, strung along a single rope like a bead necklace, are lifted, dangling, out of a Toyota truck. A goat is dragged along by its neck bristles protesting indignantly. The buyers and sellers, all men of course, are assembled beneath the market tree. Hawk-nosed beneath their turbans, ascetically thin, some of them are blinded in one eye by trachoma, and all of them exude an intimidating dignity in their noble and aristocratic bearing. Nothing much has changed here in the last two or three thousand years. Young boys in *dishdashas* and prayer caps may be seen bumping along the dry course of the wadi on their Vespas, but this in no way detracts from the age-old solemn stateliness of the holy old town.

As it is already mid-day, and we want to visit the *souq* before everybody goes off to pray, we whip briskly through the dark narrow streets, past the vegetable and spice booths, and the potters and the silversmiths crouched over their work, drenched in the heavy scent of cloves and cumin and all the various spices which go into Oriental foods. In the meat market, under its low medieval arches, whole carcasses hang from hooks on the ceiling, complete with liver and various other bits of interior furniture, all dangling and dripping with blood. The butcher indiscriminately hacks away at it all, handing over bleeding morsels into the customers' bare hands. An old man I had seen earlier marching briskly along the wadi is now skipping from one shop to another with a bunch of rusty desert swords clenched in his fist, peddling them round the *souq* in the hope of making a few *baizas*.

Here in Nizwa they produce the famous halwa, which was described by an early missionary as tasting like 'sweet wagon grease', while the explorer Theodore Bent advised his readers to forgo the pleasure of watching it being made. According to him, 'niggers' feet' were pressed into service for mixing the brew.

The huge fort, a solid lump of masonry sixty feet high and 120 feet across, looks like the great tower of Windsor Castle and is being patched up. Covered with mud, their hectic turbans at all angles and their beards stiff with dry clay, workmen shin up and down the usual erratic scaffolding, made up of whole dead trees, boards, rope and wire. Like scraggy old birds they cling precariously to their perch, scooping mud out of a plastic bucket a handful at a time. This they pat into a ball, spit on it once or twice, then squeeze it into whichever spot in the wall looks as if it could do with a bit of strengthening. Down on the ground at the base of the fort, an army of little grey men scrape dust into great heaps, while colleagues pour water on top until the right mixture is obtained. With the resulting mess they repair the fort. And this treatment will probably last for the next thousand years or more.

As we approach the main gate, the *askar* hops off his bed (a high stone ledge just inside the porch) with his rifle in his hand, and surveys us with a neutral kind of look in his eye. Without too much trouble he lets us in and leads us up a very indifferent staircase with a lot of gaping holes where steps are missing. Taking this in our stride as best we can, we reach the main part of the tower, an enormous space open to the sky, surrounded by a wall twenty feet high. Here the rebel garrison lived and fought in the 1950s, until finally conquered by the Sultan's forces. And the holes which are being plugged in the walls were made by Venoms of his air force towards the end of the tribal rebellion.

A tree grows out of the sandy floor of the tower, with a bored goat tethered beneath it. A few huts stand about here and there. Great piles of ancient cannon-balls are scattered around, obviously moulded by hand out of the molten metal, as they are every shape except the usually accepted one. Very ancient Portuguese cannon poke out of the gun holes in the wall from which the entire village can be seen clustered around the fort. The *falaj* complex runs through the oasis like an elaborate bloodstream system, splitting up the date gardens into neat irregular shapes. The narrow streets are lined with tall mud houses, most of them fortified against their neighbours, for the people of Nizwa are a suspicious lot who trust nobody, least of all the folk next door. All around in the trees, flocks of little grey ring-doves utter their haunting three-note cooing. At this height there is no other sound, not even the hubbub of the *souq* below. Walking along the road away from Nizwa towards Bahla, we follow the wadi's arid bed on one side, with its desiccated palm trees, brown and crisp as breakfast cereal. Bug-ridden by a new pest, the date palms of Oman are sadly afflicted this year.

On the other side of the road are the *tabsils*, tall mud buildings in which the *mabsila*, or dry dates, will be boiled in huge cauldrons at the time of the harvest in July. These dates, which are not fit for human consumption, are cooked, then spread out to dry on the wadi stones before being parcelled and sewn into grass bags to be sold as animal fodder.

And so we leave holy Nizwa. In the days of the great medieval explorer Ibn Battuta, Nizwa was much the same as it is today, except that the tribes just now are not actually at each other's throats. 'A brave and bold race,' he described them, 'and the tribes are perpetually at war with each other.'

12 Oman Proper

Rimmed with green scum, a thick hairy lip curls disdainfully above the wooden bar of its stall as a handsome cream-coloured camel watches us clambering up the central rock of the fortress of Bahla. Alone in his rickety shelter on the topmost part of the fort, he is the only living thing to be seen, the place is otherwise totally deserted. The *wali* who lives in the turret is out, presumably drinking coffee in the *souq* with the elders of the town and diligently minding the affairs of his territory. It was with the vengeance of this redoubtable man that we were threatened by the infuriated *askar* at Jabrin.

An enormous sandstone outcrop, part of the Hajar range, has been incorporated into the fortifications of this extraordinary town. Precariously perched on the battlements above the camel's home, we can see from where we stand the great white wall, eleven kilometres long, running up and down the surrounding hills and hugging within its confines the cornfields and date gardens of the settlement. Defensive turrets crop up at frequent intervals along the ramparts, where sentries kept a sharp look-out for envious neighbours on the war path and marauding desert tribes. Outside this magic circle, the stark wild mountains all around look like a dead planet. The contrast is dramatic: it was from here that the kings of

Nebhania ruled Oman for 500 years, until dethroned by the imams of the powerful Yaariba dynasty.

As we clamber about inside the fort over the rocks and tottering masonry, we come across some ancient battered cannon lying in the dust, one of them with its muzzle blown off.

'This is a museum piece,' remarks Captain Bruce, bending over what looks to me like a bit of old scrap iron. As an artillery man he knows what he is talking about. Among the litter of undistinguished weapons, he has identified a quite rare hand-swivel gun.

'Why not take it back for the Muscat museum?' I suggest.

'I would never get out of here alive if I tried,' he answers grimly.

As we leave the fortress, the *askar* at the gate scrambles up to his shelf. Hunting about among the bedding, impatiently shovelling his rifle and his camel-stick aside, he pokes around feverishly, hurling away the ragged bedclothes. Suddenly, with a whoop of triumph, he produces his find. 'Sign here,' he commands, hastily turning over the pages of a Harrods visiting book. When we have complied, he reluctantly lets us leave the fort. Not too sure what his *wali* will say, he would have preferred to shift the responsibility for our visit on to *him*. In no way anxious for such an encounter, I am all for an instant departure, and so off we trot to visit the town.

The potters of Bahla are famous all over the Middle East. They have been baking their wares since the beginning of recorded history. The fine white dust of the oasis which seems to come in inexhaustible supplies is ideally suited to pot-making. Scratched and shovelled together into several troughs, it is sifted, mixed with water, and kneaded into clay. A damp tunnel, leading down to the level of the water at the bottom of a nearby well, has been scooped out of the mud by hand. Crawling into its deliciously cool depths, we reach the water where a very ancient pump sucks it up to the surface. From there it is hosed into the troughs where the dust is churned into clay. As soon as the mud reaches a nice, smooth, sticky texture, just the way it has to be, the chief potter spades it into a wheelbarrow and trundles it along to the workshop. There four men, barefoot and with one hideously deformed big toe apiece, work a wheel each. On the floor, kneeling on a rush mat, a boy is pounding the mud into shape for the potters. Working at incredible speed, they seize a lump, dump it on the wheel, push a fist into the top to make a hole, and in a few minutes a rough kind of jar is spinning away merrily on the wheel. The bulging pot belly is quickly smoothed away with a bit of scrap metal, then a string is slapped round the middle to make a pattern, and the job is done. The new pot is carried outside to dry in the sun and await the next bake.

The kiln, constructed out of mud like everything else in these parts, has long ago been turned to clay by the innumerable firings. A deep pit, scooped out by the old potter himself, is the furnace which burns for five days at a time underneath the oven. This is kept going with any bit of fuel going, huge bundles of desert bush, old decayed palms, great piles of date stones, anything that burns will do. The potter is in the process of building a new kiln next to the present one in use at the moment. The firing trench is already dug out. The kiln itself is going up, made of mud and straw bricks. When I first came across the saying that you can't make bricks without straw, I thought it was a leg-pull. It was not until I first came to Arabia and saw with my own eyes how they were patted together with these very ingredients that I understood the meaning of the biblical saying.

The floor of the new kiln directly over the firing pit is pierced by a number of concentric flues for letting the hot air into the oven. Captain Bruce, greatly impressed by this scientifically constructed piece of architecture, hasn't noticed Hilal's increasing jitteriness. Hilal, a lieutenant in the Sultan's Armed Forces, came along on our jaunt to vouch for our good faith. Without his company we probably wouldn't have been allowed into Bahla fort at all.

Watching the workmen closely since our arrival, I couldn't help noticing that although our presence is tolerated nobody is being particularly friendly.

'They don't like us,' says Hilal in the end. 'They keep muttering that all this is being recorded.' As I am carrying neither a camera, a tape-recorder, nor even a notebook, there is no way they can possibly guess the purpose of our visit.

'How do they know?' I ask, puzzled. 'And why should they mind anyway?'

'They know everything. They are bad people,' says Hilal. 'If they don't like you they put a curse on you and you are dead in two days.'

This happened last year to a friend of his, who unwisely argued about the price of a mango in the *souq*. Although a perfectly healthy young man, he was found dead in his hut two days after his regrettable argument with the mango merchant. The people of Bahla have a reputation for witchcraft and strange esoteric powers. But they don't have quite so much influence, I am glad to hear, over pig-eaters, which is Hilal's delicate way of describing us Christians.

In the *souq*, where no woman is allowed to penetrate under pain of death, auctions of souls used to take place. Now, banned by the law of the land, the practice has been moved to caves in the mountains north of Bahla, where it goes on intermittently in dead secrecy, along with other strange customs which no European eye has ever seen. The women of Bahla have a special gift with herbs which they use for good or evil, according to how they feel. Brigadier Maxwell, when once visiting Bahla, was gripped by a violent and totally unexpected pain from a kidney stone. A couple of women who happened to be present took him in hand at once. Pounding together a handful of dates, lime leaves and a greyish kind of powder, they brewed it all up into a drink which he was made to swallow. Within ten minutes the pain had vanished and never since that day has he had another twinge from that stone. When pressed for their secret and asked what they had added to the date mixture, all the ladies would answer was 'just old dried leaves'.

The delicate silver jewellery and coffee-pots of Oman are all made by hand in Nizwa and Bahla. Captain Peter Bennett had his fashioned out of a handful of melted-down Maria Theresa dollars. The hollow lid rattles with inner seeds, a special device for frightening away jinn, and also to discourage slaves from surreptitiously helping themselves to a quick swig of coffee behind their master's back.

To watch a silversmith at work is a fascinating way of passing the time. On the main square in Bahla, before the entrance to the *souq*, a couple of workshops stand side by side. Posting myself between the two, I am able to watch them both at the same time. Squatting on the floor, each craftsman works at his own individual gas flame, over which he holds tiny particles of metal. At the back of one of the shops an ancient electric mangle throbs noisily on its cement base. From time to time, one of the men skips out of his back window and climbs in next door to feed a piece of silver through the mangle. Once this is flattened to his satisfaction, he gathers up his skirts in one hand, hops out of the window, then back the same way into his own shop. Feeding a corner of his newly flattened silver band into the flame, he begins to tweak it this way and that with a pair of tweezers. Suddenly a tiny hand appears. He drops this into a saucepan of water, then starts off at once on another. This is the famous hand of Fatimah which is used as a lucky charm, incorporated into jewellery, or stitched into clothes or head bands. All the time I am watching, a deafening sound of male voices, all bellowing together, is coming from a few doors down. A shaggy *barasti* roof balanced on four palm trunks forms a kind of shelter, beneath which a dense crowd of men is milling around in great excitement. Creeping along and keeping close to the wall so as not to be seen (for I am now in forbidden territory), I inch slowly towards the vociferous hubbub to investigate. On the floor among the throng, are bundles wrapped in woven rush matting. Shouting loud enough to rouse the dead, a man bends over with his dagger to slice off a flap out of which he scoops up a handful of squashed-up dates. An auction is in progress.

Suddenly, the tumult stops dead. The mid-day call to prayer can be heard in the distance in the sudden silence. Dropping everything, they all hurry away towards the voice. The flies, overjoyed at the unexpected treat, come down in impenetrable black clouds to settle on the open flaps of the date bundles. A blind old man, horrifyingly thin, shuffles along as fast as he can, feeling his way with his camel-stick as he goes. Just as he is about to crash into a truck, someone grabs him by the arm and drags him out of harm's way. And off they go hand in hand, the blind man and his rescuer, following the auction crowd, on their way to the prayer meeting.

Izki, Nizwa, Bahla, Hamra, Misfah and Mutti, all the main towns of the interior, form part of what has always been known as Oman Proper. Awabi and Rostaq, although on the ocean side of the Jebel, also consider themselves as belonging to this exclusive inner sanctum. It is the fanatic centre of Ibadhism, which accepted the imam as their spiritual and temporal leader after the death of the Prophet.

Further in, closer to the mountains, is another group of towns, Ghafat of the Beni Hina, Hamra of the Abryins, and Tanuf and Birkat al-Mawz, through which the Beni Ryiam control the approaches of Jebel Akhdar. Birkat al-Mawz, at the end of Wadi Muaydin which comes pouring down the mountainside when in spate, consists mostly of a wide avenue shaded by date palms and banana trees. There is something curiously companionable about water flowing waist-high, above the ground. Cut out of the mountainside, a lively *falaj* runs through the tranquil contented little oasis, wriggling with the usual small fry and almost cool.

Wadi Muaydin provided a convenient escape-route up the mountain in case of emergency whenever Suleiman felt worried in his fort at the foot of the gorge. As we climb about among its dilapidated remains (it was flattened by the Sultan's air force during the rebellion), half a dozen boys are playing football in the courtyard.

Tanuf, once the capital of the Lord of the Green Mountain, is now a ghost town haunted by rats, sand vipers, scorpions and camel spiders. As we scramble about among the ruins of the once prosperous city, a flock of crows, squawking protestingly, takes off towards the mountains, and a fox peers furtively round a pile of crumbling mud houses. The scene of destruction and desolation, left as a permanent reminder to the treacherous tribes, is devastating – all the more so as all this dilapidation is surrounded by flourishing fields of lucerne, wheat and corn.

The Abryins of Hamra and Misfah live on the south side of the mountain, while the Beni Kharus overlook the northern end. When all these tribes decided to sink their differences and join up together, it became obvious how difficult it was

132

for the Sultan's forces to capture the mountain fortress and quell the rebellion.

Ghafat, the Beni Hina's capital, gave its name to the Hinawi faction of the Civil War. Tucked away in a sheltered corner between Jebel Kaur and the Green Mountain, it is another magical village full of rippling *falaj*, date gardens and well-built mud houses.

At Manah, where Malik dug the first *falaj* before his battle with the Persian Marzaban, a goat auction is in full swing under a tamarind tree as we arrive. Immediately dropping their business, the sheikh and his men come forward to welcome us, with pressing invitations to coffee. But it is getting late so we have to refuse their hospitality, much as we would like to accept it, and all the local gossip which would be thrown in for good measure. Described by Wellstead as a smiling picture of contented peasants, with 'verdant fields of grain and suger-cane . . . and streams of water flowing in all directions', it presents a very different face to us today, with its desiccated vegetation, dusty streets littered with cans of sweet-corn and Pepsi-cola, and Malik's *falaj* no more than a romantic memory. As we hurry through the narrow streets, looking for an entrance to the castle and ignoring the ever more pressing invitations from the men of Manah, I suddenly become aware of our appalling rudeness and our unforgivable behaviour. Reversing the roles, it would be as if someone walked into your drawing-room and stalked all over it, staring at your treasures, meanwhile totally ignoring your presence. Instead of being incensed by our intrusion, these people are actually inviting us into their homes. Feeling hot with shame, I dive back into the car, hoping to be forgotten as soon as possible.

A twitter of budgerigars, the last thing I would ever expect to hear in interior Oman, greets us next day as we arrive at the army camp of Izki in time for lunch in the Officers' Mess.

Deep inland, at the inner end of the Sumayl gap, Izki, a group of very ancient villages, so turbulent and troublesome that they are still divided into two hostile sections, sits astride and along Wadi Halfayn. Starting at the watershed, the stream runs as far inland as it can, before its water (when there is any) evaporates into the scorching air or sinks into the parched sand of the interior desert. Rather than rely on this erratic water supply, the people of Izki have always enjoyed the benefits of a very ancient *falaj* system, supposed to be even older than the one Malik built at Manah. This is Falaj al-Mulki, originally amounting to 370 channels, but nowadays making do with a couple of well-maintained ones running ten feet below the ground. Stone steps lead down at regular intervals, to the cool clean water. During the Jebel War, Izki was a Very Bad Spot indeed. The tribes, living up to their reputation for constant anarchy and turmoil, were a thorn in the flesh of the Sultan's army, as they sided with Suleiman bin Himyiar against him. As soon as the war was over, a military camp was built on the vast gravel plain at the foot of Jebel Akhdar.

Hearing of my mission, Captain Richard Morley kindly offers to drive me to the camp, where I will spend a couple of nights, and from where he will take me to visit the distant town of Ibri, and the vast Dhahira desert in the west.

The army camp, which is a model of its kind and more like a holiday resort than a military base, is laid out like a toy fort, with its Officers' Mess and sleeping quarters, squash and tennis courts, a pool, barracks, parade ground, filling station and gun pound, where the long murderous muzzles, smothered in their khaki canvas hoods, stick straight up in the air beneath their *barasti* shelters. At the moment the camp houses the Artillery Regiment, which is taking its turn at Izki before moving on elsewhere. Continually shifting about to carry out manoeuvres in various parts of the country, the regiments are perpetually on the move.

Serenaded by budgies in their aviary in the centre of the Mess, the British Officers are enjoying a sandwich and a glass of beer as we arrive, while an Oriental lunch is being served for the Omani contingent in the dining room.

As the Commanding Officer is in Dhofar at the moment, I am billeted in his house, which is tucked away behind the swimming pool among oleander shrubs, banana trees, eucalyptus, bougainvillaea and the feathery fronds of tamarisks. As Captain Morley escorts me to 'my' house, Baluchi gardeners paddle about barefoot among their plantations. I have seen this miracle occur in many parts of the various deserts

I have been through. Wherever water can be found, it seems that anything will grow in the most unpromising of soils and climates. Attracted by all this greenery, ring-doves glide about among the trees; magpies sail overhead, trailing their long tails behind them; standing over it all is the craggy, denuded range of the forbidding Green Mountain, brooding away invisibly up there in the clouds.

Early next morning we set off for Ibri. Hilal, who is a native of the place, has agreed to drive us there in his own car. His presence will ensure that we are allowed into the town.

After all I have heard and read about Ibri, I half expect to be stoned on arrival, as Lieutenant Wellstead had been on his visit to the notorious bandit stronghold in 1836. James Morris describes it as a 'thieves' market' to which the brigands from the surrounding desert bring their loot for sale. When Colonel Miles was Consul-General in Muscat, he very nearly had all his luggage stolen in 1905, and even the intrepid Thesiger thought it more prudent to by-pass the place in 1949, even though he was romantically travelling in disguise.

There was a time when tribal rivalries were so ferocious, with non-stop blood feuds, that people preferred to sleep out of doors rather than wait at home for their enemies to come and cut their throats in bed. As the main town of the Dhahira desert, owing allegiance to neither sultan nor imam until the accession of the present monarch, the people of Ibri had a free run of their territory, and nobody could bring them to justice. As a result, wholesale lawlessness rampaged exuberantly over the entire area. But because of its closeness to Fahud, the most prolific oil station of Oman, both the Sultan and the PDO people began to take an interest in the pirate town's free-for-all affairs. It was essential to keep foreign interference and bribing away from these high-spirited, riotous outlaws, and so a garrison was planted nearby to keep an eye on the place.

Having expected, as I said, a shower of stones and a howling mob of thugs, I feel slightly let down to be totally ignored on arrival. Hilal, on the other hand, is greeted effusively by his friends all round.

'Wait here,' says he, jumping out of the car at the entrance to the town. Crossing over to the other side, he opens a tiny, brightly painted iron door in the wall, through which he disappears.

'He's gone to see his uncle, who is also his father-in-law,' explains Captain Morley. And we sit in the car for the next half-hour, patiently roasting in the sun, until he eventually reappears.

'Come along,' he says, 'it's OK to visit the town.'

And so off we set in his wake on our sight-seeing tour, basking in his reflected glory. From every doorway, from the tiniest chink in the wall, friends pop out to hug him and rub noses. Now that he is a soldier, he doesn't come home very often.

The square mud fort at the entrance to the town is a shambles. Inside the crumbling walls, among the dilapidated ruins, the usual football practice is in progress. The destruction of this particular castle, we are carefully informed, was caused by an earthquake and not, as usual, by marauding tribes.

'They are planning to build another one,' Hilal explains, 'but now somebody thinks there was once a graveyard at the new place. So they can't go ahead.' A graveyard means the ground is sacred land till Kingdom come, and can never be built over. 'Perhaps they will find another place,' Hilal continues vaguely. And perhaps they won't. My guess is they will never build another fort. The time for this kind of warfare is over . . . unless, of course, it is a matter of pride.

The narrow sandy streets, covered with palm thatch, dappled with sunlight, are deliciously cool. 'Nothing here ever changes,' complains Hilal morosely. 'It is very old-fashioned.' He is all for progress. But the Captain and I like it just the way it is, untouched by tourist hand, the real thing, the way it always was. Obviously, nobody ever comes as far as this. It is like going through the time machine and coming out at the other end, thousands of years ago. I hardly dare breathe, in case it all blows away in a puff of smoke.

In the *souq*, a cool, shady market covered with *barasti*, there are very few people about. It is Friday and not many shops are open. Here are no fluorescent flowers or plastic slippers or rolls of linoleum or cheap mats from Bombay. And there isn't a single corrugated-tin roof in sight. Spice booths line the streets with rolled-back sacks of beans, lentils, melon seeds, date-pulp and all manner of pulses and grain and bits of desiccated twiglets. Goats and hens help themselves to favourite titbits, and nobody minds them in the least.

Hilal progresses through the streets like a visiting monarch. With happy little squeaks, people jump up along the route and fall in behind, joining the party. We are an imposing cortège by the time we reach the silver *souq*.

In a tiny hutch, not much bigger than a hen-coop, a very small bearded man in turban and ragged tunic is mending an old brass coffee-pot, obviously somebody's much-loved treasure. From time to time he turns a crank which presumably puffs air into the charcoal fire in front of him. The fire, nestling inside a hollowed-out stone and no bigger than a saucer, glows as he turns the handle. As soon as he stops, the ashes go white. With a pair of tweezers he picks out a shapeless little lump of metal which is heating up in the tiny furnace. He squeezes this into a ball with his fingers and pats it into place on the coffee-pot. Leaving him to his laborious fiddling, we walk on past several others like him.

Further along, against the wall, a length of butter muslin, dyed dark-blue, is hung up on a string to dry. 'This is a kind of scent,' says Hilal, holding up the cloth to my nose. 'Ladies wear these clothes in bed at night. Come and look.'

Across the street is the dyers' workshop. Firq and Ibri are famous centres of indigo dyeing: the leaves of the plant are crushed and mixed with water in stone troughs, and the cloth is steeped in the liquor for a few hours. Cautiously we creep into the dark cave, sniffing our way towards the stinking wells in which the dark-blue liquid is doing its stuff for the ladies of the town.

'I don't like it,' says Hilal, wrinkling up his nose in disgust. 'It is old-fashioned and horrible.' And on the subject of the smell, we heartily agree with him.

Coming out of the *souq*, we bump into Ali, a friend of Hilal's and also a subaltern in the Sultan's army. He invites us at once to lunch at his house 'just a little way outside Ibri'. Hilal tells him that we are lunching with his uncle. An acrimonious argument starts up. Taking no part in this, the Captain and

I stand aside, as the two friends raise their voices, gathering a crowd. Soon everybody joins in, taking sides. In the end a compromise is reached. We will go and have coffee with Ali who wants to show us his new house, and come back to lunch with Hilal's uncle, as animals have already been slaughtered for the feast.

So off we set along a dusty track, leading into a desert of black gravel. After half an hour spent bouncing and bumping about, we reach a clump of sumr trees in the middle of a great field of stones. Here is Ali's pride and joy, his newly built house, surrounded by a breeze-block wall with a brightly painted iron door. The little house, which is waiting for a wife, is totally bare. In the *majlis,* where coffee eventually appears, we sit on the usual plastic mats on the floor. Bright-pink linoleum with custard-yellow flowers lines the ceiling, and the walls are painted raspberry and cream.

After coffee our host offers to take us for a drive. Only too anxious to get away from the pink linoleum ceiling, we accept with alacrity. The stony black desert through which we set off is now valuable agricultural land, and we learn with astonishment that it is worth a great deal of money. When Ali bought his property a few years ago, he paid 5,000 *ryals* for it (a wife in Ibri is worth 3,500) – now he could sell it for 35,000.

Through the desert we drive on to Tan Am, the capital of the fierce Duru tribes of the Dhahira country. Roaming the desert like wolves, the Duru are tall, powerful, independent men who accept no authority of any kind. A law unto themselves, they refused to sign the Treaty of Seeb, and are the only tribes to know the way across the treacherous quicksands of the Umm as-Samim.

At Tan Am the settled life of Ibri stops, together with any civilizing influence which might have trickled through. From here onwards is unremitting desert, and you can drive on relentlessly for 800 miles all the way to Salalah without seeing a single town or village.

In the sky three vultures are gliding in a circle. These are small Egyptian vultures, not like the huge creatures which Captain Morley came across not long ago picking the bones of a dead donkey by the roadside. 'Great enormous things like skyvans. From a distance I thought they were eating a dog,' he said, 'that's how big they were compared with the donkey.' Now that everybody who can afford it has a Toyota truck, donkeys are just turned loose into the desert, where they have to shift for themselves. Unadaptable and helpless as they are, they soon die of boredom, loneliness and thirst.

When we finally get there, Hilal's house is perfectly delightful. Through the tiny door in the wall we step into a courtyard like a small London mews, surrounded on all sides by mud huts, each with its own little painted door. The summer *majlis*, into which we are led, is painted a heavenly blue, with the usual rugs on the floor, television at one end and a large poster of Mohammed Ali on the opposite wall.

After more coffee, dates and oranges, a servant staggers in with a huge brass tray piled with Oriental rice and grilled chickens cut in half. Then come vegetable curry, tomato salad, chopped lettuce and sliced raw cabbage. A dish of yellow liquid (cow oil, Hilal informs us) finally arrives, for pouring over the chicken. Mercifully he forgets all about it, so that we are able to enjoy our delicious lunch without having it soaked in cow oil. As it is bad manners to talk during meals, we consume our feast in appreciative silence.

The uncle, who was so very insistent on entertaining us, never appears at all. Instead, we have the company of the servant who sits rocking on his heels as he chews his way through the chicken bones. Hilal's wife is at school. I ask if they have any children.

'No,' he says, 'we have only been married one year.' But even so, he already wants to buy another wife. Hilal is rich, with many houses and shops and various obscure businesses. If he weren't so well off, he couldn't afford another wife so soon – at 3,500 *ryals* apiece, quite a high price. I ask if he will keep them both in the same house. 'No,' he says, 'in one house they fight. No good.' In Ibri, he informs us, marriage customs are different. A girl is *asked* if she wants to marry the man who is chosen for her. She will not be forced to if she doesn't like him. As women in Ibri are known all over Oman for their outstanding good looks, they can presumably afford to be choosy.

'Does the girl you want to marry agree to it?' I ask.

'Yes. She says if she can't marry me, she doesn't want anybody else. It is my wife who doesn't agree.'

I can't help feeling sorry for the poor little schoolgirl, already faced with a rival wife. And what a rival! On the way home after lunch, Hilal takes us to call on her. Driving off the main road, we bump across the wide bed of a dry wadi until we hit a small cluster of mud huts huddling under a clump of date palms. 'There she is,' says Hilal proudly, as a sinuous, exotic creature of about fifteen willows slowly across our line of vision. Moving with unconscious grace, she wears a gold band around her head; her black hair hangs loose down her back, floating on the deep gold of her dress. Speechless with surprise at the unexpected apparition, we stare in silence. Turning round, she suddenly sees us and, bending low, dives into one of the mud huts. Hilal sighs resignedly, and we drive off across the arid countryside towards Izki, the comforts of the Officers' Mess and a delicious army dinner.

13   The Frolicsome She-Camel

'If you show a Bedu the entrance of your house, then open wide the door that his camel may also enter', enjoins an Arab proverb.

There is no doubt that a camel takes first place in her master's heart. A wife has to put up with coming second, which seems perfectly normal to the patient, long-suffering females of Arabia.

A blonde, blue-eyed English girl was once much admired by a Bedu gentleman. 'She looks just like my favourite camel,' he informed her friend, 'I want to marry her.'

'But she is married already,' answered the friend, rather taken aback.

'In that case, how many camels does her husband want for her?' queried the enamoured Arab, in no way disconcerted and quite prepared to part with several of his precious beasts in exchange for his love.

This is not an unusual attitude among the Bedu, who regard the camel as the greatest gift of God to man on earth. 'The best of women is like a frolicsome she-camel,' they say fondly. It is claimed that there are several hundred words in Arabic to describe the age, sex, looks and condition of the beast, so great is their love for the creature.

The story goes that when Allah decided to create a horse,

he informed the south wind that he planned to fashion from it a new being. Then, powerfully blowing the breath of life, he brought forth the first horse, a 'drinker of the wind'. (It would be interesting to know if there is any connection between this story and a curious fact related by Pliny about the mares of Lusitania, who give birth to incredibly fleet-of-foot progeny, fathered upon them by the west wind blowing down their throats.) But lo and behold, no sooner was he on his feet than the new animal created by Allah gracelessly objected to his shape and so-called shortcomings. His sharp hooves sank into the soft sand. The saddle slipped about on his back, and his neck was far too short so that the best grazing was always out of reach.

To show him what he might have been, Allah then created a camel, whereupon the discontented animal, horrified at the sight, regretted his ingratitude and trotted away, reconciled to his fate after all. Meanwhile the poor camel, despised and abandoned, promptly sank into a decline and went off to gloom by himself in the desert. To cheer him up, the Lord kindly produced a wife for him. The delighted animal smiled so broadly at the sight of his beautiful spouse that his nose split down the middle, and has remained so to this day. Ever since then, the camel's incomparable beauty has been recognized and appreciated to the full by the people of the desert. Encouraged by all this adulation, the creature soon began to grow too big for his boots. Taking his good fortune for granted, he became arrogant and supercilious, with a permanent bad smell under his nose – which, if he but knew it, is nothing but his own foul and stinking breath.

The Arabs put this notoriously supercilious smugness down to the fact that the camel is supposed to know the hundredth name of God, and so thinks himself justified in despising everybody else.

No one really knows where camels were first domesticated, but it is thought to have been somewhere in central Oman, from where the first caravans set off across the great empty wastes of Arabia, thus shaping the future way of life of the desert. By 1100 B.C. the Midianites in north-west Arabia were mounting the first camel raids ever in history, and of course the Queen of Sheba set the fashion once and for all by leading the first great camel-train across the desert, when she travelled north on her famous visit to King Solomon in Jerusalem. According to other sources, the camel was already in use at the time when the Qatabian irrigation system was installed in Wadi Beihan in southern Arabia between 1600 and 1200 B.C.. But at this distance in time, there must be a certain amount of conjecture – and nobody really knows anything for certain. Myth and legend apart, it is a fact that, because of their peculiar spongy two-toed feet, camels can run on sand or snow without that awful sinking feeling which the horse was complaining about. Their normal walk, pretty uncomfortable until you get used to it, is because both legs on each side move together. By careful timing, Wellstead reckoned their cruising speed to be between 2½ and 2¾ m.p.h. On a desert trip, they jog along 'at a quick hard trot' at 6 to 8 m.p.h. for as long as twenty-four hours on end. If pushed, a good Batinah she-camel can reach 13 to 14 m.p.h; then she stretches her neck full out like an angry goose and throws her legs about in all directions, giving her passenger a very chaotic ride indeed. The best among all camels is the Batinyiah from the Batinah coast, known all over the Middle East for her breeding, elegance and speed. And the Dhahira camel from the Duru country, an altogether tougher breed, holds the record for endurance, if not for looks. Without undue effort, one of these animals can average 100 miles a day over a week. The Bedu always prefer females, whatever the breed. Just as robust as males, the load they can carry nevertheless differs according to their diet. It is a matter of perpetual astonishment to me that a creature like a caterpillar needs several thousand times its weight in food a day, whereas a large and cumbrous animal like a camel can make do with a few desiccated thorns and a handful of dates (if they're lucky) for several days on end without complaint. Anyway, when fed on the fat of the land, a good beast will carry up to 1,000 pounds but, on a desert run where food and water are short, 250 to 500 pounds is as much as they can take.

Truly well-designed for their environment, they have a double row of eyelashes to keep out flying sand, and hairy earholes like old men. The nose battens down completely, and goodness knows how they breathe during a sandstorm.

Horny pads on their chests and knees protect the skin when they are being loaded or mounted; and they have a keen sense of smell and very sharp eyesight. But even then, nobody knows whether their morale is kept going on the march by the constant mirages we see retreating in the distance. They can see further than we can but we have no way of guessing *what* they do and don't pick out.

Tough though they are, Arabian camels none the less occasionally go down with one or other of their more horrible diseases, and when this happens, it can't be ignored. Mange, which will ravage a herd in a very short time, is treated with lime and arsenic. When the last hair has been ripped off the beast, a soothing mixture of butter, sulphur and red pepper is patted all over the naked skin to help the new growth along. Foot rot is a particularly nasty affliction which strikes in damp situations – petroleum works wonders in this case. Swollen neck glands will kill the victim in three to four days, and colic seems to carry them off in an even shorter time. Branding, which is usually practised for these complaints, is not always effective. Worms on the brain is another of their less appealing afflictions and these are blown out by inducing violent sneezing.

The low water-consumption of the camel is its chief virtue. When on the trail it can keep going with only a drop or two for up to a week or more. When the temperature reaches 120° in the shade, this ration should be doled out every other day. When only a few drops are available over many weeks, these should be dribbled down the nose, to cool the fevered brain and keep the poor brute going a little longer.

The Bedu, the parasite of the camel, will survive as long as his beast does. Any water she drinks will be transformed into milk for his benefit, quite apart from anything which she will gladly regurgitate for him in times of dire emergency, from one or other of her numerous stomachs. And as day after day goes by without a drop to drink, her fat hump will break down and turn to water, to keep her going a little longer. For this reason if no other, it is worth keeping the precious hump in good condition, when it should reach thirty to forty pounds in weight.

Rather than drink brackish water, a Bedu prefers to kill

one of his herd, and drink its urine, which he will mix with female's vomit if troubled with digestive disorders. The dried meat of a camel is supposed to retard a woman's delivery. Every bit of the animal is used up, but only women will eat its brains, for they make men feeble and floppy. Dried dung is used for fuel, for plugging wounds and for making nice dry litters for babies. For a reliable aphrodisiac, you dip a camel bone into the juice of the Eclipta Prostata plant and burn it. If you want make-up, mix the ground black powder of a calcinated blade-bone with antimony and paint it around your eyes. And of course impotence is cured by drinking a blend of milk and wild honey, every bit as effective as the infallible shark's fins or powered oryx horn.

The camel's well-known chronic indigestion, which manifests itself with perpetual belching and an unappetizing green scum around the lips, is due to the complicated, though primitive, alimentary tract, consisting of seven different stomachs, all working away at their own job in their own time, taking little trouble to synchronize their activities. The bad temper, no doubt due to this perpetual bilious condition and complicated internal arrangement, is notorious.

When his allotted span is drawing to an end, and a camel can't stand up any longer, the Bedu reckon that the time has come for him to wander off to happier grazing grounds, and there is no point in trying to get him on his feet again. So they leave him to his fate and to the vultures of the desert. As Arabs only take life in self-defence or for sustenance, they never think of putting the poor brute out of his misery; instead they leave him to face a slow and agonizing death through thirst and starvation. This is Allah's job, not their own, and they happily go off without a twinge of pity for the abandoned animal. In spite of their deep love for their camels, their tough realism, which excludes all sentimentality, protects them from unnecessary grief.

The hair of the beast, which is shed on the march, is collected by certain tribes after a caravan has gone by. In a good year 300,000 pounds' weight is picked up and taken to the coast, where it is sold to visiting merchants and eventually comes out as expensive camel-hair coats. Some of it is used on the spot for ropes and tents, although goat-hair is stronger for that purpose.

A man mounted on his camel, more or less tucked up on his knees, looks very precarious perched on the tiny saddle, strapped behind the hump. In Hijaz and Syria, a superstructure is raised high above the hump, gaining a special sway and momentum of its own at high speed. In this giddily rocking cradle travel the women and children of the tribe.

In Oman, a camel's nose, which is unpierced, is attached by a chain to the headstall, and the bridle, which has only one rein, is (naturally) made of camel-hair. A stick is used for steering by gently tapping the neck on the appropriate side. Branded with their owner's *wasm*, as are the bulls of the Camargue, they rove at will in the desert until needed for work or racing. The owner then repairs to the spot where he loosed his treasure and tracks him down to base, unless he has been kidnapped by camel rustlers, always a potential danger. When on his own like this in the desert, a thirsty camel will hike over to the next well and patiently await the arrival of some kind-hearted Bedu to turn up and water his own animals.

Nobody who has had any experience of the filthy temper of the living beast will ever take liberties with a camel. Visitors from the West are sometimes surprised at the length to which drivers will go to avoid a patch of road on which one of them is sitting. They have taken a great fancy to the new desert roads, which they will plod through miles of scorching wilderness to reach. Some say tarmac cools down quicker than sand at night, when the creatures are a dreaded menace to motorists. There is a company in England which manufactures fluorescent braces to make camels visible in the dark, but no Bedu in his right mind will go to the expense and trouble of importing this equipment for his animals. It is very much to his advantage anyway to get them killed on the roads, as the compensation for such a casualty is £500 apiece. In the daytime, when the highway bubbles and froths in the noonday sun, there can be no other reason for camels to sprawl across it than sheer bloody-mindedness. And I have seen one of them lying on the road – we only avoided it by careering off into the *sabkha* in a wide loop – glaring at us with bloodshot yellow eyeballs, full of venom and loathing. When we returned a couple of hours later he had left his pitch on the highway and was standing on top of a pile of rubble, craning in our direction to make sure he didn't miss us this time. As we sped rather nervously past, he charged with a furious roar, and only just missed the car by inches.

I later read a horror story of a camel who, for some dim reason of his own, suddenly turned on his master without warning. Seeing the danger signs, the man swiftly shinned up the side of the cliff, but the camel was faster. Pouncing forward, he grabbed a foot with his teeth, dragged the man down and proceeded to trample him to jelly. Long after his victim was squashed completely flat, the vindictive animal went on relentlessly turning the body over and stamping about on the remains. All through that day he stuck close to the corpse, going back from time to time for another go. The moral of the story is: nobody should ever hang around when a camel is on the warpath.

Tracks and footprints are the books and newspapers of the desert. An Omani will tell you: 'Take a Murra tribesman on a three-day journey blindfolded, have him bury a dollar in the trackless sand at night. Ten years later he can return to reclaim his dollar with no difficulty.' After only a few days in the sands, you begin to realize how this can happen. To the Bedu there is a language of the desert which the tribes use to communicate with their friends. Bits of rag tied to trees are used as signposts. Just as tramps on the roads of England chalk up squiggles on the pavements and walls of certain houses as useful hints to following colleagues, so these scraps of coloured rag can tell long and complicated stories in code, according to the height of the branch and the kind of knot and the colour . . . a regular morse-code of the desert, in fact.

Nobody better knows or loves the desert than Thesiger; he wrote:

A few days later we passed some tracks. I was not even certain that they were made by camels, for they were much blurred by the wind. Sultan turned to a grey-bearded man who was noted as a tracker and asked him whose tracks they were, and the man turned aside and followed them

147

for a short distance. He then jumped off his camel, looked at the tracks where they crossed some hard ground, broke some camel droppings between his fingers and rode back to join us. Sultan asked, 'Who are they?' and the man answered, 'They were Awamir. There are six of them. They raided the Junuba on the southern coast and took three of their camels. They have come here from Sahma and watered at Mugshin. They passed here ten days ago.'

A much-quoted incident, which I can't resist including here, is the following, taken from St John Philby's writings.

Some Arabs, said Mubarak, were riding across a plain, when one of them, a sheikh of the tribe, called the attention of his fellows to the tracks of his own daughter crossing their path in the direction of a strip of Nafud in the distance. 'There goes my daughter' he said, 'to gather *nassi* (grass) for the camels against our return.' They rode on and in the evening they returned crossing the girl's tracks. 'Ah woe is me,' cried the sheikh, 'see ye not that when she went forth this morning she was a virgin, and she is such no longer? By God, she shall die for her unchastity, and with her I shall slay the man who dishonoured her; come, help me search him out, for his tracks are not with hers.' And so the party, greatly perturbed by the shame that had come upon the tribe, rode off towards the Nafud along the girl's tracks, searching for those of her paramour, but nowhere finding them. On they rode some distance into the sands until they came to where the tracks ended near by a desert plant, the curious Tarthuth, vulgarly known as the Desert Penis – Zubb al-Hamad. The old sheikh wept for joy to know that, though his reading of the tracks was correct, he had wronged his daughter by his too-ready suspicions and had wronged her even more by keeping her so long unwed.

In the hard-edge life of the desert it is only the toughest and most enduring, both among camels and men, who can manage to survive. They are the ones who can read the signs in the sand and the sky. The immense wastes, the crucifying marches under the blazing furnace of a noonday sun, the fearful cold and the desolate solitude of the night, the loneliness, all promote introspection and a constant awareness of a life beyond. For the Arab, Allah is everywhere present, and is brought into almost every sentence. The Bedu are religious fanatics, steeped in a faith which controls everything they do and which they never for one instant forget. Personally, I can never understand why so many people regard the desert as a vast boring expanse of unrelieved monotony. You have only to look around to see that every dune is different, with a character of its own. The colour of the sand alone changes every few feet, and its quality and density is never the same from one spot to the next. At sunrise, when it is firm and crisp, the tracks made during the night are sharp and clear cut. As the heat of the day increases, the consistency of the sand undergoes a total change, its texture swelling out and loosening up in the intense heat of noon, when it runs like liquid glass. Tracks made then are loose and blurred, with the edges falling in. The grains themselves, perfectly visible through an ordinary magnifying glass, differ from place to place, white and spherical like minute fish eyes around the Gulf, sharp and angular and lemon-yellow in the Empty Quarter around Liwa, blazing red in Al-Khatam. The *sabkha* itself, which everybody despises so, glistens like snow with its salt crystals reflecting the fierce rays of the sun.

Sand devils are delicate little whirlwinds, sometimes travelling alone, often in procession as they waltz past, zig-zagging haphazardly in the breeze. Skipping merrily away into the sunset, they are the most light-hearted manifestations of the spirit world you could ever wish to see. According to desert lore, these little devils are spirits of the dead coming back on a visit to the land of the living. Jinn on the other hand are not so jolly. Floating invisibly around the place, they pounce when least expected, invading your personality and playing havoc with your soul; and it takes all sorts of complicated practices and elaborate ritual to get them finally out of your system.

Desert roses are among the curiosities which you may come across if you are lucky. But they are rare, and I have never found one myself. Geodes on the other hand are frequently picked up in the desert adjoining the South Yemeni border. Round as cannon-balls, I have seen them used as doorstops; when split open, each half reveals the crystal-encrusted interior, filled with topaz, amethyst, or whatever else was lying around at the time of their creation.

14   The Wilder Shores of War

To Marco Polo, when he visited these shores, Dhofar was 'a great and noble and fine city', which went in for shipping and horse dealing and the harvesting and export of frankincense. The town of Dhofar to which he referred was probably the ruin which is now known as al-Balid. To Ibn Battuta, that other splendid medieval explorer, the city of al-Balid was 'the dirtiest in the world', swarming with great clouds of flies, particularly in the *souq*. Already at that time, much to Battuta's surprise, the local cattle were fed on sardines. And Idrisi, the Arab geographer at the court of Roger II of Palermo (those Norman kings of Sicily), claimed that Dhofar had been annexed from Hadramaut and made into a dependency of Oman. Earlier still, Pliny had expressed surprise at the writer Juba's credulity in believing that the dragons which landed on the shores of South Arabia should have crests! He then continued in the next sentence to describe how these dragons, leaving Ethiopia, the land of their origin, wrapped themselves around one another, sticking their heads up in the wind and sailing along towards the coast of Arabia, where they hoped for a better life.

Apart from these incursions of Ethiopian dragons, poor Dhofar also came under the destructive attentions of the Portuguese and even of the Turks, who bombarded the town with unusually large cannon-balls. Then came the Persians, followed by the forces of the kings of Hormuz, from 'the city-state which controlled the entrance to the Persian Gulf'.

So much for the early history of the province, whose people now largely consist of the wild cavemen of Jebel Qara who still regard themselves as intrepid warriors. And this despite a relatively peaceful existence now spent roving about the mountainside with their cattle and goats.

These round-headed tribes, who look very different from the people of the north, are believed by the archaeologist Dr Costa to be Arabs none the less. According to him they speak southern Arabian, which resembles Ethiopic more than Arabic, and is in fact Hymiaritic, which used to be a written language but is so no longer. The same tongue is spoken in Socotra where it is, not surprisingly, known as Socotri.

There are still nine illiterate tribes of primitive aborigines in the Qara. The Bell Report recommends a system of education and modernization which is being put into effect as speedily as it can be without upsetting age-old customs too abruptly. What the tribes will do with their education is another matter. These grand, pastoral, cave-dwelling noblemen have never worked with their hands. All menial tasks, such as the recent building of Government centres, schools and clinics, have had to be performed by Baluchis, who have taken over from the slaves of yore, while the helicopter service is operated by British pilots. The Jebel covers an area of 20 by 150 square miles, with about 20,000 people on it, all waiting for a miracle.

In the plain, between the Qara mountain range and the sea, live the Bait Kathir who regard themselves as the most important tribes in Dhofar and who now employ as slaves the last three hundred aborigines of the eastern range. And all these tribes, whether from the mountain or the plain, are constantly at daggers drawn with one another. Many long-standing blood-feuds hang compulsively over their heads. These were made illegal by the Sultan at the time of his accession, but such immemorial hatreds will take a long time to dissolve. On three occasions while I was in Oman, men have been shot dead over grazing rights. My guess is, the grazing is made an excuse for the settling of far more ancient vendettas, particularly as someone always springs forward at once to claim responsibility for the deed, even though the murderer knows perfectly well that he will spend the rest of his days as the guest of His Majesty in the State prison in Salalah.

Longing for some first-hand information about these tribes, I meet Miranda Morris who works in the new model hospital in Dhofar. Married to the doctor in charge of Civil Aid, she is an intrepid and dedicated young woman, well able to look after herself and cope with the hazards of life in Oman. A few weeks ago, as she was flying back from the Jebel in a Defender, the little aircraft, unable in the heat of the day to get the lift it needed, glided straight down into the sea, where it was submerged immediately. Three passengers who couldn't find a way out were helplessly drowned. Miranda wriggled out of the aircraft and thrashed her way back 300 yards to the shore, through the sharks, the barracudas, the stinging jellyfish and the giant breakers of the Indian Ocean.

As an anthropologist, she is writing a thesis on the tribes of the Jebel, and is trying to build up a grammar and dictionary of their languages and dialects. These differ from wadi to wadi. The task is colossal, and she gets very little co-operation from the tribesmen themselves. 'They won't help me,' she says gloomily. 'They won't tell me anything.' This puzzles me, as she gets on with them so well, and they quite obviously admire her gallant spirit, her fearlessness and plucky independence, all qualities which these resolute mountain warriors rate very highly.

'The language of each tribe is its secret weapon', explains Miranda who believes that their obscure tongues are symbols of their freedom. They want the benefits of progress and civilization (meaning guns, education, medical help), but they refuse to be absorbed, disciplined or even understood. As long as they keep their secrets, including their numerous dialects, their poetry and their lore, they can deliberately remain the wild savages that they are as long as they wish. Living in caves when they want to, or wandering about with their flocks whenever the spirit moves them, is the kind of existence they demand.

Just back from a three-day camel trip among the Jebalis,

Miranda is suffering from acute frustration at being torn away from her tribes and finding herself back once more in the civilized comforts of Salalah.

Even though she hasn't got her great tome together yet, she is nevertheless making progress. A witch-doctor whom she has managed to tame a little, is beginning to part with some of his secrets. Since he was made to swallow a comprehensive cocktail of snake poison as a child he has been immune to their bite, and is now chief snake caller of his tribe. Scorpion charmers, all equally invulnerable, are other essential members of the establishment in these parts. The tribes, it appears, are entirely controlled by their witch-doctors, who keep them fit with the practice of *wasm* (branding). This is done with large or small, round or square-headed nails, according to the nature of the complaint. Unlike Jo in Khaboura, Miranda is convinced that, if properly done by experts, the benefits are indisputable. Where an infection develops, the treatment has been carried out by a charlatan, or a well-meaning old granny.

Female witches practise black and white magic. Hardly anything is done without consulting them. The safety of relatives on a journey, the milk yield of a cow, or a spell to be cast on a rival or an enemy and many more everyday problems are handled with stones or clay figures or bones. But in all cases it is incantations and the words which matter. Plants, such as the ashgar (Sodom apple) are used as anaesthetics or to draw an abscess. The colocynth (bitter apple) is a purge. The juice of the milk bush lifts off diseased skin in layers. The calatropis, with its pretty little pink flowers, is a reliable poison. Nebek, the seed of the tamarind under whose shade it is dangerous to sleep, is a powerful tranquillizer. The powdered horn of the oryx, if you can ever get hold of it, makes an effective love potion, and will also cure snake-bite.

The province of Dhofar first became involved with Oman in 1829, when some of the tribes asked the Sultan of Muscat to come and help them against their enemies. From then on, until 1970, the sultans have regarded Dhofar as their own private property. In 1880 more help had to be sent down to sort out another tribal squabble. This time the sultan dispatched a *wali* as well to keep order, once it had been restored.

From 1958, apart from his flying visit through central Oman, Sultan Said bin Taimur, father of the present monarch, settled down and lived in Salalah for the rest of his reigning days.

After the defeat of the three rebels of Jebel Akhdar, the Communists infiltrated into Dhofar, subverting the tribesmen with bribes and threats, then sending them 'to school' in reliable Communist States. And when they returned from their brain-washing establishments, the new converts bullied the tribal elders and their families to give up Islam. A couple of old sheikhs of the eastern Mahra who protested indignantly against the new doctrines had their eyeballs scooped out with red-hot knives heated in the fire. The nephew of one of these ancient chiefs had been to 'school' in Iraq and perpetrated the deed. Having acquired a substantial following with these methods, the new commissars turned their recruits into a tough mountain guerilla force. On their own terrain, which they knew since earliest childhood, these men were invincible. The only way to deal with the situation was to cut off infiltration routes and starve the new enemy of food and ammunition.

It was in 1972, at the height of the rebellion, that Vanya Kewley chose to visit the battlefield and produce a film of the war for Thames Television.

Vanya (006½, as she is known to her friends) is about four foot six, and proportioned to perfection all the way down to her toes. Like a Dresden figurine she has bird bones, a wasp waist, tiny hands and long heavy blonde hair which swings about whenever she moves her head – the last person you would ever think of in connection with the blasting of mortars and twenty-five-pounders, the rattle of machine-guns and the screaming of jet-fighters overhead. Yet this is exactly where she was, bang in the middle of it all, with British officers and Omani soldiers, on top of the Jebel, in the midst of the Dhofar War. Having unfortunately missed the war myself, the next best thing I could do was to go and see the film which Vanya had made of it; so off to Thames Television studios I trotted on my next visit to London.

The war had actually been started in 1964 by one man, a useless loafer, one Musallim bin Nafl who had been sacked by the oil company which employed him for petty thieving and general bloody-mindedness. A shiftless, bitter, dissatisfied layabout, he took up crime as a hobby after he lost his job. Stealing guns, ammunition and hand grenades, he ambushed and shot up a lorry, killing its passengers on the spot. From that moment on, the die was cast and he was an outlaw. Others of the same ilk soon joined him, and together they founded a brotherhood of crime which they disguised under the pompous name of the Dhofar Liberation Front. In September 1968, this movement held a solemn congress and announced a change of name to the 'People's Front for the Liberation of the Occupied Arabian Gulf'. The ponderous P.F.L.O.A.G., now backed by powerful friends abroad, went from strength to strength. By 1970 the Sultan's Armed Forces had a job to keep their end up on the Jebel. The town of Salalah, with the Sultan in his palace, was surrounded by barbed wire. Outside that area, the rebels roamed about freely all over the place.

Until then, the S.A.F. had always retired from the Jebel as soon as the monsoon fogs came rolling over the hills from the sea. During those three valuable months the rebels had plenty of time to hump in the supplies needed for the next season and also to swarm back into the positions which they had lost in the previous campaign.

In 1970 came the coup which deposed Sultan Said bin Taimur and placed Qaboos on the throne. Straightaway the new ruler offered a general amnesty to all rebels who were prepared to surrender, plus a handsome cash hand-out which was made even greater if they gave up their arms as well. After this, they would be reinstated as members of a newly formed tribal militia, the Firqats. Given back their arms, they would be allotted a regular salary and shipped back to their own tribal areas. There they were to keep the peace and report on any enemy activity which might come to their notice. At first a faint trickle of men came over which soon swelled to a couple of thousand and turned out to be an important help to the Sultan's forces. From then on, they decided to stay put on the Jebel during the muffled, fog-bound months of the monsoon. These heavy mists, which completely blotted out the landscape, were an added peril to the S.A.F. who were now plagued by cold miserable nights and perpetually drenched equipment, as well as the unnerving menace of an invisible, omnipresent enemy. But the new policy helped to tip the scales. More and more rebels, lured by the handsome rewards, began to surrender in earnest to the Government forces. Gradually the army was able to set up new positions across the enemy supply lines. At Sarfait, a permanent fortified base perched on top of an enormous peak overlooking South Yemen was supplied by helicopters.

Thoroughly put out by this new turn of events, the enemy hit back with non-stop bombardment from Russian-built 85mm guns in Hauf on the other side of the border. From then on shells and rocket bombs rained over the gallant S.A.F. positions day and night. In May 1972 the People's Democratic Republic of Yemen launched an attack across the frontier, which was promptly nipped in the bud when the R.A.F. swooped down over Hauf and plastered the enemy position.

Entrenched above the Communist supply line, perched 4,000 feet up the mountainside, the British colonel in charge of hammering the infiltration route was interviewed by Vanya. Joining him in his *sangar*, under intermittent mortar fire and to the sound of a twenty-five-pounder blasting off a yard away from her right ear, she asked him for his views on the enemy.

'They fight by the Red Book of Chairman Mao. They use their country well, and they are well led by their hard core,' was his opinion.

The primary objective of the Communists was to get rid of the remaining monarchies in the Arab world, beginning with Oman, and grabbing its oil revenue. The message they put over to the people was that once the Sultan was gone, there would be vast riches to distribute among the many, and everybody would be set up in wealth and comfort for life. Though illiterate, the Jebalis are clever, quick-witted and shrewd, and they may well not have swallowed all this moonshine wholesale, but they had no choice. Terrorized and browbeaten by the military 'hard-core' Communist rebels, the entire population of the Jebel were forced to co-operate. The women would scuttle about with giant bundles on their heads, usually food for the men hiding in the caves during daylight hours, or it could equally well be consignments of hand grenades, or small-arms ammunition. As no one in Arabia would ever dream of searching a woman, they invariably got away with everything. Ragged old shepherds would drive their flocks right up to S.A.F. *sangars*, rapidly tot up the number of heads and guns, then shuffle back to report to the enemy what they had seen. Vanya's film shows rows of children, kidnapped from their families and sitting in line in the dust of the 'Lenin School' four miles over the border in South Yemen, being taught how to become ruthless little Communists and preparing them for a life-long future of guerilla warfare.

Units stationed near the front line, at least those closest to enemy pockets, were completely cut off from the rest of the world and were supplied twice a week by helicopters bringing in ammunition, food, the all-important mail and water. As huge moving targets, they were terribly vulnerable, and so they tipped out their load without hanging around to wait for trouble. Hardly touching down at all, they then swooped off again as fast as they could.

The water ration, being very restricted, was used for drinking only. A young Guards officer, interviewed at his post by Vanya, had been up there on duty for the previous ten weeks. 'I haven't had a wash since I last went down to Salalah,' he told her. 'I suppose I stink a bit, but still.' That was inevitable. Water was too precious to waste on washing on the Jebel.

About the Adoo he had this to say: 'Their field craft is superlative, we very rarely see them moving into position and, once they are in position, it's very difficult to tell where they are.' His hands and face were baked like terracotta by the sun, his head exotically swathed in the all-purpose *shemag*, the very picture of a romantic Beau Geste warrior. He enjoyed his job, which was straightforward and uncomplicated, unlike Northern Ireland, where he had been stationed the year before, and where soldiers had their hands tied behind their backs because of the constant danger of injuring civilians. 'They're all enemy. And therefore one can get on and do the job, mortaring the area, returning small-arms fire without worrying about hurting innocent people.' Asked about the perks he got from his job, this irrepressible young officer replied, 'The job is the perk. I really love it. You're on your own, fighting your own war, and you can fight it how you like.' The fact that many of them were killed (one of them had his head cut off by the Adoo) and some were injured for life (I met one who had lost his leg, and another whose arm had been blown off by a mine) didn't deter these British officers in the least. James Morris said, 'Soon it would only be in a few remote corners of the Arabian peninsula that Englishmen could still serve as soldiers with Arabs, relishing the particular pleasure that stems from living with desert people in conditions of shared hardship.'

Major Peter Bennett also took part in one of the major raids on the enemy's infiltration route. The attack took place at night. The S.A.F. outposts, in ambush beside a wall, fell upon the unsuspecting caravan bringing in the supplies. There was a general engagement, in which the enemy were killed to a man. Their booty, which included gold, money, jewellery, food and ammunition, was captured. It was quite a haul. One camel, which had somehow escaped the massacre, ran amok, and went quite mad with rage. When they finally managed to catch it they tried to sell it in Salalah. 'But nobody would buy it,' said Major Bennett. 'They knew it had come from the Adoo, and they were too frightened to be seen owning it.' Talking of ambush techniques he added, 'The hardest thing in this world is to stop the Arab soldiers getting carried away with enthusiasm and firing as soon as they see the enemy coming over the horizon.' Not surprisingly, this impulsive approach gives their position away to the enemy who simply walk past the ambush twenty yards away. 'So the thing to do is to lure them into the killing zone,' continued the major in matter-of-fact tones, 'and fire only when they are in the trap.' At either end of this are machine-gun groups. The idea is to allow the rebels to move in right up to the furthest artillery posts. 'That fellow opens up when they are coming towards him.' And only after that the guns at the rear end let fly as well. The rebels, trapped between the two positions, are then lost.

The Leopard Line was the code name for a chain of blocking positions along the supply routes. In his book *Where Soldiers Fear to Tread* Ranulf Fiennes has drawn a haunting picture of the infiltration areas, the long nights, and false alarms, the loneliness of the desert wastes which it was his lot to patrol. On an improbable airstrip lost in the wilderness, a dozen live goats were landed once a week for himself and his men. The patrols followed lone camel spoor, but there was no water, as there had been a drought for fifteen years. For several months they camped in a barren field of volcanic stones and gravel, the only trail along which the rebels could bring in their supplies. The Nejd desert was full of unfriendly life: large green, black and white scorpions strolled about, a menace to bare feet. For once, Captain Fiennes was wearing shoes when he trod on a six-inch specimen. Camel spiders crept in for warmth under his blanket at night. Deadly African puff-adders and horned vipers were numerous and there were desert monitors and various other large lizards. Fred the guide knew about plants: kfeeter seeds, tied in a rag and hung around the neck, would keep evil spirits away; the gh'ader was good for colic; the Sodom apple, cut in half and heated, could draw poison out of an abscess. Further north, where the sand takes over from the Nejd, petrified ostrich eggs had been found.

Sometimes, in an ambush the men had to lie dead still for twenty-four hours on end. When pack camels loaded with arms came past, an occasional prisoner was caught for questioning. Hyenas loped by, wolves prowled, gazelle and ibex would pick their way among the stones of the wadi, searching for a trickle of water.

It was not till a year later, when the war was over and the caves were more or less cleared of remaining rebels, that I got a chance to inspect the battlefields.

It is March, and already very hot. In a comfortable air-conditioned palace Mercedes, we dash up the Midway road, now tarmacked, which had to be cleared of mines every day before the supply trucks taking men, food and ammunition could get through to the warriors at the top. As soon as a stretch was safe, off they pelted hell-for-leather, hoping to drive between the bullets which came flying through the air from both sides of the track. As we climb into the mountains, the Brigadier points out particularly vicious ambush spots. The formation of the Qara, with its crags and crevices, its canyons and its innumerable caves, makes it an ideal background for guerrilla warfare. As Colonel of the Muscat Regiment which was fighting on the Jebel at the time, he knows practically every stone of the area. *Sangars*, those special features of the Dhofar War, were continually changing hands. With the enemy in front, behind, in the cave next door, on top of the rock above, there was no front-line to this war. Hills were taken, lost and retaken. Only once was battle actually joined when a bunch of Iranian troops, crouching in a *sangar*, were overrun by the Adoo leaping upon their backs and sticking bayonets into them. Otherwise, they shot up passes, roads and convoys, then melted away into their caves or the safety of the Grand Canyon which was their headquarters. We stop and get out of the car to lean over the edge and stare into its depths. Now, apart from the racket of the cicadas, all is quiet down there. It is difficult to imagine it as an infernal arsenal only a few months ago. From here, roads and tracks were mined every day 'and everywhere that they expected the convoys to drive and the men to pass'.

Never once did the Brigadier see an Adoo face to face, until one of them eventually lay on a mine and was brought in to him, tattered to shreds. 'At all costs the man had to be kept alive. If he would talk, he would be an invaluable source of information,' but first of all he had to be patched up, and there were no surgeons on the Jebel.

Casting around for help, he approached an Indian doctor. 'It's a long time since I've done any operating. And we're not really supposed to do amputations, and anyway I am not an anaesthetist,' said this gentleman unhelpfully. Then the Brigadier remembered another Indian, a dentist this time, whom he knew in Bahrain. And of course dentists know how to deal with anaesthetics, he said to himself. So he got the men down, and between the two of them they made a first-class job of it.

After this, the Adoo got better and stronger every day. 'But the man would never talk. Nothing on earth would induce him to open his mouth,' says my companion disgustedly. The next thing was what to do with him. Was he to be locked up? 'No,' decreed the Brigadier, 'we'll fix up the bugger with a wooden leg and send him back to his mates. They always say we're a lot of bastards. Now they will see what a decent lot we really are.' Needless to say, they neither saw nor heard anything of that man again. I could have told them myself if I had been there at the time.

We pass Mount John, where an officer of that name was occupying the hill for quite a long time. Here he had settled down comfortably in his dugout, lined with ammunition tins, all as civilized as could be, with a little garden outside and all. When he was wounded, his chest ripped open by a burst of shrapnel, it took many long agonizing hours to get him down to the plain on the back of a mule, and that without the benefit of the mildest anaesthetic. The heroic young man, I am glad to say, is still very much alive today.

Having passed Ambush Corner, a particularly nasty spot, we finally reach the top of the Jebel. From here we can see right across the bare, flat plain of Dhofar, with the indigo blue of the Indian Ocean beyond.

'When the monsoon season starts, you can stand here and watch the clouds of the Khareef rolling in from the sea and over the plain,' my guide informs me. 'And by the time it gets here, you are in the middle of such a thick fog you can't even see a few feet in front of your nose.' This was ideal weather for the Adoo, whose very feet knew every inch of the terrain from memory so that, even in the thickest of cloud when visibility was nil, they could still find their way around without the slightest trouble.

At the very top stands the Special Services Station of Thumrayt, where a handful of carefully selected men are trained in the less orthodox arts of warfare. This force, which doesn't form part of the army, comes under the Sultan's personal command.

The Officers' Mess is as comfortable as a modern hotel. The Commanding Officer, Colonel Seeger, gives us coffee. On the floor of the dining room stands a telescope. In a matter of seconds the Brigadier is flat on his belly, his eye glued to the lens. 'This is just the thing,' he exclaims, 'I've got it trained right on the udders of that old cow over there.' Peering hopefully around the horizon, I can't even see the cow, let alone its udders.

15   The Flying Doctor

A week later I am back in Salalah, having winged my way over the desert in a dashing little aircraft of the Sultan's flight. Martin Robb, who meets me at the airport, drives his stripped-down Landrover right on to the runway. 'I see you've got travelling down to a fine art,' he remarks, swinging my shoulder-bag into the back of the vehicle.

We cruise along the coast road, with coconut trees swinging lazily on one side and the huge white beach on the other. Camels, grazing in the dunes, don't even bother to look up as we roar past. The Sultan's palace is on the seashore, with only a low wall in front to keep the beach from blowing in through the front door. On this wall, the late Sultan used to line up empty bottles and take pot shots at them from the palace windows. The story goes that he never missed.

The Robbs live in a comfortable bungalow draped in bougainvillaea, on the seashore. We have tea on the verandah with baby Lucy and a much loved, pulpy, stuffed animal of obscure identity. Jenny, who has a full-time job, has made a delicious chocolate cake. When does she get the *time*?

I stare out over the Indian Ocean as Martin fills me in on the situation in the Province in general, and the Jebel in particular. As soon as the war was over, it was of vital importance to convince the rebels that they had made the right decision in changing sides. Civil Aid went into action at once. Flying into areas where some of them still lurked in caves, unsure which side to back, Martin and his colleagues dropped supplies and essential equipment. 'Government centres' sprang up overnight, clinics were established, and much-needed wells were drilled as a matter of great urgency.

After tea we set off once more on the sea road, with Lucy on my lap, to visit the Sultan's model farm. Here a magnificent herd of Jersey cows, shuffling about in clean sand instead of straw, produces milk for the whole of Salalah. The enormous shed where it is sterilized and bottled is cool, pin-tidy and absolutely up to date in modern equipment – a model dairy such as I have never seen before. Lucy is enthralled. 'Mummy cows,' she squeaks in delighted surprise, pointing at the full udders swinging under the huge bellies.

On the way back we stop just past the Sultan's palace for a walk on the beach. The tide, far out, is on the turn. Lucy, who is still happier on all fours than upright on her podgy chubby feet, beetles off towards the waves with an escort of crabs on either side. Snatched up just in time by her father, she rushes back every time she thinks nobody is looking, magnetically drawn by the lovely splashing salty water. Etched out against the huge blood-red globe of the setting sun, that plump little behind waddling down the deserted beach is an unforgettable sight.

The next day, in the cool breeze of the early morning, we are at the airport once more. The flying doctor's helicopter is being loaded with supplies for the Government centres and isolated tribes. Doctor Catherine is busy elsewhere today, and her place is taken by an Indian orderly who climbs in with a heavy medicine chest. Her husband Shaun, who is in charge of our party, gets in beside the pilot. I squeeze in among a bunch of hairy tribesmen who are hitching a lift up to their home caves on the Jebel.

The engines roar, the great blades shudder and thrum and begin to whirr. In a matter of seconds they are beating so fast you can see nothing but one enormous blurred halo throbbing around the rising sun. We are off.

At this time of the year, arid and mustard-brown, the Jebel looks from the air like chewed-up gingerbread. We cruise over it, peering down into the cracks and crevasses among the flaking rock until a flat surface appears large enough to touch down on. And we swing in to land.

There is a clanking of rifles as the tribesmen scramble out (no nonsense about ladies first in these parts). They instantly disappear into the cloud of red dust, flying twigs and dead leaves whipped up by the beating of the great pulsating blades.

This is our first port of call on the Qara. Shaped like a vast boomerang, it forms a kind of barrier, sealing off the coastal plain from the interior desert, and creating a micro climate unique in Arabia. The vacuum caused by hot air rising out of the scorching Nejd desert behind the Jebel sucks in the moisture-bearing winds which blow all the way from the east coast of Africa. When these swirling, soggy mists hit the mountain they condense and fall as a continual drizzle, lasting for the whole of the monsoon season from June to September. During this period, visibility is reduced to nothing, as a permanent fog envelops the plain of Salalah, shrouding the uplands in heaving, rolling cloud. These raging African winds churn up the Indian Ocean which can be heard pounding away invisibly on the beach like rumbling thunder, When the monsoon clouds disperse, a marvellous change has taken place, and the whole Province is covered with lush, tender, emerald-green grass. Similarly, the usual bleak, dried-out-gingerbread look of the Jebel has also turned to a green carpet spreading beneath the fig trees, the camel thorn and the other scrub of the hills. Deep down in the mountain wadis, entire ravines become luxuriant oases with gushing brooks, pools and waterfalls, exuberant tropical vegetation, a tangle of soaring lianas and hanging orchids, squirming ferns and spongy mosses. Among all this, humming birds hover over the purple banana flowers, dragonflies dart over the pools, great yellow wasps swing from side to side, and clouds of butterflies arise from the water's edge at the slightest disturbance. It is hard to believe that this little paradise was for so long the battle area of a war which hardly anybody has ever heard of, and which started three months after the then Mr Harold Wilson decided to withdraw the British Army from Aden.

The fighting has now been over for more than a year and,

to mark its end, a National Day parade was held in Salalah in 1978. As a victory celebration it was a triumph, unspoilt by any acts of terrorism, a sure sign that all that side of the affair is over for the time being. But it would be folly to be smug about the present lull. On the other side of the border, carefully watched by the observation post of Sarfait overlooking Yemeni territory, Russian-trained troops are mounting guard twenty-four hours a day. In Aden, the Russian joint military headquarters, working with Cubans and East Germans, is up to no good. There are several thousand men, armed to the teeth with Russian weapons, either fully trained or being taught guerrilla methods and infiltration tactics. An important pile of arms, tanks, light bombers and MiG fighters is dangerously standing by in Aden, waiting for the right moment to strike. All this is backed by a fleet of nuclear submarines, a cruiser and three destroyers. The area is undoubtedly a fertile anarchists' breeding ground. And the reason for this impressive concentration of military power is OIL. A simultaneous attack, moving south from Iran and north from Aden through Oman, would meet at the Straits of Hormuz, effectively stopping the flow of oil to the West.

As soon as the rebels surrendered in one area of the Jebel, the Government moved in at once with supplies and medical aid. In order to discourage guerrilla activity for good and all, the idea was to install an official centre with all possible speed, including a clinic, a shop, a school and the drilling of a well. By now there are thirteen such centres in operation on the Jebel. In order to drive home the advantages of liberation, whole prefabricated units were flown in and clamped together on the spot. It was quite a usual sight for school desks, beds, cooking pots and other domestic gear to come swinging through the sky in the great helicopter net. Although Oman is not one of the very rich oil States, there are enough revenues for a robust policy of reform. Sultan Qaboos was determined from the start to wrench his country out of the Middle Ages and bring it into the twentieth century as soon as it could be done tactfully and practically. And the end of the Dhofar War was a God-given opportunity to move right in with much-needed medical aid and education at a crucial moment in time, a turning point in the history of these primitive, underdeveloped parts.

As no female doctor could at first be found, a male of the species who was regularly flown up to the Jebel would have to crouch behind a portable wattle hide, while a couple of nurses 'took' the clinic. As the women of the tribes gradually gained confidence and came along with their ailing infants, one of the nurses would describe the nature of the complaint in a loud voice over her shoulder to the doctor behind his screen. Rapidly computing the symptoms, he would shout back the relevant treatment and drugs to be administered.

Then, in the fullness of time, came the appointment of the first woman doctor who now covers every spot on the Jebel, flying hither and thither in a hired army helicopter every day of the week. Things have improved and confidence grown to such an extent that she is now openly accompanied by a *male* medical orderly who is universally accepted by those very women who confined the original doctor behind his screen during the first consultations.

And now, a year later, we are landing on the Jebel: the same medical orderly carrying the medicine chest, a Civil Aid employee whose mother came from a local Jebali tribe and who acts as co-ordinator, and myself as 'observer'.

Having decanted us, the chopper flies off to sort out pressing problems elsewhere. Later it will return to pick us up and ferry us to another spot on the Jebel.

When the dust storm has settled, we find ourselves on a wide plateau backed by a high mountain range. Camel-thorn scrub grows here and there, and under the only sumr tree sits the sheikh. Above his head, stretched among the denuded branches, are mats and brightly coloured rags to give shade to those below.

The Jebali are not Arabs but, according to one theory, are of Hamitic origin, descended from North Africans; and they are among the most primitive tribes of the Middle East, still clinging to their caves and mud huts as they have always done. They speak languages of Semitic origin, such as Shaari, Mahri, Batahri and Harsusi, all of which are quite incomprehensible to the Arabs. Apart from these main divisions, there are innumerable variations on the main themes, such as sub-tribes, sections and clans which are themselves divided by various blood-feuds, each one speaking a different dialect.

The pre-Islamic Shahara tribe, of whom about only three hundred survive, are the slaves of the late-comers, the powerful, domineering Kathiri people from the Hadramaut, who have managed to impose themselves as the leading tribes of the Qara range. Of medium height, they are as tough as mountain mules and as nimble as goats, illiterate but as sharp and bright as you could wish and, like our own distant ancestors, they frequently paint themselves blue all over. In many, quite unconnected parts of the world, this colour is used as a protection against the evil eye. In Greece and North Africa, for instance, the windows of peasants' and fishermen's huts are painted blue all round the edge. In Turkey it is a lucky colour. In the Camargue, the gardians' shacks are decorated with chips of blue glass embedded in the plaster above the front door. And in present-day western countries, baby boys are often dressed in blue as a matter of course.

The clinic is about to start. A couple of plastic mats are spread on the ground and the women, who are beginning to come along, are followed by an earnest little troop of toddlers, all bearing a pink card aloft. This is injection day, and they want to know if they are due for another jab. The mothers, small and quick-moving as sparrows, squat on the plastic mats, and the orderly opens his medicine chest.

Collecting together a few empty shell cases (the ground is littered with these relics of past battles) I construct myself a little stool to keep out of reach of the scorpions, red ants and camel spiders of the Jebel. As a woman scuttles past with one of the local pigmy cows in her arms, I grieve at not being allowed to take photographs. But the night before in Salalah, the flying doctor had declared very firmly, 'I will not have my women upset by photographs so they don't come to the clinic any more.' And that, alas, is that.

A few yards away on the right is a large wattle and mud hut shaped like an igloo, with a small round door screened by a sack. Crows, hopping about on the roof, snap up an occasional beetle or lizard, and the pointed whiskery face of a rat suddenly pokes out of the wattle wall of the hut.

Sweeping the sackcloth curtain aside with her foot and

bending low, the cow-bearing woman disappears behind it. I whip round, as someone's hot breath is panting down my ear, to find myself face to face with another of those tiny cows, no bigger than a dog. Intrigued by the visitors, a herd is cantering towards us, skipping and scampering around, trampling the rush mats and leaping over the medicine chest, all as agile as goats; the noble-looking sheikh is having his face licked by one of these affectionate creatures. Nobody seems to mind them in the least. These little cows are prestigious possessions. The more of them a man owns, the more respected and highly regarded he is. For this reason, among others, it is difficult for Civil Aid in Salalah to convince the owners to breed larger animals, their idea being to have not a few big handsome animals but a multitude of pigmies, amounting to a large herd. It is very much a question of quantity versus quality. Experiments in cross-breeding with Anglo-Saxon cows have been tried, with disastrous results. So now new schemes are being hatched, with infinite care and regard for the Jebali's preferences.

Each much-loved cow has her own name and is milked only by her owner, an honour denied to the women, who have to content themselves with milking the goats. Any fall in the yield is of course due to the evil eye, and this is often put right by the burning and swinging of frankincense. When this remedy fails, the owner applies his mouth to the cow's vagina and blows into it for all he is worth. Soon the stimulation turns her thoughts to milk, and she obliges.

As more and more patients gather under the tree, a woman suddenly appears with a calabash brimming with milk. This is handed round, and all take a swig. Remembering what I have been told in Muscat – 'That Jebel milk – instant T.B.' – I just wet my lips and pretend to swallow.

I notice with regret that the pernicious bottle-feeding practice has already spread to these parts. With the shortage of water, it is impossible to wash out these plastic bottles between feeds, let alone sterilize them, so that they become lined inside with a lethal green scum, causing diarrhoea and dysentery. It is difficult to make the mothers understand the principle of cause and effect. Having discovered bottle-feeding which allows them to become pregnant again as soon as they have weaned the last infant, nothing will persuade them back to breast-feeding at the moment. In time, of course, this problem will be sorted out, along with many others, by the spread of education on the Jebel.

Gradually more women appear from behind the rocks, carrying a child on one hip, with several others trotting behind. Scrutinizing the toddlers' pink cards, the orderly pats them on the head and says, 'No, next time,' and then to me, 'Too bad, because next week the card will be lost or eaten by a goat, and then we won't know where we are.'

By the end of the hour there are about fifteen women squatting under the tree. Most of them are wearing black *abbas* (cloaks), their handsome faces are unveiled and most of them sport a gold ring through the nose. Their fingers and toes are covered with rings, and they are shy, easily disconcerted by a sharp word from the sheikh. Children mill around, hugging first one woman then another, and it is impossible to tell who the mother is. The little cows skip around merrily, poking their noses into everybody's business unchecked.

Suddenly there is a great roar in the sky, and we all look towards the east, where our helicopter appears, slowly floating towards us and trailing a huge rafter in its wake, wrapped in the meshes of the chopper net. 'Moving building materials,' remarks the orderly, handing out a bottle of cough mixture. Children are brought to him with sore eyes and ears, chest colds, skin trouble, festering sores. In each case the diagnosis is swift and sure. The drugs are handed to the little patient in person. When he has received his tube of ointment or bottle of syrup, he toddles off, clutching his prize in his right hand, and disappears behind a rock, leaving mother to gossip with her friends.

Squatting on my home-made stool of shell cases, I watch and hold my peace. As the only female of our party and knowing my place (I am probably the second or third European woman these people have ever seen, Dr Catherine and Miranda Morris being the other two), I try to be as unobtrusive as possible. But the orderly, who knows my mission, has kindly taken me under his wing and is bent on helping me. The clinic is over, and he speaks to the sheikh. 'Kittab,' he informs the old man, pointing at me and writing in mid air. The sheikh rises and walks gravely towards his hut, inviting me to follow. Feeling rather like Alice, I squeeze through the tiny doorway behind him.

This house is very old, he explains. He built it twelve years ago, and always spends some time in it every year with his family. After that they move off, sometimes one way sometimes another, according to the year, the mood and the grazing. It was not until long after that I began to wonder how we ever managed to communicate and understand each other. At the time, the problem didn't arise and, although we hadn't a single word in common, we chatted quite happily without difficulty.

Inside the hut it is surprisingly spacious. You can even stand up quite comfortably. Solemnly we face each other, then he moves to the far end of the hut, obviously his domain. Here are reed mats and leather cushions on the floor. We sit down. Enthroned on a goatskin pillow, his back ramrod straight, his legs crossed and his camel-stick laid out before him, he looks as regal as any king.

It is quite awesome. With undiminished dignity he whacks away at the rats which come poking through the wattle wall of the hut. I look around with increasing surprise. Outside, the heat was becoming uncomfortable. Here it is cool, fresh and remarkably unsmelly, although the little cow is happily chewing the cud in a corner and half a dozen goats skip around on the sandy floor. Water-skins hang from the ceiling, rifles are stacked around the central kingpost. The kitchen quarters are not divided from the sheikh's apartment by a curtain, as is the custom with the tribes of the Empty Quarter; they are neat and tidy. The tin cauldrons and trays are clean and shiny, standing in a row against the mud wall. A goatskin cradle, hanging from a roof beam out of the way of ants and scorpions, contains a sleeping infant. Hanging below the cradle are curious racquet-shaped objects made of cow-fur. Intrigued, I ask my host what they are. He explains that they are held out for licking purposes to the cows who are being milked, so that they will be tricked into believing that they are suckling their calf and so more readily let down the milk.

The chopper appears once more in the sky, this time to pick us up. Shrinking into ourselves and crouching low, we huddle away from the rising dust-storm. Then with eyes half-closed and faces shrouded in scarves and *shemags* (those all-purpose head-cloths worn by Omani men, used for everything and anything from making a tourniquet to straining water), we run for it. The blades don't even slow down as we scramble in. Being such vulnerable targets, helicopters touch down for a few seconds only, and you have to get a move on if you don't want to be left behind. There are still sixty known rebels hiding away in caves, and it goes without saying that the 'friendly' tribes know perfectly well where they are and keep them supplied with food, if not with arms as well. The Jebali are only subdued up to a certain point.

Only a couple of Firqats are getting a lift this time; they sit opposite me, stony-faced, their rifles between their knees. These men are the ex-rebels who surrendered at the end of the war, and are now being paid by the Government to keep watch over the Jebel and report any sign of untoward activity. The Firqats are in fact a kind of unofficial police, well looked after, well paid and provided with as much ammunition as they wish.

When the tribesmen were under the sway of the guerrillas in the Yemen, they were kept under control by terrorism and sheer brutality. If they didn't spy on the Sultan's forces and report on the movement of his troops, if they didn't provide the rebels with food, milk and ready women, they were beaten up, crucified on trees or submitted to various other refinements of torture. Those who refused to give up their faith were made to regret it, and anyone found praying was burned with red-hot coals applied to the soles of the feet, the back and the genitals, and then usually pitched over the edge of a precipice.

We are now dropping on to the Jebel again, and once more there is a clanking of musketry as the Firqats shuffle towards the door of the chopper. As soon as it touches down they hop out and are gone.

Our second port of call is a wadi bed full of scorpions and camel spiders. These unattractive creatures inject you with a shot of pain-killer so that they can eat you up alive undisturbed. Another of their disconcerting little ways is to leap straight into the air from a sitting position, like a suddenly uncoiled spring. We settle down under a thorn tree, open up the medicine chest and wait. Soon a few women begin to trickle along. They are larger here, more confident, very grand, assertive and arrogant. They demand medicine and treatment as of right. One thing in their favour is the absence of the dreaded feeding-bottle. Most of them are very handsome, with enormous kohl-lined eyes and full lips. None is veiled or masked, but some have lines of indigo running over the cheekbone, from the nose to the ear-lobe. They look like large, exotic, brightly coloured moths fluttering with orange, purple, emerald and buttercup-yellow veils and scarves, as they settle in a circle on the ground around us. The nose ring seems to be universally worn. Gold coins tinkle around their necks and silver bangles filled with seeds jingle on their wrists and ankles. There are rings on their fingers and their toes, and even the left nostril of baby girls is encrusted with silver flowers screwed into the nose. The boys have a pathway shaved right through the hair, going over the top of the skull from one ear to the other, with a cropped fringe in front and a wild natural tangle hanging down the back.

As the medical orderly begins to delve into his box, a young man comes loping along, holding his rifle by the business end like a walking-stick. Dressed in a short skirt with one end of it slung over his shoulder like a Greek shepherd of classical times, his long oily hair hangs in ringlets round his neck. His face is painted blue in zebra stripes, and a little tuft of wiry bristles decorates his chin. He joins us without a word and sits cross-legged with his rifle across his knees. Our orderly addresses him with his usual cheerfulness, but the youth hangs his head, nods once or twice in an absent sort of way and remains obstinately silent.

'Is he drugged?' I ask.

'No, no,' says the orderly, 'they don't go in for that sort of thing around here.'

'What's the matter with him then?'

'That's just the way he feels. They are not very friendly around here. Whatever you do, don't let them see your camera.'

Crouching on top of another hastily gathered stool of shell cases, I sit as still as I can to fade into the background. I am obviously not entirely successful, as a boy of about ten begins to throw stones at me, watched impassively by his mother. After a while I pick up a stick and bat the stones away, and the thing turns into a game. The mother relaxes and asks if I have any boys. When she hears that I have three she thaws at once, and all the women become very friendly. It seems to be as easy as that to make friends in these parts.

The atmosphere having now improved considerably, the women forget about me and become engrossed in their own problems. Little shirts are lifted and horrible sores exposed. I notice that infant boys are not circumcised. This is done later, some time before the age of ten, by a special tribe who specialize in the business. These Jebali, although they are Muslims, are still entirely influenced by witch-doctors, and many pre-Islamic rites and cults still survive. The sores are largely caused by branding, which is still widely practised as a cure for almost any complaint, from T.B. to snake-bite.

Soon the calabash of tepid milk is produced and handed round. But before I have time to indulge in my usual deception, the taciturn young man with the fixed stare surprisingly whisks out a glass which he fills to the brim and hands to me with a strict injunction to drink it down. As I comply under his stern gaze, the orderly remarks sympathetically, 'It's all right here. They drop red-hot stones into their milk and it is perfectly sterilized.'

Even though I have obediently swallowed down his offering, the young man hasn't finished with me yet. Standing up, he orders me to follow him. I glance at the orderly, who says, 'Go with him. He wants to show you his house.' And so off we go, with me stumbling after him over the rough stony ground of the wadi bed. Brilliant blue and green roller birds hop around in the camel-thorn bushes dotted about in the dry stream and heavy crows flap among them, looking for lizards and beetles. In the hot purple blue of the sky, a bird of prey cruises in a wide circle on static wings, looking for dying things.

The banks of the wadi are smothered in flowering white jasmine. I pick a sprig of the deliciously scented, thick, waxy flowers, but it is at once snatched away by my companion, who sticks it behind his ear. Still using his rifle as a walking-stick, he hops nimbly from stone to stone. Round a corner, behind an enormous rock and shrouded in smoke, a cave suddenly opens up before us, with a wide flat ledge jutting out above it. During the war, the enemy (meaning us, my companion informs me) used to hang over this and shoot at the rebels inside the cave. And in the monsoon season, water cascades over the lip, forming an impenetrable curtain through which nothing and nobody can pass, except for those inside who know the secret ways of their cave. Now it is sealed off by a screen of acrid smoke rising from a barrage of dung fires burning in a semi-circle round the entrance, in the guise of mosquito net. Behind this pall, on a bed in one corner lies an enormous Hereford cow, the only one I have seen on the Jebel. Stuck along the rock-face at various levels and reached by man-made steps cut into the stone, huddles a series of mud huts like a colony of large swallows' nests. My guide points out the homes of his brothers and cousins. This appears to be a bachelors' dormitory. There are no women or children, no cooking pots or any other signs of domesticity of any kind.

He dives into one of the mud nests through a tiny entrance-hole, and I go in after him on hands and knees, followed by a very thin black cat with a triangular skeletal head at the end of a long stalk of a neck. At first I can't make out at all why it is so light inside the hut. Then I realize that here at least we are out of the smoke-screen of the cave and, more-over, our ceiling is made of a loosely woven network of twigs, through which trickles every bit of light coming sideways into the cave.

On the floor is a brightly coloured plastic mat, from Bombay (of course!) my host informs me proudly. Down on to it we sink, sitting cross-legged side by side. He seems to have come out of his trance. In his own home he is a different person.

A goatskin water-bottle hangs from the kingpost with a rifle lying at its foot, festooned with several bandoliers of cartridges. Apart from this there is absolutely nothing around at all. It is existence pared down to absolute essentials – water and a gun.

Sitting in cosy silence, we beam at each other for I don't

know how long. I seem to have sunk into a trance myself. Eventually becoming aware of it, I stir and begin to crawl towards the door-hole. As he follows, I pick my way through the prancing goats of the cave, the dung beetles and the smoke, and we scramble back to the clinic tree as the dust begins to rise beneath the approaching helicopter.

In a glade of young ghaf trees we find our next village. In this mud and twig commune which is like all the others, goats no bigger than terriers swarm everywhere and definitely predominate. The cows are herded inside a stable made of sackcloth and branches: a few rice bags strung between the fronds of an ancient ghaf tree. The communal kitchen is in another tree, from whose branches hang the pots and pans.

Settling down half-way between the two departments, the orderly opens up his box of tricks which is instantly pillaged by half-a-dozen ravening goats. One of them deftly consumes a tube of Latycin and, before anyone can take action, he has swallowed the whole thing. A large and beautiful butterfly settles on a bottle of aspirin, while a couple of plastic mats are hospitably unrolled for our benefit. Women in black *abbas* begin to arrive, followed by the usual platoon of toddlers. Pills are handed out, and each child bears away his own medicine, one of them chewing his on the spot, carton, wrapping and all. The mothers, who are all conferring together, seem quite unconcerned. A very old man, judging by the raddled state of his skin, exhibits a grey rash on the dark hide of his back. Another ancient warrior with a fearful scar across his chest, which appears to have been stitched together with bootlaces, is telling the orderly his business and speaking for the women before they have a chance to utter.

'Any pictures here?' I hiss into the orderly's ear.

'Wait a minute, I will ask,' he answers, and addresses the chief who is infuriated by the suggestion. Flinging his arms about, he shouts indignantly, protesting against such an unmannerly intrusion.

'Do point out I haven't taken any,' I urge. 'I was only asking his permission. Of course I won't if he doesn't like it.'

At this he simmers down at once, grins at me and grabs a minute calf out of the stable. Carrying it tenderly, he strokes the little head, padding off to a ghaf tree a few yards away.

There, still stroking and murmuring soothingly, he slits the calf's throat, then slices the head right off. Blood spurts in a great gush as I stare, horrified. Working with all the toes of both feet, his powerful white teeth and his right hand only (the left being exclusively consigned to other duties) he ties the hind legs together, and hangs up the carcass on a branch. Sinking his teeth into the gory neck stump, with blood pouring into his mouth he expertly pulls the little heifer's robe inside out like the vest off a child. With the carcass now hanging limp from the tree, he nicks choice bits of meat off here and there and pops them, dripping with blood, into his mouth. Are we all going to have to eat it raw, I wonder, shuddering apprehensively. But no; much to my relief, a fire is being lit by the women.

Abdullah, the Civil Aid co-ordinator, whose mother came from this tribe, strolls over to the butcher's corner to give a hand with the chopping up. The guts are wrenched out, carefully squeezed of their loose green spinach-like contents, stowed into a gory plastic bag and hung up on a branch. This will presumably return with us to Salalah on the chopper. Meanwhile a cauldron of water has been placed on the fire. 'They have to walk three miles for every drop of water,' the orderly informs me.

'Why don't they camp nearer the well?' I ask, puzzled.

'The land around it probably belongs to another tribe, and anyway they like it up here. In time, the Government will drill them another well.' That is one of the good things about the Jebel. Almost anywhere you dig there is water.

A tin tray is brought over, brimming with gory, tattered bits of veal; splinters of hacked bone stick out here and there. The whole lot is tipped into the boiling water, and soon it is all bubbling away, with grey scum milling around the surface. Last of all the chief throws in the choicest morsel, the liver of the beast, which sits on top, quivering in the steam above the level of the boiling water.

'It will be ready in twenty minutes,' remarks the orderly. We sit in silent expectation, staring at the boiling pot. Now that I know I won't have to eat it raw, I quite look forward to this *blanquette de veau*, Jebel-style. The pangs of hunger are clawing at my middle. We are lucky to have veal on the menu today. The Jebali have very definite ideas about what can and can't be eaten. Lizard, as well as hyena (whose jaw muscles, like trout's cheeks for us, are a delicacy), are much appreciated. But they won't touch eggs or chicken flesh, or the meat of wolf, birds of prey or fox.

Time is up, and the contents of the stewpot are hooked out with a stick and flicked into the waiting tin tray, which is still gory and caked with dried blisters of blood. The chief, coming to squat beside me, skewers the raw liver with a twig and flips it into my hand. Overwhelmed by such generous hospitality, I somehow manage to persuade him to split it and have half himself. Stoically I gulp down my share. It goes down like tepid jellyfish. The women have retired to another tree, and a child comes to collect the bones for them. We chew on and the chief continues to press delicate morsels, which he tears off the bone with his teeth, into my hand. It is all infinitely touching, but I can swallow no more. In desperation, I suddenly remember my manners and manage to produce an enormous belch, to convince him that I have had enough and have thoroughly enjoyed the feast. He is delighted and his large wrinkled belly quivers with mirth.

At last, a distant roar in the sky announces the chopper's return. We shake all the gory, greasy hands of our hosts, and double up with shrouded faces through the rising dust-storm, towards our waiting transport.

Our last call of the day is to the new school on the beach of Rakyut, close to the Yemeni border. There on the white coral sands, facing the blue immensity of the Indian Ocean, sits the little prefabricated school in which the clinic is now going to be held. It is one of the latest ventures installed in this deserted area by the Ministry of Education and is run by a dedicated Egyptian teacher. Hastily the benches are pushed aside against the walls; the mothers, who seem to have been expecting us, troop in and squat on the floor, with their children draped around them.

The orderly kneels beside his medicine chest and begins to dole out his wares. There is such a crowd today that he can't manage to keep the register, so, using an upturned plastic dustbin as his desk and sitting on an empty ammunition box, his revolver sticking out on his hip, Shaun writes down the name, diagnosis and drugs handed out to each child. However busy the clinic may be, this record is always kept up to date.

A chorus of crying babies makes it difficult to hear anything at all. A young man of classical looks and distinction, in a spotless sand-coloured *dishdasha* and an elegantly rolled Kashmir turban, is the self-appointed doctor's help. Patiently, he plucks the squalling infants from their mother's arms and holds them down with gentle firmness as the needle goes in. Four drops of vaccine on a piece of sugar immunizes against polio. This is achieved without fuss or trouble, but injections are another story. One small girl of about five puts up an appalling fight against her jab. The young man tries to grab her this way and that, but she is all teeth and claws, and he can't get a proper grip. The girl is quite hysterical, kicking and screaming, eyeballs bulging. Any minute now she will begin to foam, and we will have a fit on our hands. Wisely, the men give up. The injection, administered in her present state, probably won't do any good anyway. The mother, seeing they have dropped her, deals her a smart blow on the head. The girl gives another piercing yell then stops abruptly in order to look around for the next mug who is going to let himself be stabbed by the doctor's needle.

The orderly is besieged by the mothers who all know exactly what ails their offspring and inform him as to what they need. This is usually aspirin, for anything from skin disease to T.B. In one form or another, this magic drug has a long medical history. Extracted from the leaves of the willow in primitive societies, it acts as a sedative by stopping pain in the local nerves, which means cutting it out at source. Hippocrates gave it to his female patients in childbirth. But our medical orderly has other views: with infinite patience and good humour he deals with his ladies. '*I* am here to tell you what your little ones need. *You* are not the doctor,' he says over and over again with a chuckle and a wink at the delighted, giggling women.

'Diagnosis?' asks Shaun every time, pen poised in mid air and surveying the bedlam with a mild eye. The orderly squints at a tongue, feels a pulse, pulls down an eyelid and clamps the stethoscope to a narrow brown chest.

'How do you spell diarrhoea?' suddenly asks Shaun, peering from under his bright red hair and green *shemag* with a frown. As no suggestion is forthcoming, he bends over his dustbin again with a sigh, 'Ah well, I guess that will do,' he mutters as he scribbles on.

Little by little the mothers drift away with their whimpering infants, and suddenly they have all disappeared right out of sight in the bare landscape of sand and sea. Where have they all got to? No sign of Landrover or camel or donkey anywhere. They could all have been turned to stone at the wave of a wand. Just as the day's work seems to be over and the orderly is packing his box, a man suddenly appears on the scene, leaning on a biblical-looking staff, twice as tall as himself. He has come a long way, and his beard is peppered with dust. His four children have all got measles, and his cave neighbour's brood are sure to get it too. He wants medicine for them all. Shaun is worried. The treatment is complicated. Several drugs are involved, and they *must* be administered in the right order. Patiently, the orderly explains the sequence, the dosage and the nursing involved. The man listens intently as his arms fill up with bottles, powders, ointments. 'God,' groans Shaun aloud, 'how can he ever remember all that?'

'Whatever is going to happen?' I ask, eyeing the awesome armful which the man is clutching to his chest.

'*Insha Allah* they will get better in spite of it all,' he answers hopefully.

'*Insha Allah*', I piously intone.

The helicopter is beating its wings and churning up the beach into an angry white cloud which engulfs us all. We run for it and thankfully scramble aboard. The day's work is done.

Half an hour away, the Holiday Inn is awaiting us with all its twentieth-century comforts. It is a matter of straight from the Stone Age to the sophisticated life of Salalah, its shops and offices and ultra-modern television centre, its brand-new hospital equipped with all the latest medical appliances, its model experimental farm, and everything that goes with a vigorous, forward-looking, developing country which is fast catching up with the blessings of education and the more doubtful benefits of modern technology.

16   Gold, Frankincense and Sin

'Last time I was here,' said the Brigadier, 'we had an enormous picnic on the beach. The pickets I placed on the heights were furious at having to sit up there with their guns, while we guzzled our sandwiches on the sand.'

Standing on top of the Queen of Sheba's ruined city of Sumurham, known to the Greeks as Mocha, we look across at the strip of sand beyond the lagoon of Khor Rohri, where the officers of the Sultan's Army enjoyed their picnic on their day off from the war on the Jebel a couple of years ago. After months of gruelling guerrilla warfare on the arid plateaux and blistering peaks of the Qara mountains; of raids and counter-raids; of long sodden nights in ambush when the enemy, muffled and soundless in the thick rolling monsoon mists, came from all sides; of long boring weeks sitting above supply lines, hammering the invisible foe and being mortared back, the Brigadier had decreed a holiday for his warriors, and the picnic took place in one of the most romantic and evocative beauty-spots of the ancient world in south-east Arabia.

Heading east, and still using the smooth Mercedes from the palace stables, we had left Salalah after a large and jolly lunch of shark steak and grilled grouper. Speeding along the coast road, lined by the sparkling white beach on one side and coconut groves on the other, we branch off on to a rocky track, past a straggling little fishing village on the sea shore. The track leads inland into an arid desert, with a few desiccated skeleton trees sticking out here and there among the stones. Bouncing about, we lurch in and out of pot-holes, scraping along the rocks on our sensitive underbelly. 'This hurts me more than it hurts the car,' moans the Brigadier as we crunch one stone after another on the way.

Suddenly we swerve sideways and begin to climb into the thorn scrub. A camel, sprawling across the track on his huge swollen flanks, swivels a bulging, bloodshot eye towards us. 'Keep off', is the clear message, 'or else'.

After picking our way through the sumr and the prickly pears for a while, we come to a fork in the road. Turning to the right, we make straight for a mud fort, outlined like a cardboard cut-out against the purple-blue of the sky. We are heading for the sea once more, and this time the spot is Taqah where, a couple of months later, five Englishmen peacefully picnicking on the beach were to be machine-gunned to death in a matter of seconds.

At the sound of our horn, a curious-looking figure flourishing a rifle suddenly materializes on the battlements. As another pops up alongside, a rapid dialogue in Arabic starts up between one of our officers and the sentry on top of the fort. The way is barred, we are told; this much is obvious: the huge rolls of barbed wire billowing across our bows speak for themselves. To get to Sumurham, it appears that we must take the inland route, as the coastal road is still heavily mined. Since all roads were supposed to have been cleared at the end of the war last year, this sounds a bit fishy. But there is no point in forcing the issue. As the area has had a bad name anyway, we leave it at that and swing back on our tracks.

Taqah fort has been manned, first by *askars* then by ex-rebels, since the end of the Dhofar War, and the two lusty braves now shouting down at us look more like a couple of brigands than members of the militia. Only a year or so ago had we been foolish enough to show our faces, they would have shot us on sight.

As we turn tail in search of the inland trail, a handful of Firqats, all bristling with guns, come springing out of the fort.

182

Jumping into a truck, they instruct us to follow, saying they will show us the way. These now so-helpful rogues, ex-rebels from the Qara mountain range towards which we are bowling in a cloud of dust, are without any doubt in touch with the remaining rebels still hiding in the caves ahead of us. As we draw nearer the mountain and the troublesome Darbat area, I notice that the officers in the car are muttering under their breath and keep glancing towards the foot-hills. It is here that the great lake of Darbat, which winds northwards for a couple of miles among the mountains, comes to an end at the falls in a spectacular 500-foot drop called Dahaq. Loyal Muslims who were caught saying their prayers were tossed over this huge limestone shelf to their deaths on the rocks below.

At last we swing off towards the sea again, and away from the menacing foot-hills. All round us lies a desert of dust and stone. There is not a twig, not a leaf in sight. At last we reach a spot where even the Firqats' truck can climb no further. On the cliff, a great heap of sand and stone is all that is left of the ancient city of Sumurham. Here is total desolation; not even a plastic bag, the usual Arabian banner of civilization, is in sight to proclaim the arrival of progress to the area.

Scrambling up the tumbled ruins, we get a staggering view over the entire Gulf of Dhofar from the top of the citadel. Gold, frankincense and myrrh, the three Kings' offering to Jesus on Twelfth Night,came from the land of the Sabaeans which we are trampling underfoot at this very moment.

In ancient times this immense expanse of glittering, pewter-coloured sea which almost surrounds us would have been a breeding ground for pirates raiding the ports of southern Arabia, or lying in wait for the incense-bearing fleets on their way to the north. So the kings of Shabwa built the formidable fortress of Sumurham from which, aided and abetted by their moon god Sin, they controlled their lucrative trade of frankincense. As the god of Hadramaut, an enormous kingdom reaching half-way across south Arabia, including Dhofar and ruling Sumurham, Sin was an all-powerful deity. His priests exacted tribute, and constant victims had to be sacrificed to keep him in a good mood. In his temple, where ancient coins and frankincense of the time were discovered, we can see sacrificial slabs carved with little drains for the blood of the victims to trickle away, and wash-basins made of solid stone with a hole in the bottom, like a present-day farmhouse sink. A bronze bell and a basin found in the ruins proudly bear his name, SIN. Although the other bits of pottery discovered on the site look rather like some of the Nabatean ware of south Jordan, no official conclusions have been drawn so far. King Eleazus of Hadramaut, along with six others, had his name carved over the gate of the inner city, all of them being presumably outstanding monarchs in one way or another. The name of the city of Shabwa, which ruled Sumurham, also figures on the roll of honour. According to Wendell Phillips, Dhofar was the land of the Sachalites, which is Greek for the word S'KLN, another inscription found on the site.

Sumurham is still only partly excavated, having been originally discovered by that enterprising oil tycoon, Wendell Phillips. The bits he dug out saw the light of day for the first time after 2,300 years, in 1952. The southern and eastern sides of the fortress had walls eight feet thick and twenty feet high, while the north, west and north-east were protected by powerful watch-towers. All of which goes to show the great store that Sin and the kings of Shabwa set by their frankincense.

According to Pliny, the best-known tribes of ancient Arabia, the Sabaeans, were the most wealthy of them all as well. Their prosperity came from the fertility of their scent-producing forests, their carefully irrigated agricultural lands, their wild honey and beeswax and their prolific gold-mines. Around the beginning of the first millenium B.C. they had settled in the Marib plains and their first capital was Sirwa, a fortress town in the hills south of Marib. The enormous dam of that name, constructed by the famous engineer Lukman bin Ad in 1700 B.C., contributed very largely to the riches of the kingdom. The controlled irrigation provided by this fantastic feat of engineering turned the desert green; and the cultivations and gardens of Shabwa were the talk of the ancient world. The bits which now remain of the Marib dam give an idea of what it must have been like, fifty feet high and built of beautifully dressed stone. It started off with a modest mud wall then, when this was found inadequate, the upstream face was lined with stones and mortar. Spill-ways and sluice-gates for irrigation branched off in all directions. The areas known as the North and South Gardens were watered by a careful system of flooding through enormous channels which in turn fed smaller canals. Artemidorus states that 'the city of the Sabaeans, Mariaba, is situated upon a well-wooded mountain', adding that 'the masses engage partly in farming and partly in the traffic of aromats'. To collect the frankincense from Ethiopia, adds the writer, they sailed across the straits in fleets of little leather boats.

Marib was cunningly built at the junction of trade routes from Baihan and the Hadramaut, and the southern ports of Qana, Aden and Muza (near Mocha). The early trade routes in the west had followed the prehistoric salt tracks from the mines at Ramlat Sabatain.

Regarded as far too noble a beast to bear a burden, the camel was only fit, it was thought, for the glory of war – that is, until Balqis, Queen of Sheba, came along and briskly put an end to all this nonsense by firmly putting camels on the incense trail. From then on, straight lines could be drawn across the desert, as camels can easily go ten days without water, and a great deal of time between Shabwa and the north was saved along the new trade routes.

From Qana to Shabwa there seem to have been two main tracks, but under strict control, all the wadis being sealed off with huge mud walls several feet thick and fifteen feet high. This compelled the caravans to go through the only gate leading to a guarded pass between the wadi and the mountainside. From here the road led over the hills to Shabwa, where the priests clapped on a heavy duty for the benefit 'of the god they call Sabis'. It was as much as his life was worth for the owner of a loaded pack camel to turn off the main road and search for a chink in the wall to avoid the customs post. These endless caravans must have been a jolly, lively spectacle, with the colourful robes and turbans of the camel drivers and the jingling of the harness bells, the shouts and smells, the dust, the baying and prancing of excited Salukis and, no doubt, the enthusiastic support of urchin escorts galloping alongside. The wares brought through the customs, besides the precious frankincense from Sumurham and Ethiopia, also included myrrh, gold, spices, silks and cinnamon from India, precious stones and ivory from Africa, apes, peacocks and slaves from Zanzibar.

After leaving Shabwa where they had duly paid the tax, the caravans set off across the arid wastes of the desert in which lurked packs of ferocious brigands lying in wait by the waterholes. Fearful battles often took place, after which the raiders made off with all the loot, leaving the dead and dying behind to take care of one another.

Gradually cities grew up along the trade routes, enriched by all these passing caravans, and in time the desert pirates found it more lucrative to change their tactics to a system of tolls and, from that moment on, caravans could travel safely inside their territory. The expensive, exotic camel trains, in spite of all those dues, taxes and bandits' tolls, nevertheless carried on along the trail across the desert for another 1,500 years, mainly because the alternative route by sea was even slower and more unreliable. The Red Sea was peppered with treacherous reefs and unpredictable currents. Pirates of implacable ferocity patrolled the coasts and the boats, those little leathern shells, were an easy prey to winds and foe alike, as they crept along the coastline to avoid the hazards of the open sea.

Frankincense was at the root of Dhofar's fame and prosperity. Huge quantities of it were used in ancient times. When Poppea died her husband, the Emperor Nero, driven by remorse, is said to have burnt a whole year's supply at her funeral. Herodotus claims that two and a half tons of it went up in smoke every year in the temple of Bel at Babylon. Moses used it as a disinfectant when instructing the Israelites in the wilderness to fumigate themselves with incense. Aaron was told to take the censer in among the congregation during the plague, thus putting an immediate end to the pestilence. As the fumes given off by burning frankincense produce phenol, it acts as an antiseptic which may well have been the cause of its immense popularity at the time. The priests in the temples no doubt needed protection against the swarming vermin of their enormous congregations; frankincense would have afforded immunity.

Pliny wrote that eight days' journey from Shabwa was a frankincense-producing district: 'The forests measure about five miles in length and half that distance in breadth.' Herodotus was firmly convinced that south Arabia was the only land to produce the stuff, as well as myrrh, cassia, cinnamon and gum mastic. The wily Arabs, who didn't want their customers to go shopping elsewhere, did nothing to dispel that belief which was widely held around the Mediterranean. The excursions of the little leather boats to Ethiopia were kept a dark secret.

The mystique with which those forests were surrounded helped to keep prices high. Only a few families held the hereditary privilege of looking after them, with the help of a flock of winged serpents of many colours who would dart out of the trees with flashing eyes, spitting fire at anyone who had the temerity to approach the sacred forests. Those Druid-like families who looked after the trees were regarded as sacred and had to keep to strict rules of behaviour at all times, particularly during the 'incision season', when they had to shun all contact with women and even the sight of a passing funeral was enough to pollute them.

Frankincense and myrrh are gum resins oozing out of trees and bushes which grow only in southern Arabia, Ethiopia and parts of Somaliland. Queen Hatshepsut had tried, by reproducing the same environmental conditions, to grow them in Egypt. But stubbornly the trees refused to grow whereas, in their own natal haunts, they have prospered since time immemorial as they do to this day.

Boswellia sacra is a bush eight to ten feet high, and B. Carterii, which forms the only other known kind, comes as a small tree with a self-respecting trunk of its own. The leaves are long and narrow with a multitude of little notches all the way round. In both cases the resin flows beneath the bark and oozes out whenever a scratch occurs. The best quality of all grows in western Dhofar, that SʼKLN found carved on the walls of Sumurham, and on the slopes of the Qara mountains up to a height of two thousand feet, which altitude seems to suit them best. Colonel Bentall-Warner, Commanding Officer of Saiq military base, who is with us today, but is no great botanist, tells us vaguely that these precious trees do grow on Jebel Akhdar as well, but for some reason the people there call them juniper trees.

Pottering about among the ancient plantations and scratching the bark to make the milk flow, I half expect the winged serpents to come flying out, hissing their fiery breath at me. The see-through globules, smooth and shiny, soon harden in the sun like clusters of frog-spawn. Olibanum Boswellia, as the botanists call it, was recommended by Pliny the Elder as an antidote to hemlock poisoning, and the eleventh-century physician Avicenna, who prescribed it for all kinds of complaints, obviously knew about its antiseptic properties as well as Moses did.

When it begins to burn, frankincense first goes up in a thick ugly black smoke, but once it's got this out of its system, it produces a delicate silvery wisp which wafts around the fragrance which the ancients were so mad about.

Balsamodendron or myrrh, from the Arab word *murra* which means bitter, is a tree with a proper upright trunk of its own, growing up to fifteen feet. With the same general habits and characteristics as the more aristocratic frankincense, it is reddish brown instead of milky white, with a rougher and less seductive scent. The pain-killer given to Jesus at the time of the crucifixion could well have been a mixture of wine and myrrh. And he was quite certainly wrapped in linen soaked in myrrh and aloes at the time of his entombment.

Used more generally as a straightforward fumigant, it grows in the hills and mountains right through southern Arabia and west central Somaliland, with the exception of Sumurham. Consequently I have never seen the plant on the stalk, nor smelt the scent of its burning resin. My acquaintance is with frankincense alone. Although it has lost a great deal of its popularity, it is still sold in the *souqs* and used in traditional Arabian households. The Vatican and many Roman churches continue to burn it during High Mass, but in the West it is mostly its romantic appeal which lingers on.

The harvesting is done by the Kathiri tribes, each tree stamped with the mark of its owner. The Qara people around Hanun, where the trees grow well, neglect them and concentrate entirely on their cattle. As the animals need water and the trees do not, they leave the latter to their own devices without any attention and remain near the waterholes. The trees which have managed by themselves for so long are quite prepared to continue to do so indefinitely.

In the Nejd grows the variety which produces the silvery smoke; next in quality comes the shazri, from the Qara mountains; then the sha'bi from the coast. No preparation or purifying is needed, it is just stored in dry caves until winter, then sent to the coast to meet the merchants. At Khor Rohri and Hasik the trees, a lesser breed, are tapped by slaves and nomads who roam about the area with their goats and camels.

Three thousand years ago, Sumurham was a large and prosperous city and the creek on which it still stands, Khor Rohri, was a deep, well-protected harbour in which the great shipping fleets of King Solomon sheltered, while the urns of frankincense were rolled down the hill and loaded on board. This creek, which is now cut off from the sea by the sandbank on which the British officers of the Sultan's Armed Forces had their picnic, has never been excavated. Its depths must be filled with the most fascinating remains, and I would dearly love to be around when it is eventually dug up.

The voyage around the coast all the way from Jerusalem was a long and tedious one. King Solomon's trading ship, built and manned by Phoenicians, set off from Ezion Geber and took one and a half years to do the round trip to Ophir, Somaliland and south Arabia. It was the length of this tedious voyage in fact which put the idea into the Queen of Sheba's head. Why not strike overland towards the north to pay King Solomon a visit, she thought to herself, thereby showing him what could be done by camel train, and how much time and money could be saved that way. It was therefore as a kind of publicity stunt that she undertook her famous trip across the desert to call on the great king.

Balqis, Queen of Sheba, was a shrewd businesswoman, who had already cornered the market in all eastern goods coming from India, East Africa, Ethiopia and the Land of Punt. The imports from all these countries were to be put through her hands, thereby swelling the coffers of the Sabaean empire with prodigious wealth which enabled her to mount her fabulous expedition. Throughout the history of south Arabia and until the coming of Islam, the kingdom of Shabwa was always the most powerful, although surrounding countries such as Ma'am, Qataban and Ausan had already been established before the Sabaeans came down from the north and began to lay down the roots of their future empire.

As a result of this epic journey of Queen Balqis, there was an enormous boom in trade which prospered by leaps and bounds, and riches unimaginable came pouring into her treasury. Marib, described as Metropolis Sabaeorum by Strabo and the Regia Omnium Mariaba by Pliny, became the capital of Shabwa in 1700 B.C..

Solomon was the son of David, a self-made king who founded the Judaean dynasty and carved out an empire for himself from Egypt to the shores of the Euphrates. The odious Philistines, his chief enemies who controlled Palestine, managed to sabotage the efforts of the Tyrians and the Sidonians, preventing them from making their fortunes on the high seas.

Solomon was a brilliant general and owned a crack regiment of bowmen who habitually defeated enemy chariots and horses. His good relations with King Hiram of Tyre lasted for the whole forty years of his reign. When his father, King David, was beginning to show signs of age, his queen, Bath-sheba (a great court intriguer), manipulated the powers behind the throne so adroitly that they anointed Solomon king while his father was still alive – and all this in spite of mighty, plots working against her. Solomon, who was a younger son, lost no time in getting rid of his older brothers, prudently placing his friends in all the key positions.

As one of the great monarchs of the time, the Bible allotted 700 wives and 300 concubines to him, sisters and daughters of kings from all over the known world. Always on excellent terms with his numerous fathers-in-law, he had no trouble in obtaining handsome favours from them. An Egyptian Pharaoh, father of one of his wives, went to the extent of capturing a city in Canaan and handing it over to him as a gift. One of Solomon's chief aims was to control all the overland trade routes. To help along with this objective, he planted Israelite colonies all through the desert. Megiddo, one of the more successful, had stabling facilities for 1,200 horses and garage space for 1,400 chariots. With the Queen of Sheba's co-operation, which gave him an opening into the Red Sea and the

190

Indian Ocean, he built up Palestine to its greatest commercial heights in history.

The story of the great romance between Solomon and Balqis can be read between the lines of the Bible. Setting off across the immense desert with a very great retinue and an enormous caravan of camels laden with presents of spices, gold and precious stones, the Queen of Sheba presented herself before Solomon arrayed in her finest veils and robes, all embroidered in thread of gold and sewn with coins and little jingling bells, 'to test him with hard questions' and to tell him all that was on her mind. 'And Solomon answered all her questions; there was nothing hidden from the king which he could not explain to her.' When Queen Balqis had satisfied herself as to his great wisdom and had seen all the splendours of his capital, the magnificent appointment of his palaces, the very great numbers of his slaves and attendants and the glorious liveries they wore, the sacrifices which he offered in the House of the Lord, 'there was no more spirit in her'. So overawed was she by it all that she told him breathlessly, 'Your wisdom and prosperity surpass the report which I heard. Happy are your wives.' Then she presented him with a parting gift of 120 talents of gold and an enormous quantity of spices and precious stones. Eventually, after six packed and happy months, having duly been given by the king 'all that she desired, whatever she asked', she gathered up her empty bags, harnessed her camels and set off once more across the vast southern desert on her way home.

The story, which might well be turning to legend at this point, reports that a few months later a son was born to her, whom she called Menelik and, when he was old enough, she dispatched him to Jerusalem to be brought up by his wise and successful father.

All in all, Solomon was enjoying fair success all round. His friend King Hiram of Tyre had sent his fleet to Ophir (Dhofar) to pick up whatever trade was going and presented to Solomon a very great quantity of best almug timber on the return of this scavenging expedition. ('No such almug wood has come or been seen to this day', adds the Bible, to make the point.) With this excellent and incomparable almug Solomon made supports for the House of the Lord – and for his own as well while he was at it. So that none of it should be wasted, he also had lyres and harps made for the singers with what remained.

Jerusalem continued to prosper beyond all expectations. With all that gold which from then on came flooding in from the dazed enamoured Queen, Solomon had 200 large shields fashioned out of beaten gold, each of which contained 600 shekels of the precious metal. Then came 300 more, into which went three minas apiece, and these he stored in his summer palace, the House of the Forest of Lebanon. After this he commissioned the best craftsmen to construct him an ivory throne all overlaid 'with finest gold', crowned with the head of a calf. On each of the six steps leading up to this imposing throne stood lions on either side. Moreover, all his plate was made of solid gold, as 'silver was not considered as anything in the days of Solomon', being as common as dirt in Jerusalem. This was no doubt on account of all those mines on the east coast of Africa, whose cheap metal was brought over every three years by the 'fleet of ships of Tarshish', along with its load of gold, ivory, apes and peacocks. Prices at the time are worth noting. A first-class chariot, solid and well-made in Egypt, cost 600 shekels of silver, and a goodish horse could be picked up for as little as 150 skekels.

Solomon has gone down in history as infallible in wisdom, a military genius and a brilliant administrator. But I wonder how many people know about one of his other accomplishments, which may seem trifling to us now, but was of undeniable importance at the time. In those days when spirits ran wild about the land, hunting around for suitable victims to 'possess', he had a way with jinn, which he would call up, capture, and promptly stuff into bottles which he then corked up safely and cast into the sea.

17 Shihu Country

'Have you now seen everything you want? Is this the end of your quest?' asks Captain Ellery, as he comes across me crouching over a map of central Oman in the Officers' Mess.

'Pretty well, yes, except for the Musandam Peninsula. But I know I won't be able to see that, so there we are,' I say resignedly. Like the island of Das in the Gulf, I think to myself, there are places in the Arab world where no woman is allowed to set foot.

'Why ever not? Of course you can go to Musandam if you want to. Nothing easier,' says the captain confidently. 'Just tell Jonathan to ring me up when you get back, and I will fix it up for you.' I can scarcely believe my ears, but he is as good as his word. No sooner am I back in the colonel's flat than the telephone rings; I pick it up as my host is in the bath. Captain Ellery is on the line.

'Your trip to Musandam is all fixed up. Let me have a word with Jonathan,' he says.

At this point the door opens, and the colonel emerges with a towel round his middle, kicking a cannon-ball around with his bare toes. Like geodes in the Robbs' bungalow in Salalah, this is used as a doorstop. Leaving large wet footprints all the way down the hall, he pads over to the telephone. When he puts down the receiver he says, 'I'll take you to the airport tomorrow morning. I can't go with you myself, but Captain Jackson is going to Khasab too, and you can fly up together.'

At 6 a.m. the next morning as the sun is pushing up in a green sky over the ragged mountain range, we climb into his car and rattle off to Seeb. At the airport, he introduces me to Captain Jackson who is off on a couple of days' spree at the Khasab military base.

'Time to go,' says an Omani officer who comes into the passenger lounge to round us up. Jumping into his Landrover, we set off at once across the runway in search of our aircraft. All over the tarmac, skyvans are loading supplies to take off to distant parts of the land. Helicopters with their blades pulsating slowly, are waiting to take off on patrol.

'Where are you going to?' our escort asks the pilot, as we pause beside a skyvan into whose gaping hindquarters a dozen reluctant goats are being coaxed.

'Thumrayt,' answers the pilot. The top of the Jebel in Dhofar, quite the wrong end of the country. No use to us. The second aircraft we approach is off to Bahrain. 'Is this for Khasab?' we ask a third.

'Sorry, mate, I'm taking this crate to Masirah,' says the pilot. Finally we track ours down behind a group of hangars at the back of the airport. We are introduced to the pilot and to a friend of his who is riding beside him in the co-pilot's seat. On a mission from the Ministry of Defence in London, Jane has to call at Khasab for reasons she doesn't divulge.

Along with about a dozen other passengers, we climb into the aircraft. This one is fitted up for paratroops. The canvas seats, running along the sides of the cabin, are draped in curious string nets hanging from a hook above your head. Into these bizarre contraptions we have to drape and strap ourselves. Then sacks of rice are loaded in, a couple of *burmails* (oil cans) are lifted on, and a baby is handed in. Today there are no goats on board.

A couple of Omani gentlemen in brilliant turbans are carefully nursing a potted plant each. 'Do these give fruit?' asks Captain Jackson.

'No, no fruit, just to look nice,' answers his neighbour, lovingly stroking his plant with one finger. This is surprising.

194

Arabs do not usually take much interest in purely decorative vegetation.

On the seat opposite, a whiskery old shepherd, his rifle between his knees, extracts a wad of grimy, well-used cotton-wool from his frayed old turban and generously hands little lumps of it to us all. The passengers gratefully stuff this into their ears. The noise of the aircraft is deafening, *and* we will be rising to 6,000 or 7,000 feet. In an unpressurized aircraft this causes a lot of popping. For the moment the pilot, who knows my mission, hugs the coast and flies just above the waves, following the beach. Along the sand we scatter goats who don't know which way to run for cover. Tiny hens, scampering about in all directions, look like a lot of distracted ants. Here the traffic which consists of Toyota trucks and Landrovers is racing along the wet sand, which is the normal highway between the coastal villages. The huts, built of mud and *barasti*, are planted in an endless straggling line just above the high-water mark on the shore, all along the 200-mile coastline of the Batinah. Behind them cluster the date gardens, interspersed with the lighter green of lime and banana trees. Here and there in the more important villages a traditional fort sprawls across the beach like a Hollywood cardboard model. Looking down into the clear blue water, I can see fish darting about frantically, trapped inside the long loops of the nets as they are slowly being hauled ashore. And now here is Sohar, the birthplace of Sindbad the Sailor, a large sprawling area covered with little white square houses, hemmed in by the inevitable roundabouts of desert highways and a few hideous office and apartment blocks. This is surely not how it looked at the time of Sindbad. 'One of the most splendid cities of the Islamic world,' wrote a contemporary writer. Nobody could describe it as that now.

The plain is beginning to narrow, with the forward peaks of the Hajar range advancing towards the coast. Soon they are marching right into the sea like a forest of stalagmites all sticking up separately, sharp as toothpicks and absolutely bare of any vegetation. Deep inlets of dark-blue water weave in and out among these outcrops, many of them with glorious hidden coves of white coral sand. A Bedu family or two sometimes pitch a tent in these secluded lagoons, or a lone fishing dhow sits dead-still, like some curious insect riding on the flat surface of the sea.

At last we reach the Wadi Sallala, which soon changes its name to Makhus. Up to the left we shoot up Wadi Mawa – or is it Wadi Mahanis? The map gives both names, with a question-mark. Not one of these maps is a hundred per cent accurate. Drawn as they are from photographs taken at different times of the day, the shadows distort still further the already crazily jagged territory. This wide valley which splits up the Hajar from the Musandam Peninsula is our way through the mountains to the military base of Khasab on the other side. Rounding a peak, we take a sharp turn to the left and drop down on to the wide gravel bed as neatly as any helicopter. Beside a sumr tree which is obviously the airport station we pull up. A few passengers bundle out, and one of the potted plants leaves us here. Immediately we roar away again. We are now in notoriously inhospitable Shihu country, and our chubby skyvan would make an irresistible target for any trigger-happy joker hanging around among the rocks of those heights on either side. So up the wadi we go, our wing-tips almost scraping the sides of the narrowing gorge, weaving in and out among the peaks until we reach the watershed. After this spot the stream, whenever it happens to flow, would tumble down the other way, into the waters of the Gulf. Finally the wadi widens out once more into a valley and we come down on the gravel. In the distance we can see the oasis of Khasab and, beyond the palm trees, the green waters of the bay.

Here the airport lounge consists of palm-thatch walls hanging from the spiky branches of a large and handsome sumr tree. The dusty grey foliage forms the roof under whose dappled shade the room inside is dark and cool. A queue of passengers are waiting for a lift to Seeb in our skyvan, which is now unloading its bags of rice for the station before returning to base. The supply service goes on non-stop seven days a week, bringing in water, rice and coffee which is then lifted into the most inaccessible reaches of the mountains where the Shihu insist on roosting. No very determined effort is made to dislodge them as it is the policy of the Government to keep them in their own surroundings and improve their conditions in every possible way. The State of Ras al-Khaima is doing its best to tempt them away from their mountains but this, were it to happen, would be disastrous. Once the Musandam Peninsula is totally depopulated, it becomes a very attractive area from a military point of view for any invader who takes a fancy to it.

Beyond this little settlement come the oasis and the village, built mostly on the beach as usual. Apart from dates and a little fish, Khasab relies entirely on supplies brought in by land and sea. Ships nosing into the shallow bay have to transfer their cargo to beach landing craft, which dump their load on the sands, regardless of whether or not there is anyone around to pick it up. 'I once saw a whole consignment floating about on the rising tide,' says Captain Jackson. 'Nobody had turned up to collect it.'

We go to the Officers' Mess to find out if there is an aircraft of any shape or kind willing to wing us around the Peninsula.

The station Mess, light and airy with toffee-coloured leather armchairs and a lot of pale pine panelling, looks as I imagine a similar base would be like in the icy wastes of the distant north. A bar, a refrigerator – and this is where my Nordic dream-bubble bursts – a lot of old desert rifles on the walls, and the inevitable David Shepherd print. This one is of the fort of Ras al-Khaima, with a couple of warriors on top of a brace of sleepy-looking camels. One of the pilots comes in and the captain tackles him at once about an aircraft.

'Certainly,' says Flight-Lieutenant Harcourt, 'no problem. I'll take you up in a Defender. Have a drink, I'll be back in ten minutes.' When he comes back in his flying gear Captain Jackson, who describes himself as a nervous flyer, asks if it is 'a bit bumpy up there'.

'Not too bad,' is the reply. 'I'll show you where we're going,' he adds, bending over the map-table in the Mess. 'We will fly out along the coast, past Goat Island, then back through the centre of the Peninsula, over the highest part of the range.'

I get cross-eyed trying to decipher the names of the various peaks. 'I wouldn't bother if I were you,' says a helicopter pilot, looking over my shoulder. 'We don't rely too much on these maps.'

'How do you navigate, then? By guesswork?'

'By sight, mostly.'

With twelve years of service in this country, our pilot assures me that he is still as happy as the day he arrived. As one of the fighter-pilots who subdued the rebels in the Jebel War, he fell in love with Oman and never wanted to leave again. When they hear about a place like this – a military base in the middle of a dry gravel wadi, surrounded by hostile primitive tribes, in one of the hottest spots on the planet, and hundreds of miles away from civilization – most people imagine it to be hell on earth. They would no doubt expect those condemned to live in the place to take to the bottle, after the manner of Graham Greene's anti-heroes. In fact, the reverse is the truth: the officers and men stationed here are as happy as the busy day is long. There is practically no drinking in this unit: a little beer, and gallons of squash. Captain Jackson, the self-styled nervous flyer who has been in a dozen wars and was blown up by a mine in Dhofar, climbs into the Defender with a little hip-flask bouncing on his behind. 'Brandy?' I ask hopefully. But no, it is only water. As a seasoned warrior, he knows that if we crash up there in those blistering highlands, the first thing we will need is water.

Without any trouble at all we skim off the airstrip and zoom over Khasab, out towards the open Gulf. Lighter than air, we are only five on board, including the mechanic (just in case). The weather is perfect, or almost. As we swing out of the bay and turn north to follow the coast towards Iran, a huge bank of white cloud rolls in unexpectedly from the Gulf. Thick as a snowfield under our feet, it looks solid enough to land on. A few minutes later, leaving the cloud field behind, we fly over Ras al-Khaima where the coastline turns into a madman's nightmare. The highlands of the narrow peninsula project long, thin, claw-like fingers of tortured rock into the still, bottle-green sea. Deep, winding, twisting inlets carved into intricate fretwork scrolls snake their way inland. Goat Island, standing away from the crazy coastline looks almost normal compared with the fantastic surrealistic shapes spread out below. A little further on, across more green, peaceful-looking water is Iran, with all its problems. Avoiding this particular set of headaches, we veer south again and sweep into the central, highest mountains of the peninsula. Curry-coloured, crumbling rock is all we can see. It seems impossible to survive in all this aridity, but people do. Whole tribes of Shihu and their various ramifications exist on a 'subsistence economy' and anything the skyvans and helicopters can manage to deliver on the daily round.

'Look out for the little gardens,' yells Captain Jackson in my ear. These are tiny patches of soil laboriously humped over from miles around and kept together with dry-stone walls. These little acorn cups of dry dust are what the Shihu euphemistically describe as their gardens. This year, since there has been no rain at all up here, they are a light café-au-lait tint of hard-baked clay. Occasionally, in a good year, they could be green with the bright emerald of alfalfa, food for goats. What are the poor creatures eating this year, I wonder. Sand and date stones mostly, no doubt. We are now climbing up the face of a perpendicular cliff which drops hundreds of feet to the bottom of a canyon. This is Jebel Halim, the highest peak of the peninsula, the border between Oman and the U.A.E. Up and up we rise, our ears popping like mad in the unpressurized aircraft. It feels as if we are crawling up the face of the cliff on hands and knees.

When at last we reach the summit, we come face to face with the frontier post flying the Sultan's flag. As we roar over the roof of the little mud hut, it seems to explode, with hens, goats and women bursting through the tiny door and scattering in all directions. Swooping over the top of the escarpment, we fly into one wadi after another, exploring all the most secret parts of the mountain.

'I suppose you know every stone of the area,' I shout at the pilot.

'Pretty well,' he nods. 'Pretty well.'

The thermals waft us about and we float in slow circles around the topmost peak in an abandoned, prolonged, swooning kind of sweep. This must be the way hawks and eagles feel on their long motionless glides. All too soon the dream flight is over and we are back on our gravel base.

Even at noon there is a cool breeze up here, quite unlike the stifling noonday heat of Muscat. Lunch is up in the Mess, with a delicious pervading smell of Oriental spices oozing in from everywhere. We help ourselves to a curry made of little indented seed pods which I have seen growing on small bushes in the desert. An American civilian is sitting in one of the armchairs, with a plate of seed-pod curry on his lap. Although he doesn't look very approachable, I go and perch on the arm of his chair to see if he has anything to offer. Most people have, after all.

'Are you coming back to Seeb with us today?' I ask, to break the ice.

'Yes,' is all he says.

'Do you come from Saudi?' I try again and, with a sudden flash of inspiration, 'Do you work for an oil company there?'

At this he brightens up at once (don't ask me why), and he begins to open up. On holiday here from Ryadh, he has been climbing the surrounding mountains, looking for specimens. His hobby is natural history, and last year he did a survey of Jebel Akhdar. Although that was a good deal more productive, there is a surprising amount of material around here as well, he informs me with solemn round eyes, as though expecting to be contradicted. I do my best to hide my disbelief.

'Do tell me,' I entreat.

'Well, there are a lot of aromatic herbs, for one thing. Euphorbia Tiruccalla grows in cracks in the rocks. Goats love it.'

'Good,' I say as convincingly as I can. 'What else?'

'Artemesia, and Gulf almond struggles for survival (I bet it does!) on the lower slopes. There are foxes and leopards. One was shot only the other day.'

'What a pity,' I can't help saying, 'There can't be as many as all that around.'

'You'd be surprised,' he says, warming up, 'and then, the other day when a chopper took me right up to the summit of Jebel Halim, I found a snake.' This creature, which was apparently rather drowsy in the coolness of the early morning, was easily caught. Stuffed in with my friend's sandwiches into his shoulder bag, the snake travelled back to Khasab on the helicopter. 'And I never told the pilot until after we landed,' he adds triumphantly.

'Have you got one in there now?' I ask, eyeing the canvas bag suspiciously.

'No, no,' he answers, but with sufficient lack of conviction to make me move off smartly in search of another perch.

18   All the King's Horses

Seeb is where the famous treaty was signed between Sultan
Said bin Taimur and the leading tribal chiefs of the interior
in 1920. Here also are the airport and the Royal Stables. This
is where we are making for today.

Captain James Mackie, who is in charge of the Sultan's
horses, and his wife Shrimp have a cool comfortable villa in
the grounds of the Royal Stables on the coral beach of the
Batinah coast. Their garden, flourishing in the shade of tall,
rustling gum trees, is full of flowers and birdlife. As we lap
deliciously cool reviving drinks on the verandah, two little
blond Mackies are having their lunch at a small table of their
own. Luxuriously they splash their tiny spoons into plates full
of custard which plops gratifyingly all over the table. As we
watch this captivating performance, Shrimp informs us that
Clemmy (the older little Mackie) had told her this morning
in exasperated tones that she was thinking of hurling her little
brother down the loo and pulling the chain on top of him.

'And I suppose he said flush off?' suggests the Brigadier.

'They are all little sods at heart,' remarks their father
fondly.

After lunch, during which the little curly-headed angels
grind each other's fingers into the carpet with squawks of
rage and pain, we wend our way rather dopily towards the

swimming pool in the full heat of the afternoon. Brilliant roller birds glide among the branches, hundreds of finches of every shade and hue flash like brightly coloured tropical fish through the undergrowth, and grey-headed crows flop heavily to the ground. Surrounded by mango, Gulf almond and betel-nut trees, the pool looks irresistible.

Just as I am about to sink into the clear warm water, one of those hairy horrors in which Arabia specializes crawls cautiously over the edge, waving a couple of furry arms in the air. 'Oh look, a camel spider,' I squeal in alarm.

'It's only a baby,' says the Brigadier scornfully. 'But still,' he adds, 'with children around, I don't suppose we should let it hang around looking for trouble.' There is a pause, during which each is hoping that the other will offer to do the deed. After all he is the soldier, I think to myself, it's his job. At last he takes off his shoe to deal the fatal blow. Armour-plated like a tank, as these loathsome creatures always are, it takes several bangs on the head to knock it out altogether.

The children are in the water, but there is none of the usual childish whooping and splashing. Clemmy flashes past, skimming along with the grace and untrammelled ease of a dolphin. Turning round, I suddenly see to my amazement her young brother swimming busily below the surface. Hardly more than a baby, he paddles right across the width of the pool, comes up for air, his beaming face streaming with water, then down he goes again, and off in the opposite direction.

'However did you manage to teach him that?' I ask Shrimp.

'Oh, he taught himself. That's just the way he likes to do it,' she says.

After a couple of hours of luxurious soaking, the heat of the day has eased up a bit and the time has come to go and visit the stables. Beautifully clean and airy, the stalls face the sea from which cooling breezes come drifting over the sand.

Until Captain Mackie arrived, whenever the Sultan went riding in the countryside, he was escorted by the palace guard on foot, running along beside his horse, armed with rifles. There was no mounted guard. So Jamie's first job was therefore to provide a royal horseguard in the shortest possible time. It was no easy task. In days gone by, Oman, famous for horse-breeding, had exported champion stallions and brood mares in great numbers to India and Persia. But camels have now taken their place, and these are now about to give way to Landrovers. So the captain had to cast around far and wide for the best mounts he could find. Some were given to him but these had to be drilled from scratch, having only been ridden bareback, without saddle, bit or bridle, through the desert, tearing along like the wind or simply jogging, according to the mood of the moment. For Bedu have very little control over their animals, who are allowed to progress at whatever speed they fancy. Others were bought in India, Pakistan and the Sudan, but they all required time to acclimatize before training could begin. It took time to get them back into proper trim before training could even start. Then Captain Mackie went off to England where, by pure chance, he happened upon a fine sturdy pony which was to become the drum horse of the mounted band. After this, a trip to Australia furnished him with the rest of his blood-stock. For a whole fortnight he drove from ranch to ranch, selecting and trying out horses of every possible colour and size. As an extra bonus, he even came across an almost exact replica of the original drum horse. For this he offered the same price which he had paid for the first one in England, and the deal was clinched. Back he flew to Oman with thirty fine beasts in tow of which nobody need feel ashamed. Intensive training started at once while recruiting was going on. The palace guard were taught to ride and the band to play their notes and their instruments. On the whole, as none of them had ever clapped eyes on such strange-looking instruments, nor indeed heard the sounds they produce, they took to it all with remarkable equanimity. Arabs are not generally very musical. Their plaintive chants are tuneless and repetitive, and the wide range of the western musical scale is totally alien to them. Considering all this, the young (and not so young) desert recruits performed wonders.

When he finally had all the various parts of his bodywork assembled, Jamie had exactly eight months before the first great National Parade of Oman in which to get the horses into condition, teach the men to ride and the mounted band to play. To begin with, these wild desert horses, crazed and distracted by the unaccustomed noises and the terrifying objects brandished by the men, bucked and snorted in sheer panic or stampeded and bolted out of sight. The band learned to take it gradually, playing first at a distance, then creeping up closer every day like Grandmother's Footsteps, until finally the horses were sufficiently tamed to accept the whole load: men, instruments, noises and all.

Although it was all an unimaginable scramble, no anxiety, no impatience must ever be shown. In dealing with Arabs, everything has to be done with good humour and loads of fun, encouragement and praise. Irritation and asperity, apart from being Very Bad Form, cause bitter offence and kill all hope of co-operation, as well as losing all respect from your cheerful, carefree, happy-go-lucky recruits. Individualists through and through, they will only agree to collaborate if they like you, there is no hope of doing anything with them otherwise. Moreover, any form of criticism or correction is intolerable, as it gets dangerously close to that fate worse than death, loss of face. With infinite patience and unfailing good humour, with generous praise and recognition of the slightest effort or improvement, the captain achieved the impossible. In a matter of a few months of unremitting labour, he had these raw, ragged, irrepressible recruits on their mixed bag of horses taking part in the great National Day Parade in Salalah. He admits himself that his heart was in his mouth through most of the day, as he had no idea how his protégés would react under the strain of the ceremony. As it turned out, all went well.

They are now rehearsing for a Great Event. While the Queen is picnicking on the great dusty windswept plain of Nizwa, we are listening to the mounted band going through their paces. Scheduled to play before Her Majesty tomorrow, it is taking the excited horses quite a time to get into place and stop shuffling their feet in the sand. The Arab boys look resplendent and the music comes over, a little hesitant and faltering here and there, but immensely stirring under the dark-blue Oriental sky, on the whole a magnificent achievement. Inviting me to walk around with him, Jamie leads me in and out among them as he dispenses encouragement, tapping a stray hoof with his crop, shortening a stirrup, or frankly dragging back by its bridle a beast which obstinately insists on sidling up close and rubbing affectionately against his mate in the next line.

'However tone-deaf they may have been, these boys, anything from fifteen upwards, were handed a trumpet or trombone or whatever, and told they would be playing the instrument within a few weeks,' he tells me as we tramp about in the sand among them. 'And with a broad grin, they invariably answered, *Insha Allah*.' Hailing from the wilderness, they arrived with a completely fresh, uncomputered mind, totally devoid of preconceptions and prejudices. And being unbiased, they were prepared to tackle anything.

Commander Jay Frazier who is in charge of the police horses has started what he calls quite a breeding programme. As his original mounts which came from India were not up to much, his idea was to bring back to Oman pure pedigree Arabian horses bred in the U.K. for the last hundred years. The stud, which had been bought from the tribes 100 years ago by 'the Blunts of Sussex' and are still being bred now, have a pedigree going back several hundred years. Hunters and thoroughbreds and pure Arab geldings were all purchased at the same time. And now breeding the noble, aristocratic beasts has started here as well. The first lot arrived in June last year and have settled down very happily. The breeding programme includes all kinds of permutations. Some will be kept pure, while others will be crossed with thoroughbreds. A nice little Arab stallion will be given a harem of less distinguished Indian mares. The idea is to breed six to eight foals a year. Other young horses, acquired at the same time, are gradually being broken here and absorbed as remounts. Altogether there are eighty-seven animals out of which one detachment is in Salalah and two others are on border patrol; while forty-eight empty stables at Nizwa, all brand-new, are hopefully awaiting inmates. At the moment, sixteen are due for imminent dispatch there. In the summer, wherever they happen to be, they all return to headquarters where air-conditioned loose-boxes are available for those suffering from heat exhaustion. Funnily enough, none of the English horses ever succumb. The Arabs are the ones who tend to wilt in their own climate. 'It's humidity that knocks them, not the heat,' says the commander.

A marvellous smell of horse prevails as Mrs Frazier takes me round the ultra-modern stables. The Arabs are being brushed down and smartened up.

'You didn't give us much time,' says my host, 'but never mind, we had even less warning from a lieutenant-general from Saudi, who was expected at 5.15 and arrived at 4.45.'

'In my experience it is the other way round. Usually two hours late, if you're lucky – otherwise it could be two days.'

As we walk round to the back of the station, an impressive array of horse-flesh is facing us. 'This is our stallion, a nice horse, not quite four,' says Mrs Frazier proudly. 'It is his first season serving,' she adds, making it sound like a game of tennis. 'These are his ladies, or some of them anyway.'

A two-year-old with a beautiful head, bold eyes and tail sticking out well away from the body is also pure Arab. The others, who arrived from England last June, are substantially bigger animals and are in even better shape than when they came. The climate definitely suits them. 'This is a pure Arab gelding, not yet broken,' says my hostess, pointing out a handsome creature in marvellous condition. I notice with surprise that even their toenails are varnished. This is real grooming indeed!

Another one, also a pure Arab gelding, watches us with gentle, soulful eyes, very quiet, a true lady's horse. 'Except when he is about to be fed,' remarks the commander, 'when he just takes a chomp out of anyone who might be passing.'

Next to him is a docile-looking expectant mother, three-quarters Arab, and one-quarter Argentine polo-pony. A pretty little Indian mare has been covered by an Arab stallion, but there is no news about her condition yet. Another, this one a pure Arab mare from the famous breeding-ground in Sussex, 'is in foal to this little stallion, his first real success'. We stare admiringly at the little stallion, who tosses his mane with justifiable pride. The gestation period, for those (like me) who didn't know, is eleven months.

The ex-Indian Army horses, a very mixed bag, are used mostly for policing the towns and for border patrol, all of which they manage very well. Apart from that, they take part in the musical ride in the annual parade. Although this is quite a discipline, and must be an ordeal for them, 'some are worse than others' is as far as Mrs Frazier is prepared to go. One of these, leaning out of his loose-box as we pass and intrigued by my tape-recorder, breathes so hard into it that I can hardly make out our own voices when I play it back later. No hay at all is bought, I am told when I ask about the huge bundles of lucerne propped up against the stable doors. Barley and oats are imported from Australia. On this diet they all do splendidly.

We push on to a further paddock, where a curious-looking white-and-grey mottled mare with thick hocks, short legs and a massive head stands beside her foal. They are Gulf Arabs.

The Sultan, on one of his trips to the interior, came across the mare in a very bad state. As her plight upset His Majesty who is very fond of horses and can't bear to see them neglected, he had her immediately transferred to the police stables for rehabilitation, and there in due course her daughter arrived. The foal, born and bred here, has therefore had a better deal from the start, and so is a far more handsome animal. What probably happened, explains Mrs Frazier, was that the mare was presented to someone or other in the interior by the ruler of Bahrain, then let loose to fend for herself in the wild. 'She has now been covered by the English-Arab stallion, and we will see what happens,' explains my hostess. 'Apparently Gulf Arabs have always been this funny colour. And there's also all sorts of things wrong with their conformation. She's certainly lost it in the head. But she's not a bad ride.' A strong and sturdy animal by the look of her, she will be used to perpetuate the breed and also to build it up with the English Arabs. In the Sultan's stables at Seeb, I am told that half the horses are Gulf Arabs. Ignorant as I am about matters equine, that fact, I must admit, had escaped me.

In Salalah, the Sultan has imported pure-bred Arabs from the U.K. to start up a pure Arab stud down there, in his much-loved province of Dhofar.

We pass the site of an old palace with its sunken gardens. All the police buildings in the compound were put up in record time by Costain's and his super gang of expert workmen, including the lunging paddock, the men's quarters and the polo pit. As they can't find anyone else to take part, the game has sadly died a natural death.

The garden, brimming with flowers of every kind, is looked after by an Indian lady with very green fingers. The bougainvillaea come in colours I have never seen before, orange, lemon-yellow, salmon-pink and scarlet. Here are grown the floral decorations for all the police stations and the blooming roundabouts of Muscat, Matrah and 'the Cornish'.

Among the rustling scimitar leaves of the gum trees, brilliant coloured birds dart about: doves, sand-grouse, parakeets, jays and the ubiquitous roller bird. Their incessant shrieks, croaks and whistles (no melodious English birdsong around these parts), added to the racket of the cicadas, produces a deafening clatter to which Mrs Frazier is so inured that she doesn't even notice it. 'Yes, we have quite a few birds around the place,' she concedes vaguely. But her heart is firmly anchored in the stables, along with her noble, highly-bred English-Arab steeds of impeccable descent.

19 A Henna Party

'The women to their weaving and the men to their swords' — An Arab saying

In Muscat and Matrah, the women are sometimes veiled, but I have seldom seen the stiff, unattractive beak known as *burqah,* which is so extensively worn in the Gulf. This custom, which was unknown in Oman before Islam, came from Assyria where it is specifically mentioned in the 1,500-year-old code of behaviour, a kind of book of etiquette of the time, that a woman has to be veiled as an indication that she is her husband's chattel.

On the whole, women here go about much more than in other Arabian countries, where they are hardly ever seen out of doors; while it is the men who go to the *souq* and the supermarket, buy their wives' drapes and veils and jewellery, take the children to school and gossip at street corners with their friends. There is no doubt that women in Oman enjoy a good deal more freedom and even, among the tribes in the desert, quite a lot of influence as well. When a sheikh is away, his wife will rule in his place, and during tribal wars the women will leap upon the first horse or camel available if things are going badly. Baring their faces and loosening their hair, they fly into battle, leading the men back into the fray.

Indomitable, dauntless and cheerful in spite of their incredibly tough life, they go around like brilliant butterflies in all their purple, green, or yellow and scarlet veils. Their wrists and ankles jingle with bells and silver bangles, heavy Maria Theresa dollars made into necklaces hang around their necks and gold coins dangle on their foreheads. Rings in the ears are generally regarded as seductive, but when they go through the tip of the nose as well, the effect is less beguiling to Western eyes. Small girls have silver flowers screwed into their nostrils, and I have seen quite tiny ones thus adorned. With their huge eyes made still bigger by kohl-rimmed lids, they look as exotic as any fairy-tale princess from the mythical past.

During a visit to one of the other Arabian States, I once accompanied a sheikha, whose chief interest was the education of women, on one of her tours to a girls' school. Before we left the palace, the ladies of the harem arranged her veils so that not a square inch of skin could be seen anywhere. Thus smothered, she plunged into her Rolls with an agility which astonished me for one of her girth. Off we swept through the streets, driven by an equally veiled lady chauffeur. I was relieved to see however that she had allowed herself a chink through which to peer at the road and the passing traffic.

In some of these countries, the ruler's wife keeps open house, and the ladies of the town call at the palace every evening to pay their respects, meet their friends and keep in touch with the local gossip. The atmosphere is entirely democratic. There you will meet the wives of wealthy merchants and foreign ambassadors, Bedu women from various desert tribes on a visit to the capital, foreign princesses from distant lands, and the palace cook, all hobnobbing happily together and exchanging the day's news. However high-born and cloistered the ladies may be, they still manage to have quite a good time in their own homes. Their dinner parties are magnificent affairs. Enormous tables groan with food of every kind: entire roast sheep and goats, curried chickens, grilled fish and huge piles of Oriental rice, as well as every type of fruit you can think of. The ubiquitous tinned peach slices, so popular in these parts, are next to luscious mangoes from the oases, pomegranates, bananas and sugar-cane from tropical Dhofar, oranges and great piles of dates, nuts and roasted seeds of every possible variety. On the floor the younger set squat around enormous brass trays of rice, while slave-girls hand round dishes borrowed from the main table. And in between serving the floor and the older guests at the table, they glide about, sprinkling scent over their mistresses' heads. When the meal is over, the much-needed rose water is poured over greasy fingers and incense is handed round, to be swung under the hair and inside the veils. The first time the hem of my evening dress was lifted for a swing of frankincense at one of these parties, I hope that I managed to look sufficiently gratified by the honour.

These enormous spreads are invariably consumed in stony silence. On one occasion, when I was a guest at the palace of a desert sheikh, his four wives sat in a row at the head of the table, each one smothered in black veils with only their eyes and fingers showing. With the left hand they delicately lifted the lower half of the *burqah* which was conveniently hinged just below the nose, and with the other they inserted small pellets of squeezed-up rice between their lips, while the younger set on the floor, unhampered by veil or mask, were chewing their bones in their fingers and tossing them away with hearty abandon.

After dinner, a professional entertainer equipped with a tambourine sings the old traditional songs of the desert but, judging by the lively rhythm, my guess is that these have been considerably jazzed up to fit in with a more contemporary tempo. Soon the young people take to the floor, and veils swirl and hair flies to the stamping of feet and the clapping of hands of the older ladies of the party.

The sheikh usually comes in at midnight. The music and the dancing instantly stop as he progresses majestically through the room. The ladies dive back into their abandoned veils, and all those flushed, laughing faces disappear like the sun behind heavy black clouds. As soon as he has settled down on his throne at the top end of the room, the music starts up again, and so does the dancing. Soon the veils are slipping away once more, and the lively excited faces are as bare as the day they were born.

212

'I don't have to ask you if you're happy,' one of these sheikhs once remarked with a wink as he walked past me. 'I can see it on your face.' And so of course I was, like everybody else in the room. The life of the harem is a carefree, breezy and cheerful one. Totally exempt of material worries, it suits those women who have no wish to do anything else down to the ground. But all the educated girls I spoke to emphatically said they would much rather face the loneliness and insecurity which inevitably go with freedom than continue in the cosseted, restricted, unthinking existence of the harem. At the Zara school in Muscat, some of the top girls, already married, are allowed to continue their studies by special permission of the Ministry of Education. After three years in this class, they are ready to go to university abroad. Looking at these graceful, small-boned, doe-eyed creatures, all swathed in white muslin veils like vestal virgins (the school uniform!), I asked what their favourite subjects were – thinking the answer would be poetry, or music, or painting, or perhaps even philosophy. But in each case it was either mathematics, physics or chemistry. They are all determined to get a degree and come back to a life dedicated to helping develop their country and set it on a firm course of enlightened progress and general all-round improvement.

Young girls go unveiled until their marriage. On the eve of the great day, the relatives of the bride and all her friends, wearing their traditional clothes and covered with jewellery, arrive looking tremendously colourful for the henna party. I have unfortunately never been present at one myself, but I heard it minutely described by a couple of ambassadresses who had seen it with their own eyes. I also saw the ceremony enacted by Egyptian film-stars on television in Oman.

The rooms are absolutely packed. You drift around, picking your way through the assembled company seated on the floor, until you spot a friend, then you go and squat down beside her. The invisible bride is concealed inside a brilliantly coloured tent made of costly silks, satins and taffetas, damasks and cloth of gold. Entering one by one, members of the family and friends add some dazzling piece of jewellery, or string of pearls, or cluster of gold coins to the sparkling tent arrangement. After hanging up their offering, they join the throng sitting cross-legged on the floor throughout the various rooms. The entire gathering is an absolute blaze of colour. A slave is beating a drum, the guests clap their hands and everybody chants a fairly repetitive tuneless song. Another serving-girl pads around with a large jug of mango juice, followed by a colleague bearing a plastic thermos flask full of cardamom coffee. The tiny bowls are handed round one by one, and so deftly is all this service carried out that the chanting and clapping are never interrupted for a single instant.

After a while, a senior member of the family comes forward with a bowl in her hand. The rest of the equipment is brought to her and placed on the floor outside the tent. Having signalled her presence and attracted the bride's attention, she kneels on the floor; soon a pair of bare feet come poking through the draperies, then out of a couple of slits higher up appear the hands as well. At once the senior lady begins to work on them: with a tiny instrument she scoops up minute quantities of henna paste which she smears, first over the nails, then on to the skin of the hands and feet, in complicated arabesques and traditional designs which go back thousands of years. The paste is applied up to three times, according to the depth of the colour desired. Each application is allowed to dry and crack and peel off before the next layer is smeared on. Black henna, or *saumr*, is made of powdered lime and crystal ammonia. When painted over the orange variety, this turns black and lasts about a month. It is supposed to stop blistering; pearl fishermen used it to toughen their skin for rowing and handling the ropes to haul up the divers. Henna comes from the Persian word for Egyptian privet, from which the paste is made. The dye comes from the leaves and is used for colouring hair, beards, horses' manes, morocco leather and, of course, the hands and feet of brides. The fingernails of mummies at the time of the Pharaohs, were also dyed with henna, known as camphire in the Bible. The leaves, pounded to a paste with catechu or alfalfa, are mixed with water, and the resulting mess is then known as *hinna*.

The ceremony goes on for hours, with layer after layer being painted on, dried off and repainted, while the chanting, the drum-beats and the clapping continue without stop. Sometimes, in more modern households especially, this is replaced by ear-splitting piped music coming through loud-speakers in every corner of the room.

When the henna painting is finally over, an enormous feast is brought in for the guests. I can't help wondering if the poor painted lady trapped inside her cage is provided with any sustenance. The sounds of her friends and family carousing and stuffing themselves all round would be bitter indeed if she wasn't.

In Africa, fat women are much prized. Livingstone wrote that a king he knew kept a harem of wives of such vast proportion that all they could do was roll about on the floor like seals. Over them stood eunuchs, force-feeding them with milk with the help of a whip.

But the men of Oman like their women slender and sinuous as serpents, with a small waist and high breasts and long shapely legs, all of which must be concealed from sight beneath the billowing veils in which they are perpetually bundled.

20 Water Gardens

Half the space of the huge drawing-room is taken up by a swimming pool whose clever concealed lighting contributes to the illumination of the room. Long, green, exotic fronds trail and dangle from the gallery above. The ladies, in chic Western evening dresses or sparkling saris in costly Eastern see-through muslins and cloth of gold studded with semi-precious stones, glide about the room or wander up and down the stairs. Men in dinner jackets, *dishdashas*, Omani tunics and daggers and colourful Kashmir turbans stand about, chatting to one another and switching from English to Arabic with the greatest of ease. Our host is Yahia Nasib, one of the richest and most successful businessmen of Oman. Everybody who is anybody is here tonight.

Upstairs, where a fabulous buffet of hot and cold, Western and Oriental dishes are spread out on a huge table, I meet Sylvia, as we are both digging into an enormous salad bowl.

'What a marvellous lettuce!' I can't help remarking as I help myself lavishly to the crisp, tempting, emerald-coloured leaves.

'It is Yahia's very own home-grown salad,' says Sylvia proudly. As she works in Yahia's firm, and looks after his horses as well, she feels justified in taking a certain amount of personal pride in the products of his fertile acres with a difference.

The huge expanse of land under cultivation in Oman (including the immense green belt along the Batinah coast, parts of the interior and the plain of Dhofar) are the main agricultural regions of the country. Watered by wells and *aflaj*, these areas are divided into family plots, growing just about enough for their own needs. Only occasionally is there a surplus for the local *souq*, with a very little left over for export.

Of course, all the work is done by the women who moil and toil in their dusty patches, coaxing into growth a few peppers, lettuces, ladies' fingers, sorrel and cress. This is how it has been done since time immemorial, and new scientific methods are only slowly creeping in. A good example of progress in this connection is sesame, a great favourite in the Middle East where it ranks as an important foodstuff. Its oil, moreover, doesn't go rancid and the plant, which shoots up to ten feet high, bears fruit after only six weeks. Until a few years ago, its age-old custom of scattering its seed to the winds made harvesting a nightmare. Now that a new strain has been developed, in which the plants are forced to hang on to their seeds until the pickers come round, life has been much easier for the sesame growers.

Among the local crops grown by the Batinah tribesmen, sorghum durra is another favourite. Also called Egyptian corn or Indian millet, it is a tough kind of grass which leaps up to sixteen feet high in a very short time. It sometimes has a sweetish pith, though not so much as that of sorgos, which is made into syrup. Cassia, the bark of the very popular cinnamon tree which is less delicate than its seed, is used as a purge. The sumr tree, which grows wild everywhere, produces gum arabica, and the ghaf is a kind of acacia. Its bark is used to tan goatskins and gives a disgusting taste to the water contained within them. The male seed of the date palm is regarded as a delicacy, but I am told it is an acquired taste. As I haven't tried it myself, I can only speak from hearsay. The tarfa, or tamarisk, is much appreciated by camels. The stem of the Sodom apple contains saltpetre and is used by the Bedu for making gunpowder. Notoriously unreliable, it is likely to blow up in the user's face when least expected. The Gulf almond, which produces delicious if very small nuts, doesn't seem to be harvested by anyone in particular. Dates of course form the greatest part of the agricultural product of the entire country. Together with limes, this was about the sum total of the produce of Oman until a couple of years ago when a new venture, which was set up on the coast near Seeb, turned out to be a major success. The amazing thing about Gulf Growers is the rate at which their vegetables actually grow. A cucumber plant, for instance, thinks nothing of pushing up ten inches a day. Two weeks from the moment of planting, a lettuce is ready for picking.

In five acres of running water, underneath a special kind of netting which looks like chain mail, all this greenery flourishes on a liquid diet alone. Sheets of corrugated asbestos, set at a slight angle, form rivulets of running water. Over these comes a covering of plastic, through which are quantities of tiny slits. Into these slits the seedlings are inserted, with their little hairy roots dangling in the water below. Nourished by the fortified liquid in which they dabble, the plants instantly begin to thrive and prosper. Their needs, which are carefully studied, are scrupulously catered for and each variety is fed with its own favourite juices. There are five different mixtures flowing through the station. The water, which is constantly on the move, returns to base where it is recharged with chemicals then sent off again on its life-giving course. The system is inspired by the circulation of the bloodstream in a living body, with the pump in the control room acting as a huge beating heart.

At eight o'clock one morning, Sylvia picks me up on the oil-stained dust patch outside the colonel's flat where I am staying, and off we set to Yahia's pride and joy, the largest and most modern hydroponics station in the Middle East. The director, John Pilcher, is awaiting us in his office with his partners. Impeccable in their well-pressed casual cottons, they look more like pure scientists than agricultural experts. In fact, they all started life in a variety of other careers. John himself is an estate agent by profession. 'I can't grow a thing,' he says as we walk around his thousands of flourishing lettuces, cucumbers and tomatoes.

One very hot August day he was sitting in Dubai Airport, patiently waiting for his connection and sweltering from every pore, when a small headline in an English paper caught his eye. 'Feed the Arid World' urged the advertisement. And that is how it all started. Back in England he made inquiries and very soon he had the whole operation together. Yahia Nasib and several other Omani businessmen agreed to back the venture, and land was made available on the beach near Seeb, about 300 yards away from the edge of the sea.

Prudently John decided to try out the project on a small scale first to make sure that it was a viable proposition.

'We started off on a little quarter-acre site, and grew a lot of different things, experimenting for the first few months with all vegetables, quite a few kinds of fruit, flowers and herbs', he said. 'All right, we had a lot of problems with temperature-control and different types of shading.' The sun's blistering rays had to be deflected from the tender plants. In this climate it is all so different that everything was a new discovery and was in fact pioneering with modern methods. Of course, there was the question of having to bring every bit of equipment out from the U.K. 'And also the problems involved in setting up this sort of thing here. You know, you can't just trot round the corner to buy something you've forgotten.'

Looking around at this huge orderly area of flourishing greenery, I can hardly believe that it has all been done in one year. 'Yes,' says John, 'we've had to work quite hard, really.' This seems to me like an understatement. In March 1978 the first container of equipment arrived. 'It was like a military operation, and I'd never done one of those before,' he adds, 'I had great blisters all over my hands.'

'You didn't build it all yourselves?' I gasp.

'Oh yes. The steel for the packing shed (this is an enormous hangar the size of a church) we bought from Croydon Gas-works while they were pulling it down,' he says. 'The asbestos roofing-sheets, which were substandard British, cost one pound each, and the lights came from Lewis County Council.'

Having constructed their station in record time in March, they picked their first lettuce in August. Now, exactly a year since the operation started, they are in full production with two and a half acres of tomatoes, two acres of lettuce, half an acre of cucumber, and another area experimenting with all sorts of other things, as well as a section dedicated to that tricky herb, parsley. 'Very specialized is parsley,' says John. 'It takes a terrible long time to come up.'

'Don't you pour boiling water over the seeds first?' asks Sylvia.

'Yes, we do. But even then . . . Funny thing, parsley,' he says musingly, obviously knowing more about it than he lets on. Then there is lovely mint, which proliferates lavishly; in fact they have quite a job keeping it from taking the whole place over.

Desalinated water is brought in great barrels and fed into the storage tanks. From these it is pumped to the control room where fertilizers and chemicals are added, before being sent off into five different centres catering separately for each crop. 'You have to add different fertilizers for each thing you are growing,' my guide informs me. This is one of the things they had to learn the hard way. Tomatoes, for instance, would split when fed on lettuce or cucumber fare.

The carefully doctored stock then flows to the top end of each separate growing area, from where it is gravity-fed down to the end of the row, washing over the hungry, greedy roots. After this, it trickles back to its original tank, where more fertilizers are added to the depleted brew. Monitored by the control-panel, it doubles back on its way. But as John says, although the control-panel does a great job, they still have to keep a sharp eye on the plants themselves. Sometimes, for no apparent reason, they suddenly look peaky, and an extra dash of this or that cheers them up at once. This is the personal touch.

Having been revitalized, the water returns to the roots once more, back and forth, round the clock. There is no waste, and evaporation is minimal. Only what the plants drink is taken out of the little running stream. As this is perpetually recycled, running costs are low. It is the original setting-up which is expensive – but this always is. In England a glass-house costs £40,000 an acre.

'Do you find they take a lot of food out of the water?' I ask.

'They only take up as much as they can absorb. The thing

to do is to develop better strains capable of digesting more nourishment.'

The seeds are started off in little peat pots in the germination area. As soon as they are large enough to handle without dissolving to the touch, they are inserted into the plastic slits. Within two weeks they are ready for picking.

John tweaks a lush beauty, shaped like some delicate Chinese jade-carving, out of its nest. 'Taste it,' he says, breaking it up with a crunching sound. 'This is the Ethica variety. For some reason it won't grow in the U.K.'

'It tastes very sweet,' remarks Sylvia appreciatively. Like the one I had at Yahia's party, it is crisp and delicious. Normally I am bored to death by an undressed lettuce. This one is different. Its delicate flavour would be swamped by the usual olive-oil salad dressing.

In summer, under the intense light and the high temperatures, they grow so fast that the staff have a job to stop them bolting. Five to six thousand head of lettuce are picked every day, for seven days a week. At the end of the first season, Gulf Growers are already beginning to export to Bahrain and Dubai. They have contracts with airlines, hospitals, hotels, the police and the army; and they are supplying *Britannia*, which is at the moment lying in Muscat Harbour. Consignments are dispatched every day to Salalah, Thumrayt on the Jebel and the island of Masirah. And they have been approached by Saudi Arabia who want them to start over there as well. As a success story, it would fit into an up-to-date *Arabian Nights* saga.

We pass the flower plots, where a powerful scent of carnations comes wafting over. 'They have small heads, but a strong scent,' John tells me. 'We grow them for the palace, and now British Airways are interested as well.' And he picks one for me which I stick into a buttonhole of my shirt.

In the packing shed, which he put up with his own hands, he shows us the grading grids. 'Tomatoes are graded with very tight quality-control. If one goes bad we replace the whole box free of charge.' At the moment they are grading for size. In the summer they will control colour as well. Ships need ripe ones for immediate consumption, medium-mature for the next few days, and quite green ones which will colour up during the voyage to be ready for the last few days of the trip.

Lettuces go into plastic bags, lovely clean roots and all. 'If you don't want to eat it right away, you pop it into a bowl of water and it goes on growing.'

Another of Sylvia's interests is Yahia's stable. This has been quite a challenge. When racing stopped in Pakistan, the horses were turned loose to fend for themselves. Many of them were found starving and were only brought back to life with careful feeding and a good deal of devotion. Those acquired by Yahia, and tended with single-minded dedication by Sylvia, have picked up and are improving in health and looks. One of them, an arthritic old polo pony, had been badly beaten about the front legs. Sylvia's kindness is a great comfort to him in his old age. And I see a palomino whose original washed-out shade of old palm thatch is fast improving through correct diet to a rich auburn chestnut. A great slice of cornea had somehow been nicked out of one of his eyeballs. With careful treatment, this is now filling in nicely again, and the vet claims that he will be able to see quite well in due course. As far as I can judge, his sight is good enough already for him to spot my carnation and nip it smartly off my bosom as I walk past his stall. To the vast amusement of his groom, he wolfs it down with a greedy snuffle before I've had time to realize what happened.

21   Of Ships and String

In Oman the living take precedence over the dead, which means that medical services, civil aid and education are racing ahead at the expense of less pressing pursuits such as, for instance, archaeology. This is very properly taking second place in the 'progress programme' for the country.

Buried in the depths of the soil and sands of Oman there is a great deal of pre-Islamic past waiting to be brought to light. When this has been done, some quite unexpected and interesting facts may be revealed but, until then, a good deal is still conjecture. All of which doesn't mean of course that no work at all is being done in that field. All excavations are now under the firm control of the Ministry of Heritage and Culture, so that freelance enthusiasts, however well-meaning, can no longer charge about the countryside digging up any little bump or ruin which takes their fancy.

As a result of the work which has been done to date, an exhibition is opening (after the Queen's visit, to avoid crossing wires), planned, designed and set up by this inspired department. As soon as I hear about it, I telephone the Ministry of Information to find out the date and place of the event. Since they have had nothing to do with the project, they advise me to get in touch with the Ministry of Culture, whose concern it is entirely. There I am told that the show will be opened on 7 March by the Minister who has drawn up the list of guests himself, and it will be a very crowded affair. Tentatively I explain that my interest is not vulgar curiosity alone. The next day I am flying north and then back to London, so that I will have no other chance of seeing it. Finally the secretary at the end of the line rather doubtfully agrees to have a word with the Minister, and returns a few minutes later with a cordial invitation from His Excellency himself.

In order to reap the full benefit from this show, I call on Dr Paolo Costa, chief archaeologist at the ministry, who kindly agrees to see me in his office.

His department, he informs me, covers everything on the administration side but, from the research point of view, the main excavations in progress at the moment are concerned with the Islamic past. Near Salalah, the huge mosque of Al-Belid, the ancient city of Dhofar visited by Marco Polo, sprawls over an enormous area. In the north, at Arja, the greatest copper mine in the Middle East is being systematically excavated. The suggestion that it might have been an ancient ziggurat is laughed off by Dr Costa as pure fantasy. There is no doubt in his mind that it has always been a mine. According to geologists and specialists in this field, there is no ore anywhere in the world which was unknown to our most distant ancestors. There isn't a single deposit which hasn't been worked at one time or another.

'Most interesting to us,' Dr Costa tells me, 'is to find small mines with very little original ore available to the ancient technology, so that the mine was worked for a certain time only, and then finished.' In such a case, as soon as the ore was exhausted, the miners moved off, and there are no subsequent remains of a more recent culture on top of the old one. When the explorer Carsten Niebuhr was here, some of the mines were still in operation, and these of course have an enormous amount of slag, covering layers of settlements going back to the dawn of history. One of the older sites near the present dig is covered by 100,000 tons of slag – and that takes a good deal of shifting. It is a lovely spot, surrounded by rocks of every colour in the rainbow, red, green, yellow, purple and violet. The whole heart of the mountain, which was scratched out by the miners, is now one huge crater. This, taken with all the other mines in the country, leaves no doubt in his mind that Oman is the land of Magan, which produced copper for the whole of the ancient world. So far, seventeen settlements dating back to the third millenium B.C. have been located, though not yet uncovered.

The landscape of Oman is littered with these typical bee-hive-shaped tombs, made of beautifully dressed stone. To me they just look like hundreds of ant-hills on the horizon but, discoloured as they are by the centuries, they hardly show up unless you know what you are looking for.

'Imagine how beautiful they must have been, the white domes of the tombs standing out against the dark bare rock of the mountain,' says Dr Costa dreamily. Yes, I *can* imagine it.

On the subject of the Marib dam's collapse, he is full of enthusiasm about a marvellous lecture he has recently attended by an eminent lady scholar. For the first time he has heard clearly expounded the theory which he himself has held for a long time, that the bursting of the dam was not the cause of the population's dispersal but a result, and a symbol of the civilization's advanced state of decay.

Marib is only one of the great many dams which occurred all over Yemen at the height of its prosperous civilization. Dr Costa himself discovered one measuring 650 metres in length. Another common misconception is the date of the catastrophe which, according to him, occurred in A.D. 570. He himself found inscriptions on some of the stones of the dam in south-ern Arabian characters. And this of course is the language still spoken by the Mahra tribes of the Qara mountains.

It is the only Semitic language with four different variations of the letter 'S' he says, thoroughly warming to his subject now. 'Hebrew, Arabic and Aramaic, all have only three,' he adds scornfully. Nobody quite knows how that fourth 'S' was pronounced, but his theory is that 'they shaped the tongue in a way which is very difficult to do, then emitted the air from either side'.

A little groan escapes him when I next ask for his views on the Umm an-Nar culture, so much in evidence in the Gulf as a widely debated subject.

'Umm an-Nar is a fancy name. It is only used for want of

a better term,' he declares. 'The names we give to civilizations are always related to the stage of knowledge reached at the time.' So when the Danish team arrived in Bahrain, and heard tempting descriptions of curious piles of stones near Abu Dhabi, 'where Sheikh Shakbut was sitting in the middle of nothing', they rushed headlong to this waterless little island in a body. At that stage of knowledge, the Danes assumed it to be the centre of this early, unknown civilization. Now, as new evidence keeps coming to light, it appears that the centre is gradually sliding down well into the heart of Oman. And the arid little island of Umm an-Nar can only be regarded as the northernmost fringe of this ancient culture. The whole picture changes when you reconsider it in this light.

'How could this little island ever really be regarded as the centre of a great civilization?' asks Dr Costa in shocked, reproachful tones. Now of course the term has been accepted, but he always refers to it as the 'so-called' Umm an-Nar. 'The trouble is, you must remember that archaeological work was started in this country by people who had already worked extensively in other lands. So that they have in their minds Abu Dhabi, Iran, Qatar, Bahrain; and when they came here, they were unconsciously looking for ramifications, fringes. But in fact, the truth is that this country has been the centre all along. In Oman there are only three or four teams at work. Things have only just started. In Iraq there are forty working there every year.'

This 'so-called' Umm an-Nar culture, which was first excavated by the Danish mission from Aarhus Museum of Prehistory, brought to light an ancient world whose existence had been totally unknown in this part of Arabia before. Umm an-Nar, which is one of the 200 little islands sprinkled around Abu Dhabi, is now a totally deserted and desolate spot, apart from the unlovely new oil-refinery, which only adds to its unwelcoming aspect. But the discoveries made there prove that it was not always so, and that, about 2,700 years ago, its prosperous community enjoyed quite a high degree of sophistication. Apart from the burial mounds, which contained thirty to forty skeletons each, the excavated site of the ancient town revealed strong, well-constructed buildings, one of which, presumably the sheikh's fort, was all of 300 feet square in size. A great deal of the pottery and other finds seem to tie up with the Kulli culture of the Indus valley. The inhabitants lived on herds of the gentle, trusting dugong which still potter about in the numerous lagoons between the islands, and on gazelle hunted in the desert. Life was settled; the women spun, wove, made all the pots and pans required and grew and harvested the grain from the surrounding fertile fields. As there is no water on the island, this last fact puzzled the men from Aarhus not a little. The handsomely dressed stone of the buildings was another puzzle. In a desiccated land like this part of Arabia, dwellings are simply made of mud or *barasti*. There is no need for more permanant, waterproof materials such as stone, where rainfall barely reaches two inches a year. The scientists therefore concluded that the community they had unearthed 'was geared to a different climate, in particular to a greater rainfall than that of the present day'. This fact probably applies to the whole of Oman as well. One last point may be of sufficient interest to be worth mentioning: on one of the tomb stones were found carvings of the oryx of the desert and the camel, proving that this unlovely beast was already domesticated as early as 2700 B.C.

The Heritage Exhibition, when I finally get to it, turns out to be a joy. Beautifully designed, mounted and set up, it is light, well spaced out, with a thoroughly 'modern' feel that some of our own similar shows might emulate with advantage. The displays are clearly labelled and explained. Many of the items such as the manuscripts, the silver and the pottery, are borrowed from the museum. A huge, magnificent Arab bed, all turned and carved, occupies one corner, and a famous, fantastically carved door has been borrowed from a house in Ibra.

Blown-up photographs show the various digs, and an architectural survey gives a detailed account of all the castles, the forts and the monuments of the Batinah. Having seen the fortified palace of Jabrin makes it very much easier to follow the minutely described explanations of the copious restoration plans and diagrams.

The *barasti* compound outside is made up of genuine country huts, woven out of the usual palm thatch. Inside, craftsmen are at work on their various ploys. Fascinated, I stop by a boat builder who is stitching his ship together with string made of coconut fibre. The framework, which looks like the rib-cage of a whale, is being assembled. A little further along, his colleague is making holes in the rose-coloured timber slowly and laboriously with a hand-operated bow-drill, pulling and releasing a string which rotates the drill which bores the hole through which the string will go.

As palm-trunks are soft and spongy at the best of times, proper shipbuilding timber has to be imported from India. Great teak and sisso logs are sliced into planks, then smoothed with an adze which gives them a typical, slightly uneven surface, infinitely more congenial than a smooth, mechanical finish. In this manner the great *boums*, solidly sewn together, would sail as far as East Africa, India and China. In the nineteenth century an Omani dhow thought nothing of sailing to New York. The big powerful *baghala*, just as securely stitched together, is now very rare because of its two masts which leave little space for the new-fangled diesel engine funnels of the steam age. The Suez canal was another nail in the coffin of Oman's importance as a trading country, although trade is expected to come into its own again now, with the building of the new port of Mina Qaboos.

At the other end of the scale are the little *houris*, dug out of tree trunks, and the *shasha*, a curious, frail little craft made of palm fronds tied together at either end which takes a couple of men two days to weave into shape, fit for the open sea. Measuring ten feet in length, they have to be taken out of the water after each expedition as they get increasingly heavier with every soaking. 'Sand fishermen' set off in their *shashas* in fleets of a thousand at a time for trips of about fifty miles, expecting to catch only 'sardin'. One of the unusual features of these little boats is that they sit just below the surface of the water; so whenever you see a man up to his waist in the sea, peacefully paddling himself along without any visible sign of a boat around, you may safely assume that he is riding a *shasha*.

Standing in front of the boat builders, I take care not to let my shadow sprawl across the unfinished hull as this would assuredly bring tragedy to the crew as soon as the boat set sail for the high seas. It is a custom for pregnant women to jump over the first timber of a new-laid keel, to strengthen their unborn child. This takes virtue out of the ship, which will claim a life for a life unless a goat is sacrificed on board before the voyage starts.

Nowadays some boats are held together with wooden dowels, or so I am told. I have never seen any myself and, as for iron nails, they are never, never used. When the hull is finished, a fretwork railing, beautifully carved, is built around the deck. And finally, when all is done, a *chaise percée*, also carved and painted in beautiful colours, is slung over the edge on ropes. This is the ship's loo. Arabs have no feelings of embarrasment about their natural functions, which they quite happily perform in public; I have sometimes seen two or three crouching in a chummy circle, gossiping companionably only a few yards away from where I was sitting on the beach.

It is now my last day in Oman, and my kind host, who may well have guessed the almost obsessive fascination which the Indian Ocean holds over me, offers to take me on a last deep-sea fishing expedition as a farewell treat.

All official ceremonies are over, the Queen and Prince Philip have left and everything has returned to normal. We set off after lunch for the little cove at Qurm where the boat is beached. As it is much too heavy to push out to sea, I climb into the clapped-out old Landrover, no longer fit for road service, which is used to haul the boats in and out of the sea. As soon as the rope is fixed, I get into gear and crawl forward. When the landing ramp begins to slope sharply into the water, I have to stand with my whole weight on the foot-brake to keep the whole business from bolting downhill. When the boat is finally afloat and I have to reverse up that slippery slope, it takes every ounce of my puny strength to put the hand-brake on. A kind soul, standing by watching my antics, throws dry sand on to the slimy seaweed to reduce the skidding. 'You want to put on a bit of weight,' he advises, 'a couple of extra stone would make all the difference.'

The sea is a dark translucent indigo hue under the blazing afternoon sky. And that is actually its very own colour and not the reflection of the sky, as I used to think it was. Clear sea-water is purest blue because some of the sun's rays, which are not absorbed, are reflected back. In shallow, plankton-infested waters, the red and yellow rays, which are normally assimilated, are also reflected, and the water becomes quite green. The Gulf, which is never more than twenty-five metres deep at any point and swarms with all manner of plankton, is a typical example of this. And whenever patches of olive green appear, you may be sure that diatoms are around in great numbers. On occasion I have seen enormous expanses of white, particularly under an early-morning mother-of-pearl sky, and assumed that this was also reflected from above. It is in fact due to a certain kind of plankton which turns the surface of the sea into huge milk-white slicks which can stretch for miles around.

Once we are well away from the rocks of the coast, Jonathan rigs up the fishing lines and all his wildly expensive tackle. Two rods stick up on either side and a third protrudes beyond the back of the boat. How they don't all get tangled up together is a mystery.

We are making for the island where groupers and kingfish often rest in the deep troughs of the lee side. Tiny, neat little sea-birds no bigger than quail dart about just above the crests of the waves. The air is warm, the weather perfect, and on the skyline a procession of tankers are patiently waiting their turn to fill up at the oil station. As we navigate cautiously between the fishermen's white floats (it is pure murder getting caught in their nets), the water suddenly explodes on our left, as an enormous kingfish leaps high into the air, flies in a graceful curve for about twenty feet, and dives in again, nose first, with hardly a splash.

Spurred on by this magnificent display, I point the boat straight at the spot where he has disappeared. But the noble fish is either a mile away by now or else is too wily to let himself get hooked. Round the island we go, without a single bite. We spot a snake sunbathing voluptuously, rocked on the gentle swell; a turtle eyes us morosely as he paddles past, on his way out to the open sea.

'There is very little fish at this time of the year,' says the colonel glumly. 'They don't like the red tide.' This is made up of minute organisms which get caught in their gills and stifle them to death. No sooner has he said this than wavy lines of dark-red sludge suddenly appear a hundred yards away, floating on the surface of the sea. This blood-coloured mess heaving about among the waves is actually swarming with millions of tiny copepods, and the brown algae Trichodesmium Erythraeum, which changes the indigo colour of tropical seas to a gruesome dark blood-red.

The Indian Ocean is the youngest, in terms of Earth time, of the three great oceans of the planet; it is also the smallest. Its evaporation is constantly replenished by six large rivers, as well as by a constant flow from the floor of the Red Sea through the Straits of Bab el-Mandeb. This enormous volume of water which pours into the Gulf of Aden raises the salinity and the temperature of the Indian Ocean from a mean annual of 82° or 84° to a maximum of 88° in the summer months. The Gulf, which is hottest of all, goes up to 96°, almost blood-heat.

Land gravity, acting as a powerful magnet, draws water towards the shore so that it piles up around the continents, causing the level to drop far out in mid-ocean. The surface salinity is slightly higher than in deeper water, and its temperature always a little warmer than the air above it.

In early spring the 'vernal explosion' takes place in the seas of the world, with a huge outburst of new life, thanks to the increased sunlight essential for the growth and reproduction of these infinitesimal organisms. During the long, cold, dark months of winter, fertile feeding-stuffs accumulate in readiness for the spring explosion. The rise in the temperature of the sea acts as another boost to all this new life. All the vegetable plankton, and especially diatoms, proliferate in their millions and swarm into the shallow seas. Using energy from the sun, they soak up the carbonic acid dissolved in the water and somehow manage to grow fat on this unappetizing diet.

Animal plankton, which live and die on the surface, graze avidly all through the summer on this swirling vegetable patch. Some, like the Foraminifera and Radiolaria, go around in extraordinary shells of all shapes, each one more astonishing than the last. Some go in for tiny pill-boxes linked together with a few bristles. There are stars with uneven points, little hairy long-tailed nodules, intricately carved paperweights, beaks floating free without head or body, and the copepod Nauplius, a plump headless little body sprouting whiskers in all directions. And there is the missing link, Perdinian, a little one-cell creature which is neither vegetable nor animal and provides copious fodder for the ravening 'sardin'. At night they light up the water with their brilliant white phosphorescent fire. More radiant still, Noctiluca, a close cousin, blazes like a submerged sunset.

But for the moment, the red tide is here to clog up the gills of the poor fish, and either they have all died off, asphyxiated, or have fled elsewhere. One way or another, after several hours' cruising under the blistering sun, we have to resign ourselves to a fishless dinner tonight.

The time has come to turn tail and make for home. We haven't caught a thing, poor sport for us, but good news for the fish who don't need another problem on top of all the miseries which assail them at the moment. The sun is about to set. The sea is flat and calm. The tiny birds are still skimming over the water like swallows around a swimming pool. Suddenly, as we approach the shore, there is a tug on one of the lines. Jonathan winds it in, and a curious little grey flat-headed fish comes spinning out of the water. 'Lizard fish,' says the colonel scornfully. 'Only good for shark bait.'

And now all the lines are in, the rods lying neatly along the side of the boat. The waiting tankers look like sombre cut-outs against the lime-green horizon in the east. A delicate mist hangs about, so that the line between the sky and the sea is blurred, and the pathway streaming out of the huge smouldering blood-red ball of the sun makes a flickering orange trail all the way down to our boat.

Muscat 1979
Monte Carlo 1980

Index

233

Hormuz
  Island of, 26
  kings of, 152
  Straits of, 20, 57, 166
horses, 141–2, 143, 210, 216
  breeding and types, 39, 203, 206–7, 208
  dealing, 151
  Royal Stables, 202, 208
  Sultan's horse guard, 203–5
  Sultan's police horses 206–9
  Yahia Nasib's stables, 222
hyenas, 81, 160, 178

Ibadhi tribes, 29, 30, 31, 40, 132
Ibadhi 'the Upright' *see* Nasim bin Murshid
Ibn Battuta, 26, 126, 151
Ibra, 227
Ibrahim bin Isah, 85–6
Ibri, 19, 63, 84, 108, 119, 134, 135–8, 227
  souq 136–7
Id, festival of, 108, 110
Idrisi, 151
India, 4, 9, 10, 12, 20, 32, 36, 37, 39, 40, 45, 48, 55, 58, 104, 185, 189, 204, 228
  horses from, 204, 206, 207
  in Omani commerce, 16, 46
  influence on architecture, 12
Indian millet *see* sorghum durra
Indian Ocean, 19, 21, 26, 37, 44, 51, 98, 99, 102, 153, 162, 163, 165, 178, 191, 229, 231
indigo
  as cosmetic, 173
  dying, 137
Indus Valley, 24, 227
Iran, 19, 49, 161, 166, 198, 226
Iraq, 32, 103, 155, 226
Iraq Petroleum Company, 83–4
Islam, 6, 20, 31, 53, 74, 104, 168, 174, 189, 210, 223, 224
  and Communism, 155
  conversion of Oman to, 33
  see also Shi'a; Sunni
Israelites, 186, 190
Italy, 89
ivory, 20, 45, 51, 104, 186, 192
  trade, 46
Izki, 28, 29, 33, 39, 63, 91, 132, 133, 134, 140
  military camp, 133–4

Jabrin Castle, 39, 41, 42, 70, 119–26, 127, 227
  dungeons, 123–4
Jackson, Captain, 194, 197, 198–9
Jalali, fortress of, 7–11 *passim*, 38, 42, 86
  prisoners, 7–8, 124
Japan, 5, 89
jasmine, 46, 70, 107, 174
Jebalis, 25, 153–4, 157, 167–8, 169, 172, 174
  food: delicacies, 178
  taboos, 178
Jebel Akhdar, 19, 29, 32, 33, 44, 63, 76, 80–82, 85, 86–95 *passim*, 121, 123, 132, 134, 155, 187, 200
Jebel Halim, 199–200
Jebel Kaur, 77, 132, 133
Jebel Qara, 152–3, 155–61, *passim*, 163, 164–80, 181, 194, 221
  climate, 165
Jebel War, 20, 21, 29, 32, 77, 80, 82–95, 105, 126, 134, 198
jellyfish, 22, 153
Jemsetjerd fortress, 33
Jerusalem, 14, 143, 189, 191, 192
Jews, 20, 23, 105
Jizzi (wadi), 19, 27, 63, 104
Jordan, 184
  River, 20, 23
Juba, 151
Judaean dynasty, 190
Julanda bin Masud, 31

Kamil, 63
Kashf al-Gummah, 33
Kathiri people, 168, 188
Kawar, 47
Keir, Major-General Sir William, 56
Kewley, Vanya, 155, 157, 158
kfeeter seeds, 160
Khaboura, 63, 106–18, 153
khanjars, 13, 16, 54, 58, 78, 93
Khareef, 162
Kharijites, 29–30
Khasab military base, 194, 196, 197–8, 199, 200
Khor Rohri, 181, 189
Kilwa, 136–7
kingfish, 16, 102
Koran, 30, 122
Kulli culture, 227
Kuria Muria Bay, 5
  Islands, 21, 61

languages and dialects
  Akkad, 23